STUDENT'S BOOK

HUGH DELLAR AND ANDREW WALKLEY

PRE-INTERMEDIATE
OUTCOMES

HEINLE
CENGAGE Learning™

Australia • Brazil • Japan • Korea • Mexico • Singapore • Spain • United Kingdom • United States

WELCOME TO *OUTCOMES*

Outcomes will help you learn the English you need and want . Each of the sixteen units has three double-pages linked by a common theme. Each double page is an individual lesson – and each teaches you some vocabulary or grammar and focuses on a different skill. The first lesson in each unit looks at conversation, the next two at reading or listening.

WRITING UNITS

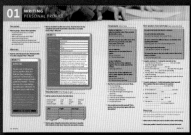

There are eight writing lessons in the Student's Book, which teach different styles of writing. Each one has a model text as well as speaking tasks to do in pairs or groups. There are also extra vocabulary or grammar exercises to help you write each kind of text. In addition, there is a lot of writing practice in the *Outcomes* Workbook.

REVIEW UNITS

There are four Review units in this book. Here you practise the core grammar and vocabulary of the previous four units. The first two pages of each unit feature learner training, a board game, a quiz and work on collocations and pronunciation (especially individual sounds). The next two pages feature a test of listening, grammar and vocabulary. This is marked out of 80 – so you can see how you are progressing.

Clearly stated communicative goals in the unit menu, supported by grammar and vocabulary.

Listening exercises provide examples of the conversations you try in Conversation practice.

Grammar taught in context, with natural examples of usage and clear practice tasks.

Visuals to help with new vocabulary.

Interesting listenings and readings. Very varied contexts .

Tasks to practise a variety of skills.

Information on interesting bits of language common to native speakers of English.

---

01 FAMILY AND FRIENDS

In this unit, you learn how to:
- ask common questions about people
- respond to questions in a natural way
- describe people you know
- recognise collocations – words that go together
- talk about how often you do things

Grammar
- Question formation
- The present simple
- Similarities and contrasts

Vocabulary
- People you know
- Character and habits

Reading
- Living well around

Listening
- A friend of mine
- Our genes or our c

VOCABULARY People you know

A Put the people in the box below into three groups.

actress	aunt	brother	cousin	businessman
colleague	dad	flatmate	friend	housewife
teenager	gran	uncle	waiter	neighbour
sister	nurse	lawyer	retired	boyfriend

Male	Female	Either

B Tell a partner about six different friends or family members and the jobs they do – or did. For example:
My granddad is a retired nurse. He was working until last year.
My cousin Hamid is a student and he works part-time as a waiter.

C Work in pairs. Check any words you don't know in the *Vocabulary Builder*. Then discuss questions 1–3.

| clever | annoying | pretty | fit | generous | open |
| patient | creative | caring | strict | religious | neat |

1 Which adjectives often describe an actress? a lawyer? a nurse? a parent? a grandparent? a housewife?
2 Do you think each adjective is more common for men or for women – or is it equally common for both?
3 Which of the adjectives describe you?

D Choose eight words from this section which were new for you or which you didn't know well. Translate them into your language. Compare what you translated with a partner.

8 OUTCOMES

LISTENING

You are going to hear a conversation between two friends, Laura and Maya. They talk about the people the photo.

A 🔊 1.1 Listen. Who are the people in the photo?

B Complete the questions. Listen and check.

| How old | When | How | Is |
| How long | What | Why | Do |

1 A: .... have you been here?
   B: About half an hour.
2 A: .... do you know her?
   B: I met her on a business trip.
3 A: .... did you do that?
   B: Year 12 at school.
4 A: .... she just visiting?
   B: No, she's working here.
5 A: .... does he do?
   B: He's a teacher.
6 A: .... did he go there?
   B: His girlfriend is from there.
7 A: .... is he?
   B: 34.
8 A: .... you get on well?
   B: No, not really.

C The answers in exercise B are wrong. In pairs, discuss what the answers should be. Look at the audioscript page 162 and check your ideas.

Justinia Lewis (Biologist)

John and Trent Simons (aged 17)

Alicia and Angela Martinez (Spain)

SPEAKING

A Read the text below. Then discuss the questions in groups.

What makes us the people we are? Where do we get our characteristics and habits? It is one of the oldest debates in science. Some say it is our experiences in childhood – the way our parents treat us, our experiences, our friends and our education; others say it's all the result of biology, it's just the genes we get from our parents.

1 How much do you think the following things are caused by genes? How much by childhood experiences? How much by other factors such as where you live? Say a percentage for each one.
   a poor sight
   b confidence
   c how creative you are
   d how fit you are
   e good grades at school
   f the colour of your hair
   g heart disease
   h criminal behaviour
2 What other causes could there be?

12 OUTCOMES

LISTENING

You are going to hear three of the people in the photos above talking about genes and childhood.

A Discuss why you think they're interested in the genes v childhood debate and what opinion you think they will have.

🔊 1.4 Listen. Do they think their character is more because of genes or childhood experience? Does anything surprise you about their opinions?

NATIVE SPEAKER ENGLISH

Keen on
We often say I'm (not) keen on something instead of I (don't) like it. For example:

I'm keen on sport.
Neither of us are keen on dogs.
He's not very keen on spicy food.

LANGUAGE PATTERNS

Write the sentences in your language. Translate them back into English. Compare your English to the original.
My friend Anna from Poland
She's a friend from my Spanish class.
This is Karen. She's a friend from university.
Do you know my friend Dan from work?

GRAMMAR Question formation

For questions in the present simple, put _do / does_ before the subject + infinitive and for questions in the past simple, put _did_.
How do you know her? Does she like it here? (present simple)
Why did he go there? Did you get married there? (past simple)

For present continuous questions, put the form of _be_ before the subject + -ing.
Where are you going? Is she just visiting?

For present perfect questions, put _have_ before the subject + the past participle.
How long have you been here? Has he seen it?

A Put the words in the correct order to make questions.
1 live do Where you?
2 know you anyone in the Do class?
3 known have How long him you?
4 you are English studying Why?
5 this school Have studied you in before?
6 enjoying you the Are class?
7 you have Did nice weekend a?
8 you did do What?

B ♦1.2 Listen and practise saying the questions.

C Ask and answer the questions in pairs.

▶ Need help? Read the grammar reference on page 136.

DEVELOPING CONVERSATIONS
Responding naturally

In conversations, we usually give short initial replies – and then explain more.
A: Really? How old is he?
B: 24
A: And do you get on well?
B: Yes. We're quite close. He's very caring and generous.

Repeating all the grammar of the question – for example, by saying _He is 24 years old_ or _Yes, we do get on. We're quite close_ – can be frustrating or annoying for the listener.

A Cross out all the words you don't really need to say.
1 A: Where are you from?
   B: I am from the Czech Republic.
2 A: Have you got any brothers or sisters?
   B: Yes, I've got brothers and sisters. I've got two brothers and six sisters.
3 A: Are you the oldest?
   B: No, I'm not. I'm in the middle.
4 A: Do you see your grandparents much?
   B: No, I do not see them much. They live in a different city.
5 A: Do you get on with your brother?
   B: No, we do not really get on. He's quite annoying.
6 A: Where did you meet your girlfriend?
   B: I met my girlfriend when I was at university. We were in the same class.
7 A: Do you like sport?
   B: No, I don't. I hate it, but I walk a lot to keep fit.

B ♦1.3 Listen and check your ideas.

CONVERSATION PRACTICE

You are going to have similar conversations to the one you heard in _Listening_. Think of three people you know. One should be a friend, one a member of your family, and one you decide.

A Either draw simple pictures of the three people or, if you have photos of them on a mobile phone, use those. Show the pictures to your partner. Your partner should start by asking: _Who's that?_ and should continue the conversation by asking at least four more questions about each of the three people.

Luis   Angela   Stefan

Many expressions and grammatical patterns in spoken english are similar to other languages. These exercises help you notice those.

A translation exercise helps you think about how sentences work in your own language compared to English.

This section allows you to put together what you've learnt.

Fuller explanations, more examples, and exercises are in the reference section at the back.

C Listen again and decide if 1–10 are true or false.
1 John's brother, Trent, isn't very keen on sport.
2 John's parents see him and his brother as two individual people.
3 John has no similarities to his brother.
4 Alicia's mother is a businesswoman.
5 Alicia is ambitious.
6 According to her gran, Alicia's parents are strict.
7 Justinia Lewis says people share a lot of the same genes as bananas and chimpanzees.
8 Heart disease is mainly a genetic problem.
9 Her parents were scientists.
10 All her family are messy.

D Read the audioscript on page 162 and find four words which are new to you and you'd like to remember. What other words go with them? Compare what you chose with a partner.

E Do you know anyone who is:
• a twin? How similar are they to their brother / sister?
• an only child? What are they like? Do you think being an only child is good?
• pregnant? When is the baby due?

GRAMMAR Similarities and contrasts

Both (of) and _neither (of)_ show that two people or things have something in common. _Neither_ is the negative form of _both_.
Both of my brothers are quite tall. (= I have two brothers)
Neither of my parents are scientists, but they both read widely. (= they're not scientists, they read a lot)

When we are talking about more than two, we can use _all_ for positive statements and _none of_ or _no-one_ for negative statements.
All my family are messy.
None of us are neat and tidy.
No-one in my family likes sport.

We can show a contrast by using _whereas_ or _but_.
Both my brothers are dark, whereas I'm quite fair.
My parents and gran go to church every week, but I don't.

A In pairs, ask questions to find things you share with your partner. How many similarities can you find in five minutes?

B Join another pair of students and explain your similarities and differences. Use _both (of us) / neither of us_ and _whereas_.

C Now explain to the class what things your group of four have in common. Use _all_ and _none_ or _no-one_.

▶ Need help? Read the grammar reference on page 137.

VOCABULARY Character and habits

A Match 1–8 (containing character adjectives) with a–h (describing habits and behaviour).
1 She's very neat and tidy.
2 My granddad's very wise.
3 Neither of us are very clever.
4 Neither of us are very calm and patient.
5 I think we're all very open in our family.
6 My dad's quite strict, whereas my mum's a bit soft.
7 My sister's very determined.
8 He's very kind and caring.

a We hardly ever get A grades. We usually only get Cs.
b We always talk about how we feel. We never hide things from each other.
c When she has decided on something, you can't stop her. She just keeps going till she succeeds.
d She always put things away and keeps things organised.
e We get frustrated quickly and start shouting.
f I always go to him for advice.
g He always thinks about others and helps people.
h I always ask her for things because she usually agrees.

B In pairs, test each other.
Student A: say sentences from a–h.
Student B: close your book and say the adjectives in 1–8.

PRONUNCIATION _and_

There are lots of pairs of words in English like _neat and tidy_ or _kind and caring_ that are joined by '_and_'. When the second word starts with a consonant sound, you hear /ən/ not /ænd/.

A ♦1.5 Listen and practise saying the word pairs.

B In pairs, write down the pairs of words you can remember. Then check in the audioscript on page 162.

SPEAKING

A In groups, tell each other about your family. In what ways are you similar to and different from your grandparents, parents, brothers and sisters? Who are you most / least similar to? Talk about your character, your habits and your looks.

Try and use language you have learnt in this unit.

Further grammar and vocabulary points presented and developed through the unit.

Pronunciation activities are integrated with the communicative goals.

Speaking activities allow you to exchange information and ideas or comment A longer final speaking task ends every unit.

LEARNING

Research suggests words need lots of revision in context if you want to be able to use them with confidence. The authors of _Outcomes_ have tried hard to make sure words reappear many different times in the course. Here are **twelve** ways to learn the word _sort out_.
• see it and practise it in **Vocabulary** p. 26
• look it up in the **Vocabulary Builder** p. 15
• practise it in **Pronunciation** p. 29
• revise it in square 17 of the game in **Review** p. 32
• read it in **Vocabulary** on p. 41
• hear it and see it in **Listening** p. 82
• use it again in **Writing** 02 p. 122
• find an example in the **Grammar reference** p. 142
• write it in **Grammar** p. 151
• check it in the **Vocabulary Builder** exercises p. 17
• listen, write, read and to it in **Workbook** unit 4
• test it with **ExamView**

Outcomes VOCABULARY BUILDER

The _Outcomes Vocabulary Builder_ provides lists of key vocabulary with clear explanations, examples of common collocations and exercises focusing on the grammar of the words.

MyOutcomes ONLINE

The pin code at the front of the Student's Book gives you access to a wide range of interactive, online exercises. We have created additional exercises to go with each unit from the book, so you can continue developing your English.
Visit **elt.heinle.com**

Grammar	Vocabulary	Reading	Listening	Developing conversations
• Question formation • The present simple • Similarities and contrasts	• People you know • Character and habits	• Living well around the world	• A friend of mine • Our genes or our childhood?	• Responding naturally
• The past simple • Comparatives • Passives	• Describing shops and things you bought	• Newspaper stories about shopping	• Did you buy anything nice? • Five conversations in a department store • Anti-shopper podcast	• Complimenting • Making offers and checking
• The present perfect simple • *too / not … enough* • Offers, requests, permission, suggestions	• Restaurants • Describing food	• Breakfast around the world	• Deciding where to eat In a restaurant	• Suggestions
• Present continuous and simple • Future plans and wishes • Past continuous and past simple	• Talking about jobs • Activities at work • Forming words	• Extract from *An Office and a Gentleman*	• So what do you do? • Unpaid work	• Questions about jobs
• *might*, present continuous, *be going to* + verb • Superlatives	• Activities, places and equipment • Sports and games verbs • Forming words	• Sports around the world	• Plans for the weekend • The reasons for football's popularity • Having a nap	• Introducing negative comments
• *have to, don't have to, can* • *will / won't*	• Cities and areas • Staying with people	• Five things you should know before leaving home	• Where are you from? • My first place of my own • Staying with a host family	• Explaining where places are • Asking for permission
• Giving advice (*should, ought to, why don't you*) • Imperatives	• Illnesses and health problems • Forming words • Parts of the body	• Not just all in the mind	• *I'm not very well* • Dealing with health problems	• Common questions about illness
• Articles (*a, an* and *the*) • Quantifiers with uncountable nouns	• Places in town • Means of transport	• *The Two Travellers and the Farmer*	• Do you know if this is the right way? • The travel news	• Giving directions

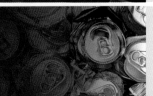

01 FAMILY AND FRIENDS

In this unit, you learn how to:
· ask common questions about people
· respond to questions in a natural way
· describe people you know
· recognise collocations – words that go together
· talk about how often you do things

Grammar
· Question formation
· The present simple
· Similarities and contrasts

Vocabulary
· People you know
· Character and habits

Reading
· Living well around the world

Listening
· A friend of mine
· Our genes or our childhood?

VOCABULARY People you know

A Put the people in the box below into three groups.

actress	aunt	brother	cousin	businessman
colleague	dad	flatmate	friend	housewife
teenager	gran	uncle	waiter	neighbour
sister	nurse	lawyer	retired	boyfriend

Male	Female	Either

B Tell a partner about six different friends or family members and the jobs they do – or did. For example:
My granddad is a retired nurse. He was working until last year.
My cousin Hamid is a student and he works part-time as a waiter.

C Work in pairs. Check any words you don't know in the *Vocabulary Builder*. Then discuss questions 1–3.

clever	annoying	pretty	fit	generous	open
patient	creative	caring	strict	religious	neat

1 Which adjectives often describe an actress? a lawyer? a nurse? a parent? a grandparent? a housewife?
2 Do you think each adjective is more common for men or for women – or is it equally common for both?
3 Which of the adjectives describe you?

D Choose eight words from this section which were new for you or which you didn't know well. Translate them into your language. Compare what you translated with a partner.

LISTENING

You are going to hear a conversation between two friends, Laura and Maya. They talk about the people in the photo.

A 🔊 1.1 Listen. Who are the people in the photo?

B Complete the questions. Listen and check.

How old	When	How	Is
How long	What	Why	Do

1 A: .... have you been here?
   B: About half an hour.
2 A: .... do you know her?
   B: I met her on a business trip.
3 A: .... did you do that?
   B: Year 12 at school.
4 A: .... she just visiting?
   B: No, she's working here.
5 A: .... does he do?
   B: He's a teacher.
6 A: .... did he go there?
   B: His girlfriend is from there.
7 A: .... is he?
   B: 34.
8 A: .... you get on well?
   B: No, not really.

C The answers in exercise B are wrong. In pairs, discuss what the answers should be. Look at the audioscript on page 162 and check your ideas.

LANGUAGE PATTERNS

Write the sentences in your language. Translate them back into English. Compare your English to the original.

My friend Anna from Poland
She's a friend from my Spanish class.
This is Karen. She's a friend from university.
Do you know my friend Dan from work?

GRAMMAR Question formation

For questions in the present simple, put *do / does* before the subject + infinitive and for questions in the past simple, put *did*.
How *do you know* her? *Does she like* it here? (present simple)
Why *did he go* there? *Did you get* married there? (past simple)

. . . .

For present continuous questions, put the form of *be* before the subject + *-ing*.
Where *are you going*? *Is she* just *visiting*?

. . . .

For present perfect questions, put *have* before the subject + the past participle.
How long *have you been* here? *Has he seen* it?

A Put the words in the correct order to make questions.

1 live do Where you?
2 know you anyone in the Do class?
3 known have How long him you?
4 you are English studying Why?
5 this school Have studied you in before?
6 enjoying you the Are class?
7 you have Did nice weekend a?
8 you did do What?

B 🔊 **1.2 Listen and practise saying the questions.**

C Ask and answer the questions in pairs.

▶ Need help? Read the grammar reference on page 136.

DEVELOPING CONVERSATIONS
Responding naturally

In conversations, we usually give short initial replies – and then explain more.
A: *Really? How old is he?*
B: *24*
A: *And do you get on well?*
B: *Yes. We're quite close. He's very caring and generous.*

. . . .

Repeating all the grammar of the question – for example, by saying *He is 24 years old* or *Yes, we do get on. We're quite close* – can be frustrating or annoying for the listener.

A Cross out all the words you don't really need to say.

1 A: Where are you from?
  B: I am from the Czech Republic.
2 A: Have you got any brothers or sisters?
  B: Yes, I've got brothers and sisters. I've got two brothers and six sisters.
3 A: Are you the oldest?
  B: No, I'm not. I'm in the middle.
4 A: Do you see your grandparents much?
  B: No, I do not see them much. They live in a different city.
5 A: Do you get on with your brother?
  B: No, we do not really get on. He's quite annoying.
6 A: Where did you meet your girlfriend?
  B: I met my girlfriend when I was at university. We were in the same class.
7 A: Do you like sport?
  B: No, I don't. I hate it, but I walk a lot to keep fit.

B 🔊 **1.3 Listen and check your ideas.**

CONVERSATION PRACTICE

You are going to have similar conversations to the one you heard in *Listening*. Think of three people you know. One should be a friend, one a member of your family, and one you decide.

A Either draw simple pictures of the three people or, if you have photos of them on a mobile phone, use those. Show the pictures to your partner. Your partner should start by asking: *Who's that?* and should continue the conversation by asking at least four more questions about each of the three people.

Luis   Angela   Stefan

SPEAKING

A **Work in groups. Discuss these questions.**
- Which part of your country – or of the world – do you think is the best place:
- to be a child? Why?
- to be a teenager? Why?
- to start a family? Why?
- to get old? Why?
- Do you like the place you grew up in? What was good / bad about it?

READING

You are going to read an article about the best countries to be a child in and to grow old in.

A **Read the article and answer these questions.**
1 What four reasons are given to explain why the Netherlands is so good for children?
2 What four reasons does Goro Taniguchi give to explain his long life?

> It is important to learn words together – and to learn common collocations. Collocations are words that often go together. They can be verb + noun, adjective + noun, etc. For example:
>
> *wear glasses, leave home* (verb + noun)
> *friendly neighbours, the middle child* (adjective + noun)

B **Cover the text. Complete the collocations Look back at the bold words in the article to check.**
1 a .... report
2 .... pressure on someone
3 .... parents
4 .... arguments
5 .... time with someone
6 a .... life
7 .... fish
8 .... swimming

C **Which four collocations above are verb + noun – and which four are adjective + noun?**

D **In pairs, discuss these questions.**
- What do you think is the main reason for the Netherlands' success? Why?
- What do you think is the main reason for Mr Taniguchi's long life? Why?

LIVING WELL AROUND THE WORLD

The Netherlands

According to **a recent** UNICEF **report**, the Netherlands is the best place in the world to be a child, while the UK is the worst! The report looked at areas like health, income of parents and education, but also did research into how children felt about their lives – and why.

Several reasons for the country's success are suggested: there are plenty of parks, play spaces and facilities for the young; the percentage of mothers who work is quite low; Dutch parents – and teachers – **put** less **pressure on** their children at school and don't worry about their children's grades; Dutch families are generally very open and they talk about everything. Because **parents** are more **liberal**, teenage issues that sometimes **cause arguments** in stricter societies aren't usually a problem in Holland. Here's what Dutch children say:

My parents **spend** a lot of **time** with me. We eat together three times a day and I often go to the park with my mum to play. We're very close. *(Margot, 6)*

I really enjoy school most of the time. I hardly ever get bored and the other people in my classes are usually really nice and friendly. If I have a problem, there's a special teacher I can talk to, which is great. *(Robin, 13)*

My parents are great. They help me a lot and they never force me to do things I don't want to do. My life is very free, so I don't need to get angry with my parents. The only problem is that now I'm older, they want me to look after myself more – and that's difficult. *(Ysbrand, 16)*

Japan

If Holland is the best place to be young, Japan is perhaps the best place to grow old. 11% of the population are retired and the number is growing. There are now more than 36,000 people aged 100 years or more – 86% of them women. At the age of 110, Goro Taniguchi is one of the oldest men in the world. He explains his **long life** as follows:

Living a long time means nothing if you're not healthy. I'm lucky I still have my health. I eat well – lots of **fresh fish**, fruit and vegetables – and I keep fit. Most days, I go for a walk in the fields near my house and **I go swimming** once or twice a week. I'm a happy, patient person and I keep busy. It's also nice for me because there are lots of women my age, but very few men!

GRAMMAR the present simple

Use the present simple to talk about facts (things that are always true) or regular occurrences and habits (things we often / regularly do). Remember to add *-s* to the verb when talking about *he / she / it*!
My brother lives in the States. (= always)
We don't really get on. (= always)
Do you see your grandparents much? (= often)

We often use adverbials of frequency with the present simple. Some go before the main verb, some go at the beginning or end of a sentence.
I *hardly ever* get bored.
Most days, I go for a walk in the fields near my house.
I go swimming *once or twice a week*.

A Make questions using the words in brackets.
1 .... married? (be / any of your brothers or sisters)
2 Who .... closest to in your family? (be / you)
3 Where .... from originally? (be / your parents)
4 .... well with your parents? (you / get on)
5 .... studying? (you / like)
6 .... good English? (anyone in your family / speak)
7 .... abroad? (anyone you know / live)
8 .... any other languages? (you / speak)

B In pairs, ask and answer the eight questions above.

C Change partners. Ask and answer questions 1–10 below using the words in the box. For example:
A: *How often do you see your parents?*
B: *Every day – I still live at home. What about you?*
A: *Not very often, really. A few times a year.*

always	usually
quite often	sometimes
not very often	hardly ever
never	every day
two or three times a week	once or twice a week
two or three times a month	a few times a year

How often do you ...
1 ... see your parents?
2 ... talk to your parents about your problems?
3 ... see your aunts and uncles and cousins?
4 ... visit your grandparents?
5 ... have dinner with the people you live with?
6 ... argue with the people you live with?
7 ... eat fresh fish?
8 ... eat fresh fruit and vegetables?
9 ... go swimming?
10 ... go running?

▶ Need help? Read the grammar reference on page 137.

Justinia Lewis (Biologist)

John and Trent Simons (aged 17)

Alicia and Angela Martinez (Spain)

SPEAKING

A **Read the text below. Then discuss the questions in groups.**

What makes us the people we are? Where do we get our characteristics and habits? It is one of the oldest debates in science. Some say it is our experiences in childhood – the way our parents treat us, our experiences, our friends and our education; others say it's all the result of biology, it's just the genes we get from our parents.

1 How much do you think the following things are caused by genes? How much by childhood experiences? How much by other factors such as where you live? Say a percentage for each one.

a poor sight
b confidence
c how creative you are
d how fit you are
e good grades at school
f the colour of your hair
g heart disease
h criminal behaviour

2 What other causes could there be?

LISTENING

You are going to hear three of the people in the photos above talking about genes and childhood.

A **Discuss why you think they're interested in the genes v childhood debate and what opinion you think they will have.**

B 🌑 1.4 **Listen. Do they think their character is more because of genes or childhood experience? Does anything surprise you about their opinions?**

NATIVE SPEAKER ENGLISH

Keen on
We often say *I'm (not) keen on* something instead of *I (don't) like it*. For example:

I'm keen on sport.
Neither of us are keen on dogs.
He's not very keen on spicy food.

C Listen again and decide if 1–10 are true or false.
1 John's brother, Trent, isn't very keen on sport.
2 John's parents see him and his brother as two individual people.
3 John has no similarities to his brother.
4 Alicia's mother is a businesswoman.
5 Alicia is ambitious.
6 According to her gran, Alicia's parents are strict.
7 Justinia Lewis says people have a lot of the same genes as bananas and chimpanzees.
8 Heart disease is mainly a genetic problem.
9 Her parents were scientists.
10 All her family are messy.

D Read the audioscript on page 162 and find four words which are new to you and you'd like to remember. What other words go with them? Compare what you chose with a partner.

E Do you know anyone who is:
• a twin? How similar are they to their brother / sister?
• an only child? What are they like? Do you think being an only child is good?
• pregnant? When is the baby due?

GRAMMAR Similarities and contrasts

Both (of) and *neither (of)* show that two people or things have something in common. *Neither* is the negative form of *both*.
Both of my brothers are quite tall. (= I have two brothers)
Neither of my parents are scientists, but they *both* read widely. (= they're not scientists, they read a lot)

When we are talking about more than two, we can use *all* for positive statements and *none of* or *no-one* for negative statements.
All her family are messy.
None of us are neat and tidy.
No-one in my family likes sport.

We can show a contrast by using *whereas* or *but*.
Both my brothers are dark, *whereas* I'm quite fair.
My parents and gran go to church every week, *but* I don't.

A In pairs, ask questions to find things you share with your partner. How many similarities can you find in five minutes?

B Join another pair of students and explain your similarities and differences. Use *both (of us) / neither of us* and *whereas*.

C Now explain to the class what things your group of four have in common. Use *all* and *none* or *no–one*.

▶ Need help? Read the grammar reference on page 137.

VOCABULARY Character and habits

A Match 1–8 (containing character adjectives) with a–h (describing habits and behaviour).
1 She's very neat and tidy.
2 My granddad's very wise.
3 Neither of us are very clever.
4 Neither of us are very calm and patient.
5 I think we're all very open in our family.
6 My dad's quite strict, whereas my mum's a bit soft.
7 My sister's very determined.
8 He's very kind and caring.

a We hardly ever get A grades. We usually only get Cs.
b We always talk about how we feel. We never hide things from each other.
c When she has decided on something, you can't stop her. She just keeps going till she succeeds.
d She always put things away and keeps things organised.
e We get frustrated quickly and start shouting.
f I always go to him for advice.
g He always thinks about others and helps people.
h I always ask her for things because she usually agrees.

B In pairs, test each other.
Student A: say sentences from a–h.
Student B: close your book and say the adjectives in 1–8.

PRONUNCIATION *and*

There are lots of pairs of words in English like *neat and tidy* or *kind and caring* that are joined by *'and'*. When the second word starts with a consonant sound, you hear /ən/ *not* /ænd/.

A ✪ 1.5 Listen and practise saying the word pairs.

B In pairs, write down the pairs of words you can remember. Then check in the audioscript on page 162.

SPEAKING

A In groups, tell each other about your family. In what ways are you similar to and different from your grandparents, parents, brothers and sisters? Who are you most / least similar to? Talk about your character, your habits and your looks.

Try and use language you have learnt in this unit.

02 SHOPS

VOCABULARY

A Label the pictures below with the words in the box.

mobile	shirt	T-shirt	top	suit	coat
skirt	camera	laptop	watch	hat	tie

B Work in pairs. Discuss these questions.
- Do you like the different clothes and things in the pictures? Why? / Why not?
- Have you bought any of these things recently?
- Where from? Are you happy with them?

C Use the extra information in 1–12 to guess the meanings of the words in **bold**. Translate the sentences into your language. Then check in the *Vocabulary Builder*.

1. Their shoes are **good quality**. They're very well made. They really **last**. I've had these ones for three years.
2. Go to World PC. They're very **reliable**. If you have any problems, they're always quick to solve them.
3. I usually go to Davy's for food. They've got a really **wide selection**. You can get whatever you want there.
4. They're open on Sundays. In fact, I think the only day they're **shut** is Christmas Day!
5. I bought this nice **thick** coat for the winter. It'll keep me warm in the cold weather.
6. They're nice shoes. They look cool, but they're a bit small for me. They're a bit **uncomfortable** to walk in.
7. What lovely flowers! They're so **bright** and colourful.
8. It's **complicated** to use and the instructions don't make things any easier. They're really hard to follow.
9. I think their clothes are really **good value**. They're very fashionable, but not very expensive.
10. I bought a **smart** pair of trousers and a couple of shirts for work. We can't wear jeans or T-shirts.
11. Yellow **doesn't** really **suit me**. I look better in darker colours like blue or black.
12. I got a really **neat** laptop. It's very light and it's got all the latest software. It looks cool too.

D Work in groups. Discuss the following.
- Use words from exercise C to describe things you have.
- When was the last time you went shopping? Did you buy anything? What? Where from?

> ### NATIVE SPEAKER ENGLISH
>
> ***cool***
> We often say something looks *cool* if it has a modern design. A *cool* person looks fashionable and attractive.
>
> *It looks cool too.*
> *I bought this really cool new mobile phone.*
> *He looks very cool with those new sunglasses.*

LISTENING

You are going to hear three friends – Keira, Claire and Dan – talking about things they have bought.

A 🔊 **2.1 Listen. Take notes on what they bought, where they bought these things and what they are like.**

B **Work in pairs. Discuss these questions.**
- Where can you buy second-hand things?
- Have you ever bought / received anything second-hand?
- Would you buy any of these things second-hand? Why? / Why not?

a car	a computer	a coat	kids' clothes
a book	a bike	boots	a computer game

DEVELOPING CONVERSATIONS
Complimenting

> We often compliment people and then add a question – or a further comment. In both cases, it is normal to reply.
>
> K: That's really neat. Where did you get it?
> C: In Jessops in town. I'm really pleased with it.
>
> C: I love your jacket. It looks really nice and warm.
> D: Yeah, it is. It's great. It's pure wool.

A **Put the words in the correct order to make questions or further comments.**
1 That's a great bag. – new / is / it?
2 I love your shirt. – really / a / design / it's / nice.
3 Nice car! – one / I'd / that / love / like.
4 Hey, neat phone! – how / have / had / long / it / you?
5 I like your boots. – comfortable / look / really / they.
6 That's a lovely jacket. – really / you / it / suits.

B **Work in pairs. Take turns saying the sentences in 1–6 and giving replies.**

GRAMMAR The past simple

> **To make verbs in the past, we normally add –ed or just –d if the verb ends in –e.**
> I *looked / lived* in about six different places.

> **However, a lot of common verbs are irregular:**
> I *went* to a market in town.
> I *bought* a digital camera.

> **Make questions and negatives using *did / didn't* + the infinitive of the verb. With *be*, use *was(n't) / were(n't)*.**
> Where *were* you yesterday? *Did* you *go* shopping?
> I *didn't see* anything I liked. The clothes *weren't* very nice.

A **Complete the dialogue with the correct forms of the verbs. You will also need to add some pronouns.**
A: ¹............................. (do) anything yesterday?
B: Yes, we ²............................. (go) round the market in Rye.
A: Oh yes. ³............................. (buy) anything nice?
B: No. I ⁴............................. (want) to get something for my parents, but I ⁵............................. (not see) anything I ⁶............................. (like). Carol ⁷............................. (get) a nice top, though.
A: Is it that one you're wearing?
C: Yeah, and it ⁸............................. (not be) very expensive either. It only ⁹............................. (cost) 20 euros.
A: Really? That's really good value. ¹⁰............................. (have) any others like that?
C: Not exactly the same, but they ¹¹............................. (have) lots of nice things.
A: Sounds good. The top's cool. It really suits you.

▶ Need help? Read the grammar reference on page 138.

CONVERSATION PRACTICE

A **Work in pairs. Have a conversation that starts:**
A: *Did you do anything at the weekend?*
B: *Yeah, I went shopping.*
A: *Really? Did you buy anything nice?*

Try to continue the conversation for as long as you can.

B **Talk to some other students. Compliment them on things they are wearing – or have. Use the sentence starters below. Continue each conversation for as long as you can.**
I like your ...
That's a nice ...
Those ... are really nice

LISTENING

You are going to hear five conversations in a shop.

A Before you listen, look at the picture above. What do you think the people in situations a–e are saying?

B 🔊 2.2 Listen. Match the conversations to situations a–e in the picture.

C Which conversations did you hear these questions in? Can you remember the answers? Listen again to check.
  a Are you sure you didn't drop it or anything?
  b Do you have one of these in a smaller size?
  c Do you have anything a bit prettier?
  d Well, do you want to go first?
  e Is there anyone serving here?

D In pairs, discuss the questions below. Then read the audioscript on page 163 to check your ideas.
Conversation 1 What is the man complaining about?
Conversation 2 What does the woman offer to do?
Conversation 3 What is the customer buying?
Conversation 4 What problem does the assistant have with the complaint?
Conversation 5 Why does the mother want to buy the sweater?

E Work in groups. Discuss these questions.
  • What polite things do you usually do or say?
  • What was the last kind thing you did for someone?
  • What was the last present you bought? Who for? What was the occasion? Did you wrap it? Did they like it?
  • When was the last time you took something back to a shop? What was wrong with it? What happened?
  • Did your parents ever make you wear something you didn't like when you were a child?
  • Did you have favourite clothes? What were they?

LANGUAGE PATTERNS

Write the sentences in your language. Translate them back into English. Compare your English to the original.
I bought this the other day and it's damaged.
I saw Kenji just the other day.
I tried to phone you the other day, but your phone was off.
I was thinking about you the other day when the Arsenal game was on.
I went shopping there just the other week.

DEVELOPING CONVERSATIONS
Making offers and checking

> **We often make offers using *Do you want* or *I'll*.**
> A: *Do you want to go first? / I'll go after you.*
>
> **Look at how to check things are OK:**
> B: *You don't mind? / Are you sure?*
>
> **We usually then say it's fine – and add a comment.**
> A: *Not at all. / Of course. I have lots of things.*
>
> **To accept the offer, just say *Thanks*.**

A In pairs, have four–part conversations like the one in the explanation box above. Start with these ideas.
1 Do you want me to carry those bags?
2 Do you want to sit down at that table? I'll wait.
3 Do you want me to drive you home?
4 I'll pay for this.
5 I'll help you with your homework, if you like.

GRAMMAR Comparatives

> **To make comparatives, add *-er* to adjectives / adverbs of one syllable or just *-r* if the adjective / adverb ends in *-e*.**
> Do you have this in a *smaller* size?
>
> **Two-syllable words ending in *-y* change to *-ier*.**
> It's a bit plain. Do you have anything a bit *prettier*?
>
> **We usually use *more* with two- or three-syllable adjectives / adverbs.**
> Their service is much / a bit *more reliable*.
>
> **To say there's a big difference, use *much*. To say there's a small difference, use *a bit*. This applies to adverbs too.**

A Complete 1–7 with the correct comparatives.
1 They're a bit loose when I walk. Do you have them in a .... size? (small)
2 It looks too complicated for my gran. Do you have one which is .... to use? (easy)
3 It's a bit tight round my shoulders. Do you have a .... size? (big)
4 You can't go to the interview like that. Have you got something .... to wear? (smart)
5 It doesn't look very strong. Have you got one which is a bit .... quality? Something which will last a bit .... ? (good, long)
6 It's a bit plain and dark. Have you got something a bit ...., a bit .... ? (bright, colourful)
7 It'll probably be .... for the baby, but it's a bit heavy and it'll be difficult to carry up and down stairs. Have you got something ...., something a bit .... that you can fold .... ? (comfortable, practical, light, easily).

B Work in groups. Discuss what you think the people are talking about in 1–7 above.

C Try to remember 1–7 above. Test each other in pairs.
Student A: read out the first sentence in each of 1–7.
Student B: close your books. Try to ask the questions.

▶ Need help? Read the grammar reference on page 138.

> **We make negative comparisons using *less* or *not as*.**
> A: Let's go by bus. It's *less expensive* than taking the car.
> B: It may be cheaper, but it's *not as quick*.

D Disagree with the statements in 2–5 below by first using a comparative and then using *not as / less*. For example:
1 Let's take a taxi instead of the bus – it's easier with the shopping.
   It may be easier, but it's not as cheap.
2 I prefer wearing jeans to wearing a suit. They're more comfortable.
3 I'd prefer to live in the country. There's less traffic and it's less noisy than the city.
4 I usually go to department stores to buy clothes. They have a wider selection.
5 I do my shopping at the supermarket outside town rather than the local shops. It's less expensive.

SPEAKING

A Work in groups. Think of two examples of each of the following for where you live:

a supermarket	a department store	a bookshop
a clothes shop	an electronics shop	a shoe shop

Then think of two different makes of:
computer	mobile phone	car

B Individually, spend two minutes deciding which one of each of the shops or makes you prefer. Make a list of reasons, using comparatives and your own experiences (using the past simple). For example:
Of the supermarkets, I prefer Fullers. It's a bit more expensive, but the food is better quality. It's fresher and there's a wider selection of things. I don't like Costsave because it's quite dirty. The other day, I went there and there was rubbish on the floor and it was messy.

C In groups, discuss which shops and makes you prefer.

READING

A Look at the headlines below and check you understand the highlighted words. In pairs, discuss what you think the story for each headline is.

> **RUMOURS OF SALE CAUSE SHOP CHAOS**

> RIOTS CAUSE DAMAGE TO CITY CENTRE SHOPS

> SHOPPING CENTRE'S 'HUSBAND PARKING AREA' A BIG SUCCESS

> POLICE STOP TOURISTS' PROTEST ABOUT 'TOO MANY SHOPS'

B Work in groups of four – Pairs A and B.
Pair A: read File 12 on page 158.
Pair B: read File 22 on page 161.
As you read, think about these questions:
a Where did the problem happen?
b Who were the crowd of people?
c Why were they there?
d Why did the arguments start?
e Was anyone hurt or taken to a police station?

C In the same pairs, compare your answers to a–e and decide which headline from exercise A goes with your story.

D Still in the same pairs, discuss any vocabulary you don't understand. Check your ideas in the *Vocabulary Builder*.

E Now work with a partner from the other pair – the pair that read a different story. Close your books and explain what happened in your story. Discuss what you think about each story.

F With your new partner, complete the collocations using the nouns from the two texts.

mixture	temple	discount	rumour
crowd	item	injury	coach

1 a ~ gathered / the ~ turned angry / control the ~
2 a Hindu ~ / visit a ~ / an ancient ~
3 false ~s / believe the ~ / a ~ on the Internet / hear a ~
4 have a bad knee ~ / a minor ~ / be treated for an ~
5 the ~ is locked / travel by ~ / go on a ~ tour
6 expensive ~s / only carry essential ~s / sell luxury ~s
7 have a huge ~ / give a ~ for students / a 20% ~
8 an interesting ~ of styles / a strange ~ / a ~ of Chinese and Portuguese buildings

G Work in groups. Discuss these questions about the vocabulary in exercise F.
- Do you know any places with a mixture of styles?
- Have you heard any rumours recently? What about? Do you believe them?
- What items do you always carry with you?
- Do you know anyone who has a sports injury?
- Have you seen any large crowds recently? Why did they gather?

LISTENING

You are going to listen to a podcast called 'The anti-shopper' which talks about the two stories you read.

A Tell a partner which of the people in the stories you think the podcaster will have more sympathy with. Give reasons for your ideas.

B 🔊 2.3 Listen and find out if you were right.

C In pairs, discuss in what ways you agree or disagree with the podcast.

GRAMMAR Passives

A Look at these two sentences from the texts. Do you know who called the police in each sentence? Which verb is in the passive?
1 Managers at the store called the police to control the crowd.
2 Riot police were called to control a group of angry tourists.

> Sentence 1 is an active sentence. The managers did the action of calling.
> ....
> In sentence 2, the writer doesn't know who called the police, so they use a passive form. The writer makes *police* the subject and uses *be* + the past participle form of the verb. The past participle often has the same form as the past simple, but some verbs are irregular (see VB pages 70–71 for a list).

B Find five more passive forms in texts 1 and 2.

C Choose the correct forms in this article.

Primark [1]*sells / is sold* fashion items very cheaply and, as a result, has become a hugely successful company. It [2]*established / was established* in Ireland in 1969 under the name of Penny's and now the company [3]*operates / is operated* 170 stores in the UK as well as in Europe. Most of Primark's clothes [4]*supplied / are supplied* by factories in countries such as Bangladesh and Indonesia. In 2008, a report [5]*discovered / was discovered* that some factory workers [6]*paid / were paid* just 8 cents an hour. It also found that sometimes children [7]*used / were used* to make the clothes. Afterwards, Primark stopped using the suppliers employing children and better inspections [8]*introduced / were introduced*.

Primark was not the only low-cost chain which [9]*accused / was accused* of exploitation in the report. The company says it pays the same as most of its competitors, but it [10]*charges / is charged* its customer less.

▶ Need help? Read the grammar reference on page 139.

D Work in groups. Discuss these questions.
- Do you know any similar shops to Primark?
- Do you shop at them? Why? / Why not?
- Have you heard or read any similar reports about how clothes are made?
- Do you worry about where things are made or issues like this?

PRONUNCIATION

When we use passives in speech, the verb *be* is usually pronounced as a weak form in the past –/ wəz / and /wə/– or a contraction in the present (I'm / it's, etc.).

A Say these sentences using a weak or contracted form.
1 I am not paid very well.
2 It is sold in most shops.
3 They are supplied by a firm in India.
4 We were charged 100 euros for it.
5 Luckily, no-one was injured.

B 🔊 2.4 Listen and compare what you hear with the way you said the sentences.

SPEAKING

In newspaper headlines, the verb *be* is often left out of the passive construction.
City centre shops damaged in riots
(= Shops in the city centre *were damaged* during a riot.)

A In pairs, explain the following headlines. Discuss what you think each story is probably about.

1 MAN ARRESTED AFTER STEALING 10 KILOS OF BANANAS

2 SHOP PAYS $20,000 TO WOMAN INJURED IN CHANGING ROOMS

3 WOMAN FINED AFTER CALLING AMBULANCE TO HELP HER HOME WITH SHOPPING

B Choose one of the headlines and write a short news report of 60–80 words about it.

03 EAT

SPEAKING

A **Work in groups. Discuss these questions.**
- Look at the different kinds of restaurants in the box below. Which do you have in your town / city?
- Can you describe where each restaurant is?
- Which of the different kinds of food below do you like? Which don't you like? Why?
- Can you cook any of these different kinds of food?

Thai	Indian	fast food	Japanese	Turkish	vegetarian
steak	Mexican	Greek	Italian	seafood	Moroccan

VOCABULARY Restaurants

A **Complete the sentences with the pairs of words.**

busy + seat	money + portions
choice + options	place + do
delicious + disgusting	service + staff
dishes + choose	terrace + view

1 The first time I went there, the food was ...., but I went there again recently and it was .... !
2 It's quite good value for .... It's quite cheap – and you get really big ....
3 The .... is great. The .... are always really friendly and polite.
4 It often gets really .... and you sometimes have to wait to get a ....
5 It's got a good selection of .... There's plenty to .... from.
6 It's OK, but there isn't much .... They don't have any vegetarian ....
7 There's a little Japanese .... near my office and they .... great sushi!
8 It's great. You can sit outside on the .... there and get an incredible .... of the city.

B **Underline** any words and expressions in exercise A that describe two restaurants you know. Then tell a partner as much as you can about each place. For example:
I often go to an Italian restaurant called Luigi's. It's really good value for money. The food is delicious and you get really big portions. They do the best pizzas in town!

LISTENING

You are going to hear two friends deciding where to eat.

A 🔊 3.1 **Listen and take notes on what you hear about each of these places. Then compare your ideas in pairs.**

the Thai restaurant	
the steak restaurant	
Sofra	

B **Can you remember why they talked about these things? Compare your ideas. Listen again to check.**

spicy food	the big department store
red meat	the bus station
dishes	phone

C **Discuss these questions with a partner.**
- Which of the three restaurants do you think sounds best? Why?
- Do you like spicy food?
- Do you eat much red meat?

DEVELOPING CONVERSATIONS
Suggestions

Look at this way of making and responding to suggestions.
A: Where do you want to go?
B: *How about* that Indian place round the corner?
A: *To be honest, I don't really feel like* a curry today.
B: *Well, we could go* to Prego *instead*.

A **Work in pairs. Have similar conversations using these ideas.**
1 sushi bar / Japanese food / Moroccan place
2 pizza place / Italian food / Mexican restaurant
3 McDonald's / fast food / seafood place
4 the cinema / watching a film / a museum
5 one of the galleries / looking at paintings / the park

GRAMMAR The present perfect simple

The present perfect simple is formed using *have / has* + the past participle. It shows something happened before the present at an unspecified time in the past.

We often use it to start conversations about our experiences.
I've seen it, but I've never eaten there.
A: *Have you been* there?
B: No. I've never heard of it. Where is it?

A **Say all three forms of each of the verbs in the box.**

be	bring	go	forget	lose	think
become	choose	have	hear	read	try
break	eat	find	leave	see	win

B **Complete the sentences using the present perfect form of the verbs in brackets.**
1 A: .... you ever .... on a diet that actually worked? (be)
   B: No. I .... lots, but I usually put on weight again once I stop them! (try)
2 A: .... you ever .... anything unusual? (eat)
   B: Yeah, I .... camel meat a few times and I had bat soup last year in the Philippines. (have)
3 A: .... you ever .... to a really expensive restaurant? (go)
   B: Yes, I have, but luckily my boss paid!
4 A: .... you ever .... a hair in your food? (find)
   B: No, never, but I once found a piece of glass in a burger. I couldn't believe it!
5 A: .... you ever .... in a restaurant? (complain)
   B: Yeah, a few times, actually. Last week I complained in a café because the food wasn't cooked properly.
6 A: .... you ever .... any of Gordon Ramsay's recipes? (try)
   B: No, I .... never .... of him. (hear)

C **Which tense does B use in answers 4 and 5? Why?**

▶ **Need help? Read the grammar reference on page 140.**

D **Ask a partner the six questions in exercise B – and give true answers. Then write five more *Have you ever ...?* questions to ask some other students.**

CONVERSATION PRACTICE

A **Think of three places you like eating in – and why they are good places to go to.**

B **Work in pairs. Have a conversation similar to the one in *Listening*. Start by asking *Are you hungry?* Reject at least one of your partner's ideas and explain why.**

SPEAKING

A **Work in groups. Discuss these questions.**
- What's the most important meal of the day for you – breakfast, lunch or dinner? Why?
- Where do you usually have each meal?
- What do you usually have?
- Do you eat anything between meals? What?

READING

You are going to read a text about breakfast in different countries.

A **Label the pictures with the words in the box.**

grilled fish	flat bread	honey
boiled egg	yoghurt	onion
fried egg	olives	toast

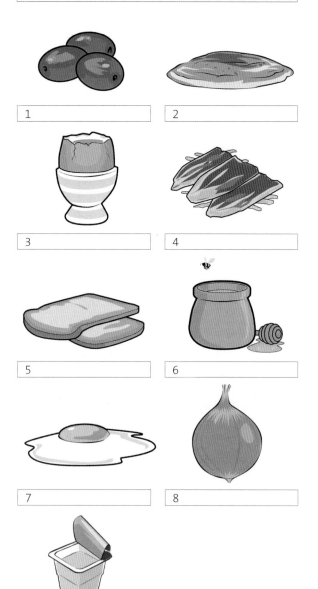

1	2

3	4

5	6

7	8

9	

B **Work in pairs. Discuss these questions.**
- Have you had any of the foods in the pictures recently? When? What with?
- Are there any things in the pictures that you've never tried?
- In which countries do you think these foods might be popular for breakfast?

C **Read the text and answer these questions.**
1. In which countries are the 12 foods from exercise A popular for breakfast?
2. What else do people often have for breakfast in each country?
3. Which breakfasts do you think sound: healthy? fattening? filling? spicy?
4. What are each of the things below?

kimchi	*kiselo mlyako*
gallo pinto	*plantain*
agua dulce	*foul medammes*

D **Work in pairs. Discuss these questions.**
- Which of the five breakfasts would you most / least like to have? Why?
- Do any of the breakfasts contain anything you can't eat? Why can't you eat them?
- Have you ever had breakfast abroad? What was it like?

GRAMMAR *too / not ... enough*

> Use *too* + adjective / adverb to explain why you don't like something or to talk about problems. Use *not* + adjective / adverb + *enough* when you need more.
>
> Most people are *too conservative* to change their eating habits. We *aren't* usually *adventurous enough* to experiment.

A **Complete the sentences using *too* or *not ... enough* and the adjectives in the box.**

big	cooked	expensive	fattening	good	hot

1 It's .... to eat at the moment. It needs to cool down.
2 The food there is nice, but the portions are .... I'm usually still hungry at the end of the meal.
3 It's a nice place, but the service is .... They take too long to bring you your food.
4 It's an amazing restaurant, but it's .... for me to eat there very often.
5 I love chocolate, but it's .... to eat very often.
6 Some of the food was OK, but my steak was .... I wanted it well-done, but they served it medium-rare!

B **Use *too / not ... enough* to discuss problems you might have with the things below. For example:**
a dessert: It's too sweet – and it's too fattening!

a drink	a dessert	a hotel	a movie
a car	an English course	a jacket	a room

▶ **Need help? Read the grammar reference on page 141.**

Need help? Read the grammar reference on page 141.

NATIVE SPEAKER ENGLISH

Grab
If you grab food or drink, you have it quickly.

Plenty of Koreans just grab a quick coffee and some cereal.
Let's grab a quick drink after class.
Do you want to grab something to eat before the meeting?
Give me two minutes. I just need to grab a sandwich.

Breakfast around the world

They say breakfast is the most important meal of the day. Maybe that's why most people don't like to change their morning eating habits. While we may be open to foreign food at lunch or dinner, at breakfast we are people of habit and we aren't usually adventurous enough to experiment. Below, we look at typical breakfasts in five different countries. Would you try any of them?

South Korea
Obviously, city life and busy lifestyles mean plenty of Koreans just grab a quick coffee and some cereal or toast, but many others still find time for the traditional breakfast of rice and soup. People then choose extra dishes such as grilled fish, vegetables and *kimchi*, which is pickled cabbage with chillies. The dish is so popular that the first Korean astronaut took special *kimchi* with him to his space station!

Costa Rica
Many Costa Ricans start their day with the national dish, *gallo pinto*, which is a mixture of fried rice and black beans. It's lightly spiced and often served with fried plantain (a kind of banana used like a vegetable in a lot of Central American and Caribbean cooking), cream and fried eggs. There's usually some strong local coffee as well – or perhaps some *agua dulce* ('sweet water'), which is made from sugar cane juice.

Egypt
Visit any town in Egypt in the morning and you'll find street stalls selling *foul medammes* – broad beans cooked with tomatoes and onions – and eaten with a boiled egg on top and lots of flat bread. Pickled vegetables are usually served as a side dish. For many poorer Egyptians, this is the main meal until dinner. They say the dish is 'a rock in the stomach'.

Bulgaria
Breakfast in Bulgaria includes tea or strong coffee, sesame bread and butter, cheese made from sheep's milk, honey, olives, boiled eggs and – most importantly – *kiselo mlyako*, a local yoghurt. Bulgaria has a lot of people aged over 100 and many believe that the secret behind this is their yoghurt, which most Bulgarians eat every day.

Ireland
The traditional Irish breakfast is called a fry and is not good for vegetarians! It consists of bacon, black pudding (a kind of sausage made with blood), white pudding (another kind of sausage), fried eggs, fried mushrooms and toast – all accompanied by strong Irish tea!

SPEAKING

A Discuss these questions in groups.

- How often do you eat out?
- Who do you usually go out for meals with?
- Do you generally order the same thing – or do you like trying different things?
- Who usually pays when you go out for a meal?
- Have you ever had any problems in restaurants? What happened?

VOCABULARY Describing food

A Put the words in the box into the correct list.

roasted	fruit	skin	thick	soft
seafood	shell	raw	bitter	herb
grilled	mild	sauce	stone	salty

kind of food	part of body / vegetable	taste and texture	how cooked / eaten
meat	leg	strong	fried
fish	seed	sweet	boiled
vegetable		hard	

B Match the descriptions to the pictures below.

1 They're a kind of seafood. They're quite big and white, not very soft, with a mild taste – not very salty. They're usually fried or grilled in the shell. They have a big shell – almost the size of my hand.

2 It's a kind of fruit. It's green. It has a very thick skin, which you don't eat, and a very big stone in the middle. The inside is green and it's neither sweet nor salty and you usually eat it in a salad, or you sometimes make a kind of sauce with it.

C In pairs, take turns describing four different foods for your partner to guess.

kiwi fruit

avocado

scallops

oyster

clams

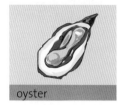
mango

courgette

aubergine

LISTENING

You are going to hear some people who are eating out in The Globe Restaurant.

A First, read the restaurant menu below. Put a tick ✓ next to the dishes that look good to you, a cross ✗ next to any dishes that don't look good and a question mark ? next to any dishes you don't understand.

B Compare your ideas in groups.

- Try and explain some of the dishes to the others.
- What would you order in this restaurant? Why?

The Globe Restaurant

Starters
Grilled squid
Country stew
Soup of the day
Crab cakes with Spanish ham and apples
Six oysters
Mushrooms with garlic
Tomato and avocado salad

Main courses
Fried chicken with potatoes (roasted, boiled or fried)
Aubergines stuffed with rice
Spaghetti with tomato and clams
Spicy scallops with noodles
Leg of lamb with vegetables
Lamb curry
Steak and chips
Courgette and potato pie with Greek cheese

Desserts
Chocolate pudding with chocolate sauce
Fruit salad
Home-made strawberry and vanilla ice-cream
Carrot cake (with cream)
Plate of cheese (with biscuits)

Drinks
Soft drinks (lemonade, orange juice, cola, etc.)
House wine (red or white)
Beer

C Below are ten questions asked in the restaurant. Put them into the order you think you will hear them in.

1 Could I just have a coffee, please?
2 Would you like to see the dessert menu?
3 Does it contain any meat at all?
4 Shall we leave a tip?
5 Could we get some water as well, please?
6 Are you ready to order?
7 Have you booked?
8 Would you like a high chair for the little girl?
9 Could we have the bill, please?
10 Could you get us a cloth, please?

D Compare your ideas with a partner. Who do you think would ask each one – a waiter / waitress or a customer?

E 🔊 3.2 Now listen to six short conversations. Put the ten questions from exercise C into the order you hear them in.

F Can you remember the answers to any of the ten questions? Discuss your ideas and then listen again to check.

LANGUAGE PATTERNS

Write the sentences in your language. Translate them back into English. Compare your English to the original.
Do you mind waiting?
Do you mind sharing a table?
We don't mind sitting in the smoking area if we have to.
I don't mind where we go.
I don't mind if you want to try somewhere else.

GRAMMAR Offers, requests, permission, suggestions

would, could and shall
We use *would*, *could* and *shall* to add meaning to other verbs. *Would*, *could* and *shall* are often used when you want to do things. For example:
Make polite offers (instead of 'Do you want ...?')
Would you like to see the menu?

Make polite requests (instead of imperatives)
Could you get us a cloth, please?

Ask for permission (instead of 'Is it OK if I...?')
Could I / we change the baby somewhere?

Make suggestions (instead of 'How about -ing...?')
Shall we leave a tip?

A Complete the questions with *would / could / shall*

1 A: .... we just have a jug of tap water please?
   B: I'm afraid not, madam. You have to buy a bottle.
2 A: .... we get the bill?
   B: Yeah, it's getting late and I'm tired.
3 A: .... we have a half portion for the kids?
   B: Of course, sir.
4 A: .... you like to see the drinks list, madam?
   B: No thanks. .... we just have two mineral waters?
5 A: .... we ring them and book a table?
   B: That's a good idea. They get quite busy.
6 A: .... you move your chair a little so I can get past?
   B: I'll get up. It's very tight in here.
7 A: .... you like me to order for everyone?
   B: Yes, if you don't mind. There's so much to choose from.
8 A: .... we get a taxi or do you want to walk?
   B: Let's walk – it's a lovely night. It's so warm.

B In pairs, take turns saying questions 1–8. Your partner should give different replies to the ones above.

C In groups, think of three suitable offers / requests / suggestions for each restaurant situation below.

1 The menu is in a language you don't speak.
2 You're allergic to tomatoes.
3 You've left your wallet at home.
4 The woman sitting behind you is smoking.
5 You've all finished your main courses.

▶ Need help? Read the grammar reference on page 141.

SPEAKING

You are going to role-play a conversation in The Globe Restaurant.

A Work in pairs.
Student A: you are the waiter / waitress. Read File 2 on page 156.
Student B: you are a customer. Read File 16 on page 159.

B Spend five minutes planning what you are going to say. Use as much language from these pages as possible. Then role-play the conversation.

04 JOBS

VOCABULARY Talking about jobs

A Look at the pictures in File 21 on page 161. Then discuss these questions in pairs:
- Do you know anyone who does any of these jobs?
- Which of the jobs would you like to do? Why? / Why not?
- Are there any jobs you could never do? Why?

B Match a–f with the words in **bold**.
1 **I work in** Accident and Emergency in a local hospital.
2 **I work** late most nights.
3 **I work for** Henning and Schmidt. It's a big law firm.
4 **I'm working on** a project for my class.
5 **I'm doing** work experience in a school at the moment.
6 **I run** my own business.

a a new product / a new film / developing social policy
b a local paper / an airline / myself / Google
c a primary school / sales / the marketing department
d night shifts / hard / very long hours
e the accounts / some research / a training course / repairs
f a hotel / a restaurant / my own studio / the sales team

C Work in pairs.
Student A: choose one of the jobs on page 161. Then say one of the collocations from exercise B.
Student B: guess the job.
Student A: If B is wrong, say another collocation.

For example:
A: I work for a local paper.
B: Journalist.
A: No. I run my own studio.
B: Photographer.
A: That's right.

D In which of the jobs might you do the following?

negotiate a price	sort out a problem
make appointments	fight for someone's rights
arrest someone	install a computer system

DEVELOPING CONVERSATIONS
Questions about jobs

> We can use some questions to ask about lots of different jobs. We often add *so* to the start of questions or *then* to the end. This shows we are continuing the conversation.

A Match the questions 1–6 to the answers a–g.
1 What do you do?
2 Where do you work?
3 So how long have you worked there?
4 So do you enjoy it?
5 What're the hours like, then?
6 Do you get on with the people you work with?

a Yeah, it's good. It has its boring moments – like any job – and we have to do too much paperwork, but basically it's fine.
b A couple of years. I joined after I finished university.
c I'm a policeman.
e In the local police department in Lyon.
f Yes, they're nice. We often go out together after work.
g Not brilliant. I work shifts, so it's hard for my family. It makes family life difficult.

B Spend two minutes memorising the questions in exercise A. Then close your books. In pairs, see if you can remember all six questions.

C Work in pairs. Take turns saying the six questions. Give different answers to the answers above.

LISTENING

You are going to hear two people talking about work.

A 🔊 4.1 Which questions from *Developing conversations* do they ask in each conversation?

B Can you remember the answers to the questions? Compare your ideas in pairs. Listen again to check.

C Work in groups. Discuss these questions:
- Who do you think has the better job? Why?
- Could you work with people in your family? Why? / Why not?
- Do you know anyone who has moved or travels a lot because of their job? What do they do? Are they happy?

NATIVE SPEAKER ENGLISH

money
We often use *money* to mean the salary or payment for a job.

I don't really mind the travelling and the money's good.
The money's awful! She only gets 6 euros an hour.
It's difficult to survive on that money.
A: What's the money like in that job?
B: Really good. He earns over 60,000 a year!

" WORK? ... ON MY SALARY? "

GRAMMAR
Present continuous and present simple

Use the present continuous when you see an action as temporary or unfinished. It is often used with *at the moment*.
I'm actually working in Scotland *at the moment.*
They're building a new stadium. *I'm working on* that.
What *are you studying*?

Use the present simple when you feel that the verb describes something that is generally true, a habit or permanent state. It is often used with adverbs such as *generally, normally, often, sometimes, never*, etc.
Where *do you live*, then?
I *usually come down* to London every two weeks.

A Choose the correct form.
1 A: *What do you do? / What are you doing?*
   B: I work for an airline.
2 A: *How does your job go? / How's your job going?*
   B: Fine, but we're very busy. *We work / We're working* on a new project at the moment.
3 The business *does / is doing* well at the moment. I hope *it is continuing / it continues*.
4 I'm unemployed at the moment. *I'm looking / I look* for a job, but it's difficult.
5 I usually work in Padstow, but *I do / I'm doing* a training course in Hendon at the moment.
6 A: What time *do you start / are you starting* work?
   B: Eight – and my office is on the other side of town, so *I usually leave / I'm usually leaving* the house around seven and *am getting / get up* around six.

▶ Need help? Read the grammar reference on page 142.

B Work in groups. Discuss 1–3 below. Use the present continuous and present simple.
1 Explain two or three things that are different to your normal habits at the moment.
2 What are you working on at the moment – at school or in your job? Is it interesting?
3 Do you know of any construction work that's happening where you live?

CONVERSATION PRACTICE

You are going to have conversations like the ones you heard in *Listening*.

A Either think about your own job or occupation or choose your parents' job or one from the list on page 161. Spend two minutes planning how to answer the questions from *Developing conversations*. Include at least one example of the present continuous in your answers. Then have conversations with some other students. Start like this:
So what do you do? You haven't told me ...

LISTENING

You are going to hear three people talk about unpaid work that they do.

A In pairs, make a list of all the different kinds of work people do for no money.

B Compare your list with another pair. Then discuss these questions in groups.
- Why do you think people do these different kinds of work?
- Do you know anyone who does / has done any unpaid work?
- Do you think people should be paid to do any of these different kinds of work? Why? / Why not?

C ♺ 4.2 Listen and answer the questions below.
1 What kind of work does each person do?
2 Why do they do this work?
3 How do they feel about working for no money?
4 What are their plans for the future?

D Work in pairs. Can you remember which of the three speakers said each of the things below – and why?
1 going on strike
2 it's a competitive area
3 got bored
4 pay us a pension
5 have a really positive attitude
6 making coffee
7 building the nation
8 my contract ends
9 the company is exploiting me

E Listen again to check your ideas.

LANGUAGE PATTERNS

Write the sentences in your language. Translate them back into English. Compare your English to the original.

I worked as a doctor in a small town in Switzerland.
I'm working part-time as a waitress in a café in town.
She works as a marketing consultant in the fashion industry.
I'd like to work as a journalist, if possible.

SPEAKING

A Work in groups. Discuss these questions.
- Do you agree that companies which don't pay young workers are exploiting them? Why? / Why not?
- Is voluntary work common in your country? What kind is most common?
- Do you know anyone who has ever done voluntary work? Would you like to? If yes, what kind?
- Do you think the government should pay housewives for their role in building a nation? Why? / Why not?

VOCABULARY Activities at work

In *Listening*, all three speakers talked about what they are doing or working on at the moment.
I'm helping to advertise a German film.
I'm advising local doctors how to improve services.
We're fighting for the rights of housewives in Kerala.

A Complete the sentences with the present continuous form of the verbs in the box.

advise	do	negotiate	organise	teach

1 I .... currently .... the government how to improve health care.
2 This week I .... some training with the new people. I .... them how to sell over the phone.
3 I .... a big party for a car company. They're going to launch a new car soon.
4 We .... a big deal with a Chinese producer.

attend	do	install	learn	work on

5 I .... some research on why people forget things.
6 I .... a new collection of dresses for Milan fashion week.
7 I .... a new security system in a big office in town.
8 I .... a training course this week. We .... how to arrest angry or aggressive people.

B Work in pairs. Discuss these questions.
- Have you ever negotiated anything? What? Who with?
- Have you ever attended a training course? What did you learn?
- Have you ever done any training? What did you teach people to do?
- Have you ever organised anything big? What? Was it OK?
- Do you know anyone who does research? What on?

GRAMMAR Plans and wishes for the future

Use *be going to* + verb to talk about personal plans / intentions for the future – things that you have already decided to do.
I'm going to start looking for another job soon!

Use *would like to* + verb or *be hoping to* + verb to talk about things that you want to do – or want to happen – in the future.
I'd like to work here full-time, but not for nothing!
We're hoping to make the government pay us a fixed salary.

Use *be planning to* + verb when you have already thought carefully about something in the future – and have a plan.
I'm planning to stay here for another year, if I can.

Use *be thinking of* + *–ing* to talk about possible future plans that are not yet certain or decided.
We're thinking of stopping work and going on strike.

A Correct the mistakes in the sentences below.
1 I'm hoping become a photographer.
2 My parents going to give me a job.
3 I like to run my own business when I am older.
4 I'm thinking to negotiate a new contract.
5 I'm planning apply for a new job next year.
6 I don't would like to work for myself.

▶ **Need help? Read the grammar reference on page 142.**

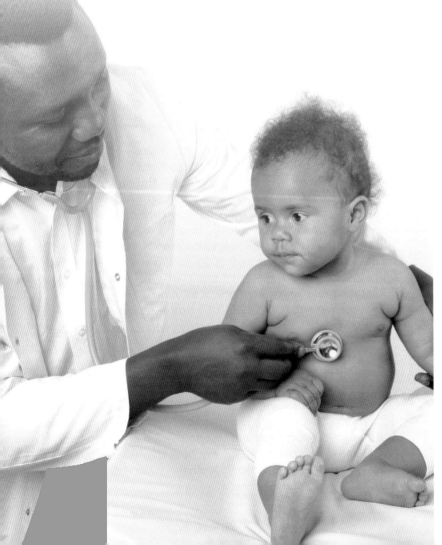

B Complete the sentences below using your own ideas. Then work with a partner and compare what you have written.
1 I'm studying Art at the moment. I'm hoping
....
2 I'm really interested in computers. I'm thinking ....
3 I'm very good with animals, so I'd like .... sometime in the future.
4 I've asked my boss for more money. If he says no, I'm going ....
5 It's hard to find work at the moment, so I'm planning ....
6 I'm thinking of doing an evening course to learn Spanish because I'd like ....
7 We're going to launch our new website soon. To celebrate, we're planning
....
8 My dad is 58 next year. He's thinking
....

C Spend three minutes thinking about the following. Then discuss your ideas in groups.
• Say three things that people in your family are planning to do.
• Say two things connected to your work / studies that you are hoping to do sometime soon.
• Say one thing you've decided you're NOT going to do any more in the future. Explain why.
• Say two things you're thinking of doing in the next few days.
• Say three things you'd like to do – or that you'd like to happen – sometime in the future.

PRONUNCIATION *Going to*

In normal speech, *going to* is usually pronounced /ɡəʊɪŋtə/. However, when people speak quickly, they often say /ɡʌnə/. However, we do not write *gonna* except in very informal text messages, emails, etc.

A 🔊 4.3 Listen and write down the six sentences. The sentences will be said in two different ways – the first time will be faster.

B Compare your sentences with a partner.

C Listen again to check your ideas. Then discuss:
• which way is easier for you to understand.
• which way is easier for you to say.

D Work with a partner. Practise saying each sentence whichever way is best for you.

SPEAKING

A Work in pairs. Look at the ideas about working in an office. Discuss whether you agree with each one. Explain why.

- It's nice because you can chat. You're never alone.
- It's not very efficient. It's hard to concentrate.
- Work's better because more people contribute their ideas.
- There's a lot of politics in an office.
- You just look at a computer or do photocopying all day.
- You don't need to wear a suit or smart clothes every day.
- It's best to work from home and communicate by email.

READING

You are going to read an extract from a romantic comedy called *An Office and a Gentleman* by Annabella Stephens.

A Read the extract and decide who the people in the pictures are. Explain your ideas to a partner.

B Work in pairs. Discuss these questions.
- Why is Marian an enemy?
- Why is the boss angry with Annie?
- What problem does she have at the end of the email?

C Find the verbs which go with the nouns in **bold**. Can you think of one more verb that goes with each noun? Compare your ideas with the *Vocabulary Builder*.

D Discuss these questions in groups.
- What do you think is going to happen in the book?
- Do you like Annie? Why? / Why not?
- Would you read the rest of the book? Why? / Why not?
- Do the characters remind you of anyone you know?

Glossary

lol is short for laugh out loud. It's often used in texts / emails.

a shredder is a machine you use to destroy documents. It cuts them up into little pieces.

Hey Sandra,

The latest news from the office:

You're still not here, of course – very empty desk next to mine. ☺

Really hope you get better soon. I'm missing having someone to chat to.

Marian is still enemy number one. Awful – more later. 😠

Today's fashion from Jilly: a huge, loose pink jersey which is big enough to camp in! Then, tight brown jeans with grey boots. Strange flower thing in her hair. 😶

Rick spoke today: 😯 his first words so far this year, I think, apart from the usual sighs and nervous laughter while he does things to his computer. The words were 'coffee's rubbish'. I'm not sure whether this was a comment on the coffee I was making or general health advice. Anyway, I think you'll agree, it shows his communication **skills** are improving!!!

Ugly Boss: He's still useless and ugly – obviously. The hair from his nose is now about 3cm long. 😯 He's also angry with me – more later.

Harry really is very attractive, but my hopes of finding love with him are disappearing fast. We were in a meeting together – Marian was presenting some **figures** for her marketing proposal. It was all very efficient and very boring as always and I was just thinking how Harry looked very smart – he was wearing a really nice new suit – when suddenly Ugly Boss asked me something. In fact, it's possible he asked me something two or three times. He certainly was quite angry and BOTH Marian and Harry looked happy about it. I stayed late to try and look a bit more serious – and found this great website. Check out this **link** – so cute! lol. https://www.funnies.com/work#_officedogs1110/gh6_85rt

I was leaving when I saw Ugly Boss standing next to the shredder. He looked very stressed and I saw a chance to impress him. I asked if there was anything I could do. 'I can't see how this works,' he said. 'No problem,' I replied as I took his papers. 'You just put them in here and press this **button** and there you go.' 'Excellent,' he said. 'Could you do two copies for me? I need one for my boss and one for the client.' 😯 I said I'd leave them on his **desk**! What am I going to do?!

Annie

VOCABULARY Forming words

The most common way to make verbs from nouns in English is to do nothing! *Sigh*, *comment*, *hope*, *link* and *copy* are all used as nouns in the extract, but can also be verbs. Many nouns are formed from a verb + *–ion* (*–tion* / *–ation*) or from a verb + *–ment*. For example: communica*tion*, improve*ment*.

A Which of these verbs are also nouns?

interview	plan	propose	repair
experience	produce	organise	arrest
research	negotiate	return	offer

B Write the verb form of each of the underlined nouns.

1 make a good <u>impression</u>   try to .... her
2 do a <u>presentation</u>   .... a proposal
3 stop <u>exploitation</u>   .... workers
4 make a big <u>contribution</u>   .... $1 million
5 have good <u>management</u>   .... a company
6 see a job <u>advertisement</u>   .... on TV
7 fill in an <u>application</u> form   .... for a job

GRAMMAR
The past continuous and past simple

We use the past continuous to show an activity was unfinished when another thing happened in the past.
I met Harry when *I was working* for a public relations company.

past	now
I met Harry	job at publisher

A Match this sentence from the extract to one of the pictures below. Explain your choice to a partner.

Rick spoke today ... the words were 'coffee's rubbish. I'm not sure whether this was a comment on the coffee I was making.

B When Annie's boss asked her a question in the meeting, which three activities were unfinished? Look again to check.

1 Marian ....
2 Annie ....
3 Harry ....

C Complete the sentences by putting the verbs in brackets into the past simple or past continuous.

1 We first met when we .... at Microsoft, and then we stayed friends after I left. (work)
2 What .... yesterday? I phoned you and sent you three emails, but you never replied. (you / do)
3 I met Julia Roberts once. I was doing work experience in a TV company and she .... to the studios one day. (come)
4 Maybe he .... very well when he wrote the email, because it was full of mistakes. (not feel)
5 I .... with my friend about our boss when he suddenly .... in. I hope he didn't hear what we were saying! (talk, walk)
6 The interview was awful. They asked me lots of difficult questions and I .... what to say. (not know)
7 I heard she .... because she was trying to send a text to her boss while she .... (crash, drive)
8 Oops! Sorry. I .... where I .... I'll pick up your papers for you. (not look, go)

▶ Need help? Read the grammar reference on page 143.

SPEAKING

A Choose ONE of the experiences below and write a short story explaining what happened – and when.

- a mistake that you made
- a famous person you met / saw once
- the first time you met a special person in your life
- a funny thing that happened at work or school

B Now tell your story to other people in your class.

LEARNER TRAINING

Vocabulary is key to developing your English, especially when you learn groups of words (collocations). Most words in *Outcomes Pre-Intermediate* are among the 3000 most common in English, so they will help you understand what you read and hear. The *Vocabulary Builder* (VB) helps you learn important words and see how they are used. To remember this language:

- read the words for the unit in the VB before class.
- after class, revise new words and the section in the VB.
- remember the collocations in the VB by doing this: look at the collocations; say the collocations; cover the list; write the collocations down; check against the list.

- use the workbook, the exercises in the VB and the review units to test yourself. They all revise key words.
- if you find some words difficult, revise them more often.
- make efforts to use the language you learn in class.
- write sentences about your life with new words.

GAME

Work in pairs. Student A use *only* the green squares; student B use *only* the yellow squares. Spend five minutes looking at your questions and revising the answers. Then take turns tossing a coin: heads = move one of your squares; tails = move two of your squares. When you land on a square, your partner looks at the relevant page in the book to check your answers, but *you don't*. If you are right, move forward one space (but don't answer the question until your next turn). If you aren't right, your partner tells you the right answer, and you miss a go. When you've finished the game, change colours and play again.

Start	**1** *Grammar* p. 9: ask six of the questions in exercise A. Use three different tenses.	**2** *Grammar* p. 11: say six habits you or people in your family have. Use a different adverb / expression of frequency each time.	**3** *Native Speaker English* p. 12: if you can say what the *Native Speaker English* note was and give an example, throw again.	**4** *Vocabulary* p. 13: yo partner will say a–h should say the corre adjective from 1–8. may need to say *no not tidy*)
5 *Vocabulary* p. 14: say eight words from exercise C to describe shops or things you buy.	**6** *Native Speaker English* p. 14: if you can say what the *Native Speaker English* note was and give an example, throw again.	**7 Miss a go!**	**8** *Developing conversations* p. 15: give four different compliments to your partner and ask a question after each one.	**9** *Grammar* p. 17: you partner reads out th first sentences in 1– exercise A. You ask *Have you got ...* + a comparative.
10 *Grammar* p. 21: ask your partner six different *Have you ever...?* questions.	**11** *Native Speaker English* p. 23: if you can say what the *Native Speaker English* note was and give an example, throw again.	**12** *Vocabulary* p. 24: say 12 of the words in the table that you use to describe food.	**13** *Grammar* p. 25: say six questions you'd ask in a restaurant. Use *would, could* and *shall* twice each.	**14 Miss a go**
15 *Developing conversations* p. 26: ask your partner the six questions about jobs.	**16** *Native Speaker English* p. 26: if you can say what the *Native Speaker English* note was and give an example, throw again.	**17** *Vocabulary* p. 28: say eight verbs + nouns to describe activities at work.	**18** *Grammar* p. 29: say four plans you have for the future using four different verbs in the present continuous.	**Finish**

For each of the activities below, work in groups of three. Use the *Vocabulary Builder* if you want to.

CONVERSATION PRACTICE

Choose one of the following *Conversation practice* activities.
Family and friends p. 9
Shops p. 15
Eat p. 21
Jobs p. 27

Two of you should do the task. The third person should listen and then give a mark between 1 and 10 for the performance. Explain your decision. Then change roles.

ACT OR DRAW

One person should act or draw as many of these words as they can in three minutes. Their partners should try to guess the words. Do not speak while you are acting or drawing!

a neighbour	neat	crash	dark
religious	fight	boiled	press
pregnant	wrap	fried	fold
grilled	a skirt	messy	a suit
a crowd	arrest	shout	a top
roasted	lock	a hat	tight

QUIZ

Answer as many of the questions as possible.
1 Who is your **cousin**?
2 How old is a **teenager**?
3 When do you get **grades**? What's a good / bad grade?
4 What might you parents **force** you **to do**? Why?
5 What clothes are often **thick**? Why would you wear them?
6 If your trousers are too **loose**, do you need a bigger or smaller size? What else could you do if clothes are loose?
7 Where do you find **changing rooms**? What are they for?
8 What's the difference between **damage** and **injure**?
9 Which adjective do you use for food that isn't **cooked**?
10 When do you need to let food **cool down**?
11 Say three ways you can have a **steak** done.
12 Say two kinds of **water**.
13 What do you do to **apply for** and get a job?
14 Say three things you could **install**.
15 In what jobs do people often have to **work shifts**?

COLLOCATIONS

Take turns to read out collocation lists from Units 1–4 of the *Vocabulary Builder*. Where there is a '~', say '*blah*' instead. Your partners should guess as many words as they can.

PRONUNCIATION Words containing *a*

The letter *a* can be pronounced in lots of different ways. For example, *gran* is pronounced /græn/, but *grade* is /greɪd/. Learning some phonetic symbols can help you because then you can find the pronunciation in a dictionary.

A ♪ R 1.1 Listen and repeat the sounds and words below.

/æ/	gran	/eə/	share
/eɪ/	grade	/ɔː/	saw
/aː/	dark	/iː/	treat
/ə/	arrest		

B Decide which four words in each of the seven groups have the same sound for the '*a*'.
1 brand / hat / value / terrace / wrap
2 behaviour / debate / creative / establish / steak
3 complicated / argue / aunt / heart / smart
4 active / annoying / pregnant / unreliable / facilities
5 airline / caring / research / repair / wear
6 cause / fault / install / warm / persuade
7 colleague / healthy / disease / steal / neat

C ♪ R 1.2 Listen and check. You will hear the common sound first, then the four words with that sound and finally the word with the different sound.

It's impossible to pronounce a word 'perfectly': native speakers often pronounce words – especially the vowel sounds – slightly differently. It is the reason we hear different accents. For example, many speakers say *staff* as /stæf/ and many others say /staːf/.

When you do exercises like this, don't worry if you don't pronounce words exactly the same as you hear on the audio. However, trying to say words is good, because it helps you remember them as well as being able to hear them better.

D ♪ R 1.3 You are going to hear eight groups of words. Listen and write them down. Then compare what you have written.

LISTENING

A 🔊 R 1.4 **Listen to four people describing different places Match places a–e to speakers 1–4. There is one place you do not need.**
a ...... a department store
b ...... a restaurant
c ...... a supermarket
d ...... an office
e ...... their home

B **Listen again and match items a–e to speakers 1–4. There is one item that you do not need. In the place they talk about:**
a ...... it is it hard to concentrate.
b ...... there are lots of things to choose from.
c ...... they always go there to buy things, eat or work.
d ...... it is good to go in hot weather.
e ...... there's plenty of space to work.

[... / 8]

GRAMMAR

A **Put the verbs in brackets into the correct tense.**
1 I see my cousin quite a lot. He .... to our house after school twice a week, because both my aunt and uncle .... late on those days. (come / work)
2 I usually have a tennis class at the weekends but I .... at the moment, because I'm injured. (not play)
3 You should see the film *The House Keeper*. It's great. I .... it about six times now. (see)
4 .... anywhere last week? (you go)
5 The police arrested him after he .... trying to steal a car. (be caught)
6 I'm sorry, what did he say? I .... (not listen)
7 I can't tell you anything about the class. I .... because I was doing the evening shift at work last week. (not go)
8 A: How long .... married?
B: Ten years this year. (they be)
9 My son .... to go travelling next year after he finishes school. (plan)
10 What .... of doing this weekend? (you think)

[... / 10]

B **Complete the second sentence using the word in bold so that it has a similar meaning to the first one.**
1 I liked both the cameras on sale, but this one was cheaper.
I liked both the cameras on sale, but .... expensive. **not**
2 How about going to that Thai restaurant?
.... to that Thai restaurant? **shall**
3 They both get frustrated quickly and get angry.
.... very calm or patient. **neither**
4 They usually make it with chicken, but this is a vegetarian version.
It .... chicken, but this is a vegetarian version. **is**
5 Do you want to eat any more of anything?
.... any more of anything? **like**
6 He's too young to be out so late.
He .... to be out so late. **old**
7 Would you mind opening the window?
.... the window? **could**
8 My parents, my brothers and I love going to the cinema.
.... in our family love going to the cinema. **us**

[... / 8]

▶ **Find this difficult? Look back at the grammar reference, pages 136–143.**

LANGUAGE PATTERNS

Complete the sentences with one word in each gap.
1 She's an old friend .... university.
2 I crashed my car the .... day and now it's being repaired.
3 I'm sorry. There are no tables available. Do you mind .... for 15 minutes? You can have a drink first.
4 You decide on the restaurant. I don't mind .... we go.
5 I'm working part-time .... a waiter in a café in town.

[... / 5]

PREPOSITIONS

Choose the correct preposition in each sentence.
1 They accused me *to / of* charging them too much, but the bill was right.
2 He paid *to / for* everything. It was very generous of him.
3 The workers went *on / of* strike.
4 The workers were protesting *about / for* their bad income.
5 According *to / of* a recent report, they earn much less than other people who do similar jobs.
6 I belong *to / with* a gym.
7 I'm working *on / in* a new project at the moment.
8 I'm afraid we don't have any coats of that size *on / in* stock.
9 I'm thinking *on / of* changing jobs.

[... / 9]

FORMING WORDS

Complete the sentences with the correct forms of the words in bold.

1 There's not much .... in that shop. **choose**
2 You made a good .... on the boss. **impress**
3 I'm sure .... is genetic. It's not something you learn. **creative**
4 Those cars are quite .... They often have problems. **reliable**
5 My parents .... a lot about silly little things. **argument**
6 He should learn to control his .... **angry**
7 I saw an .... for the job in the paper. **advertise**
8 I don't have the .... to speak in public. **confident**
9 She made a huge .... to the project. **contribute**
10 They're going to give us some .... to show us how to operate the new computer system. **train**

[... / 10]

ADJECTIVES

Match the underlined adjectives in 1–8 to their opposites in a–h.

1 a <u>pretty</u> girl
2 a <u>delicious</u> meal
3 a <u>low</u> proportion
4 <u>complicated</u> software
5 <u>soft</u> fruit
6 a <u>mild</u> taste
7 <u>sweet</u> tea
8 a <u>clever</u> idea

a <u>simple</u> to use
b <u>hard</u> cheese
c a <u>stupid</u> comment
d an <u>ugly</u> building
e taste <u>disgusting</u>
f taste <u>bitter</u>
g a <u>high</u> percentage
h <u>strong</u> cheese

[... / 8]

NOUNS

Match the nouns to the words they go with.

research	behaviour	policy	sauce
sale	repairs	disease	portion

1 do ~ / ~ into cancer / ~ shows it's true
2 good ~ / bad ~ / control kids' ~ / cause criminal ~
3 heart ~ / a genetic ~ / cause ~ / have a ~
4 get big ~s / a small ~ / do kids' ~ / a ~ of rice
5 do ~ / ~ to a building / ~ to a road / be closed for ~
6 have a ~ / buy it in the ~s / reduce prices in the ~s
7 a thick ~ / a delicious ~ / make a ~
8 education ~ / social ~ / develop a ~ / advise the government on ~

[... / 8]

VERBS

Choose the correct verb (a, b or c) below for each gap.

My family ¹...... a chain of 20 clothes shops in the UK. We ²...... over 3,000 people in our chain of shops and we also have a factory in India which ³...... most of our clothes. I think our staff are well-paid. They ⁴...... between £13,000 and £40,000 a year, but some people obviously don't think it's enough. One of our staff was arrested recently for ⁵...... £5,000 from our shop in Birmingham. It makes me angry!

In two years' time, I'll be 65 and I'm going to ⁶...... . I'm sure I'm going to ⁷...... working, but I have plenty of other things I want to do, like play golf and see more of my grandchildren. I'm trying to ⁸...... my son to work for me. I would like him to be the boss, but he doesn't want that. He says he's happy in his job. He's a teacher.

	a		b		c	
1	a belongs		b launches		c runs	
2	a operate		b employ		c offer	
3	a supplies		b charges		c establishes	
4	a earn		b fit		c gather	
5	a stealing		b dropping		c spending	
6	a end		b retire		c return	
7	a miss		b lose		c share	
8	a offer		b present		c persuade	

[... / 8]

▶ **Find this difficult? Re-read units 1–4 in the *Vocabulary Builder* for more information on these words.**

VOCABULARY

Complete the words in the story. The first letters are given.

My sister doesn't like the word 'no'. If she decides she wants something, she keeps on until she ¹suc........................... For example, when she was younger, she wanted a *PlayStation* or something similar. It was expensive and my parents didn't want to buy it. She screamed and ²sh........................... about it, but my parents still said no. They said she could do jobs and earn the money to buy it. She started doing cleaning for my family and for our neighbours. It was funny, because she's not very ³n........................... or tidy herself! It took several months and she finally had enough money. When she went to the shop there was a ⁴s........................... and the *PlayStation* had a 30% ⁵dis..........................., so she also bought two games. You see my sister is a very lucky person as well as being very ⁶det...........................!

[... / 6]

[Total ... /80]

05 RELAX

SPEAKING

A Work in groups. Discuss these questions.
- Are the activities in the pictures relaxing? Why? / Why not?
- Which of the things in the pictures do you do? How often? Which do other people you know do?

VOCABULARY
Activities, places and equipment

A In pairs, complete the table with the words in the box.

Activity	Clothes	Equipment	Place
dance classes	boots	racket	golf course

basketball	fishing	tennis court
bat	running track	golf clubs
trainers	football pitch	pool
shorts	cycling	cards
net	Pilates	walking

B Which words from exercise A could complete each question below? Notice the collocations and grammar.
1 Do you want to **go** .... with me on Sunday?
2 Are you **playing** .... this weekend?
3 Have you ever **done** ....?
4 **Is there a** .... anywhere near here?
5 Do you **have a** .... I could borrow?
6 Do you **have any** .... I could borrow?

C Ask and answer the questions. Give true answers.
A: Do you want to go *fishing* with me on Sunday?
B: I'd love to. Where are you going to go?
or
B: Maybe, but I've never been before.
or
B: No thanks. I don't really like fishing.

LISTENING

You are going to hear a conversation between Corinne and her friend, Maribel, who is visiting her for the weekend. It's Thursday.

A 5.1 Listen and tick ✓ the things they talk about doing.
- relaxing and doing nothing special
- buying a few things
- taking a flight
- watching a sports event
- doing some exercise
- going to a dance class
- going on a trip to the country
- going to a swimming pool

B Work in pairs. Discuss these questions.
- Which three reasons does Maribel give for not agreeing to Corinne's plan for Sunday?
- What reasons does Corinne give for her plan?

C Listen again to check your ideas.

NATIVE SPEAKER ENGLISH

gear
We use *gear* to talk about the special equipment and clothes you need or wear for a particular activity.

I haven't got my swimming gear with me.
We just hired all the gear when we went skiing.
He wears all the latest cycling gear.

SPEAKING

A Work in groups. Discuss these questions.
- Would you go on the Sunday trip if you were Maribel?
- What time do you usually get up at the weekend?
- Do you prefer swimming in a pool or the sea? Why?
- Where's the nicest place you've been walking, running or swimming?

DEVELOPING CONVERSATIONS
Introducing negative comments

> **We often add a short expression before stating things that are negative in some way. For example:**
> ....
> *I must admit*, I'm a bit soft.
> *To be honest*, I'd prefer a park.
> *I have to say*, I hate sport.

A Tell a partner about negative characteristics you have using *I must admit / I have to say / To be honest*. Use some of the adjectives in the box.

messy	soft	bad with money	unreliable
lazy	unfit	a bad loser	conservative

B Use the sentence starters in **bold** to tell a partner six negative things.
I must admit, I hate golf.
I have to say, I can't stand Julia Roberts.
To be honest, I think studying **is a waste of time**.

GRAMMAR *might*, present continuous, *be going to* + verb

A Match two items from 1–6 to each of the following:
a a future arrangement with people
b a definite personal plan for the future
c a possible plan not fully decided

1 <u>Are you playing</u> basketball this weekend?
2 What <u>are you going to do</u> while you're here?
3 <u>I'm going to</u> take it easy.
4 I <u>might</u> go shopping.
5 Some important clients <u>are coming</u>.
6 What time <u>are you thinking of</u> leaving?

▶ **Need help? Read the grammar reference on page 144.**

B Put the words in 1–3 a and b into the correct order to make questions.
1 We're having a picnic on Sunday, if you're interested.
  a else who going is?
  b going are where it to you have?
2 I might go to watch Halifax play on Saturday.
  a are who playing they?
  b of when tickets thinking are you getting the?
3 My friend Jane's going to come and visit.
  a long how she stay going is to?
  b you are while of what doing she's thinking here?

C In pairs, have the conversations in exercise B.

D Change words in 1–6 below so they are true for you. Use *might* if the plan is not fully decided. For example:
I'm meeting some friends for a drink on Friday.
I might meet a friend for lunch tomorrow.

1 I'm meeting a friend for a drink tomorrow.
2 I'm going to the cinema at the weekend.
3 My grandparents are coming round for dinner tonight.
4 I'm going to stay in and study tomorrow night.
5 I'm playing basketball on Thursday.
6 A friend of mine is having a party on Friday night.

E Tell your partner your sentences from exercise D. Your partner should ask questions to find out more.

CONVERSATION PRACTICE

You are going to have similar conversations to the one in *Listening*. Student A is the host; student B is the visitor.

A Before you start, decide where B is visiting and what activity A suggests. Then decide what to say using the chart in File 18 on page 159.

B Role-play the conversation.

VOCABULARY Sports and games verbs

A **Complete 1–8 with the words in the box.**

beats	drew	kicked	scored
support	throw	won	time

1 I once .... a medal in a running race at school.
2 I .... 185 the last time I went bowling. It's my best.
3 A: How fast do you swim 100, then?
   B: I don't usually .... myself, but I guess it'd take me about two minutes. I usually do about 30 lengths in 20 minutes.
4 We .... our last match 1–1.
5 My brother always .... me when we play cards. I'm sure he cheats! How can anyone have that much luck?
6 I was playing football in the street and I .... the ball through my neighbour's window by mistake.
7 Don't .... it to me – I'm terrible at catching.
8 A: Who do you ....?
   B: Slavia Prague. I've got a season ticket, so I go to all their home games.

B **Work in pairs.**
Student A: act or explain the eight verbs from exercise A.
Student B: try to guess the verbs.

C **Work in groups. Discuss these questions.**
- Are you good at sport or any games? Which ones?
- Have you ever won anything?
- How fast can you swim / run / cycle?
- Have you ever had an accident playing sport?
- Do you support any team in any sport?

LISTENING

You are going to hear a short speech discussing why football is so popular.

A **Before you listen, work with a partner. Think of some reasons for football's popularity – and reasons for not liking it.**

B 🔊 5.2 **Listen and see if the speaker mentions the same reasons.**

C **Look at the audioscript on page 166. Tick ✓ the things you agree with. Cross ✗ the things you disagree with. Put a question mark ? next to what you don't understand. Then discuss your ideas with a partner.**

GRAMMAR Superlatives

A **In *Listening*, the speaker said:**
Football is the *most* popular game in the world.
It's the simpl*est* game to play.

Do you know when we use *most* to form superlatives? And when we use –*est* (and –*iest*)? Compare your ideas with a partner.

▶ Need help? Read the grammar reference on page 144.

B **Write the superlatives of the adjectives in brackets in the correct spaces.**
1 .... is .... person I know. (tall)
2 .... person I know is probably .... (fit)
3 .... is probably .... person I know (clever)
4 .... person in my family is .... (relaxed)
5 .... is the .... building in my town. (ugly)
6 .... thing I've ever done is .... (exciting)

C **Complete the sentences in 1–6 above with your own ideas so that they are true for you. Tell a partner your sentences and explain some details about them. For example:**
My brother-in-law, Javier, is the tallest person I know. He's almost 2 metres.

PRONUNCIATION /ɪ/ for weak sounds.

We usually pronounce –*est* as /ɪst/. We also use /ɪ/ in other weak sounds, especially words ending in -*age* such as *advantage* /ædvɑːntɪdʒ/ and *manage* /mænɪdʒ/.

A **Mark the /ɪ/ sounds in these sentences.**
1 These days, people are married on average for 11 and a half years, but the longest marriage lasted 80 years!
2 English must be one of the easiest languages to learn.
3 We wanted to go there because they said it's the nicest place to eat.
4 It's the prettiest village round here, so there's often a shortage of places to stay.

B 🔊 5.3 **Listen and compare your ideas. Then listen again and practise saying the sentences.**

READING

A Read the texts about three different sports and match each one to one of the pictures in a–f.

a

b

c

d

e

f

B Of the three sports,
1. which is the most popular?
2. which is the oldest?
3. which is the newest?
4. which was the most dangerous?
5. which is the most dangerous now?

C Match the words in **bold** in the text with the meanings below. Then check your answers in the *Vocabulary Builder*.
a. how fast you do something
b. the result of something
c. people who watch a sports event
d. try
e. made illegal by the government
f. try to win money by guessing who will win

D Work in groups. Discuss the questions and explain your choices. Which of the sports you read about do you think:
- is the most fun to do?
- is the best to watch?
- needs the most skill to do?
- requires the most fitness?
- needs the most strength?

Although it's doesn't attract big crowds or money, *Pato* is the national sport of Argentina. It was invented in the 17th century and originally involved two teams on horses trying to prevent each other from carrying a duck (*pato* in Spanish) to their farmhouse. The sport was **banned** for a while because of violence – not only to the duck, but also to other players. Some were killed in fights or from being kicked by the horses. The modern game (sometimes also known as Horseball) is a lot safer. Teams of four riders fight for the 'duck' (now a ball with handles) and throw and catch it to try and score in their opponent's net.

Since 1948, Keirin has become one of Japan's biggest **spectator** sports with over 20 million a year attending events. People now **bet** over $15 billion dollars on the **outcome** of the races. Keirin is like horseracing, but with cyclists. Nine competitors ride round a track following a cyclist who sets the **pace** at about 50km/h. He then leaves the track so the riders can race each other for the remaining two laps, reaching speeds of 70km/h. There are often crashes as there is so little space to race in. Riders have to train 15 hours a day in special schools to be able to race and can win millions of dollars.

Bossaball is a new game with a small but growing support. It was invented in Belgium a few years ago. It's played on a special inflatable pitch and is a mixture of volleyball, football, gymnastics and dance. Players bounce up and down and **aim** to pass, kick and head the ball over the net. The rules are a little complicated, but you basically lose a point when the ball touches the floor. The referee is also a DJ who plays Brazilian music as the teams play.

LISTENING

You are going to hear a radio feature about napping.

A Read the dictionary definition of *nap*. Then discuss the questions below with a partner.

> **Nap /naep/ V and N-COUNT**
> If you **nap** – or if you **have a nap** – you sleep for a short period of time, usually during the day.

- Do you know any countries where napping is common?
- Do you ever have a nap? Where? When? For how long?
- Which of the things below do you think are the results of napping? Why?
  - people can go out and enjoy their social lives more
  - people feel happier and more creative
  - people get lazier and lazier
  - people are less productive and do less work
  - people lose concentration and make more mistakes
  - new business opportunities are created
  - people are more likely to have heart attacks

B ⏺ 5.4 **Listen to the radio feature. Decide which of the seven ideas above the speaker says are the actual results of napping.**

LANGUAGE PATTERNS

Write the sentences in your language. Translate them back into English. Compare your English to the original.

More and more people are working longer and longer hours.

I'm spending more and more time at work – and less and less time with my family!

It's getting harder and harder to buy tickets for games.

You get more and more beautiful every year!

C Listen again and complete these notes.

> SPAIN:
>
> People usually work from 9 till [1] ....
>
> They often eat dinner at [2] .... and stay out till as late as [3] ....
>
> Research says naps should last between [4] .... and an hour.
>
> Best time is between [5] .... in the afternoon.
>
> Can increase energy levels / improve your [6] .... and [7] ....
>
> Spanish habits changing. People going to start [8] .... from lack of sleep.
>
> BRITAIN:
>
> National Nap at Work Week campaign
>
> Aims to inform people of [9] ....
>
> BUSINESS OPPORTUNITIES:
>
> Metronaps in NYC create [10] .... for business people to nap in the Ready Bed in Europe is specially designed so you can easily [11] .... and [12] ....

D Compare the notes you took with a partner. Did your partner hear anything you missed?

E Work in pairs. Discuss these questions.
- Do you think 'National Nap at Work' week is a good idea? Why? / Why not?
- Does tiredness ever affect your work? How?
- Do you like either of the business ideas – Metronaps or the Ready Bed? Why? / Why not?
- What percentage of your time is not spent working, studying or sleeping? What do you do during that time?

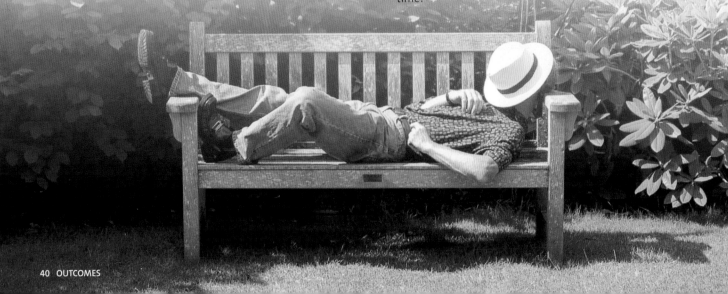

VOCABULARY Word families

> We can make nouns from some adjectives by adding **–ness.**
>
> tired   ➔   tiredness
>
> ....
>
> If the adjective ends in **–y**, remove the **–y** and add **–iness.**
>
> happy   ➔   happiness

A Complete each pair of sentences below by adding either an adjective from the box or a noun based on the adjective.

aware	conscious	fit	homeless
ill	lazy	mad	weak

1 a I don't really like doing exercise. I'm quite
....

   b Having a nap is not a sign of ....

2 a Bossaball has really improved my general
....

   b I try to keep .... by going to the gym twice a week.

3 a I have a real .... for chocolate! I eat too much of it.

   b I can't use my phone here. The signal is too
....

4 a I can't come out with you tonight. I'm too
....

   b More and more people are suffering from mental
....

5 a I think the whole idea is completely ....!

   b The bank lent her £100,000! It's complete
...........................!

6 a A lot of people become .... after losing their jobs.

   b One of the biggest problems in my city is
...........................!

7 a The pain was so bad that I lost ....

   b I was .... during the whole operation.

8 a We're .... of the problem and we're trying to sort it out.

   b The campaign aims to increase .... of the benefits of napping.

B In pairs, think of two other nouns that end in **–ness.** Compare your ideas with another pair. Then write four sentences showing how to use the adjective and noun forms.

C Work in groups. Discuss these questions.
- Do you have a weakness for anything?
- Why do you think people suffer from mental illness?
- Is homelessness a problem in your country? What do you think causes it? How should governments sort it out?

SPEAKING

A Read the Fact File and put an exclamation mark **!** next to any facts that surprise you.

- On average, we sleep 6.9 hours a day – almost an hour less than a few decades ago.
- 33% of adults surveyed would nap at work, if allowed to.
- 24% of adults wake up several times during the night – and find it hard to get back to sleep.
- Sleep problems are now thought to be the biggest health-related problem in many countries.
- Tired workers cost the American economy $150 billion each year.
- 30–40% of traffic accidents are caused by tired drivers.

B In pairs, compare the things that surprised you.

C Check you understand the words and expressions in bold below. Then discuss the questions in groups.
- How many hours a night do you usually sleep?
- What time do you usually **go to bed**?
- And what time do you usually **get up**?
- Do you ever have **trouble** sleeping?
- Have you ever **fallen asleep** in class / on the bus / on a train? What happened?
- What's the latest you've ever been to bed? Why?
- Do you usually remember your dreams?
- Do you ever have **nightmares**? What about?

In this unit, you learn how to:
- explain where you are from
- describe your hometown and area
- ask useful questions when staying with people
- ask for permission to do things

Grammar
- have to, don't have to, canff
- will / won't

Vocabulary
- Cities and areas
- Staying with people

Reading
- Five things you should know before leaving home

Listening
- Where are you from?
- My first place of my own
- Staying with a host family

SPEAKING

A Work in pairs. Discuss these questions.
- How well do you know your country?
- Which places have you visited / lived in?
- Do you have any family or friends in other parts of the country?
- Do you know anyone who has lived abroad? Where did they live? Why?

LISTENING

You are going to hear three conversations about these three places:

Treviso   Muscat   Port Isabel

A Before you listen, discuss with a partner whether you have heard of them – and where you think they might be.

B 🔊 6.1 Listen and find out where each of the places is.

C Listen again and take notes on anything else you find out about the three places. Compare what you heard with a partner.

D Work in pairs. Discuss these questions.
- Which sounds like the best place to live? Why?
- Have you ever experienced a strange coincidence like the one you heard about in the last conversation?

NATIVE SPEAKER ENGLISH

Whereabouts?
We often say whereabouts to ask which part of a country, city, town, etc. something is in.

A: Texas.
B: Whereabouts?
A: I doubt you'll know it.

A: I'm from France.
B: Whereabouts?
A: Paris.

DEVELOPING CONVERSATIONS
Explaining where places are

A Decide which of the places on the map of Germany are described in sentences 1–8.
1 It's a big port in the north-east. It's on the Baltic coast.
2 It's a tiny village in the centre of the country.
3 It's an old city in the north-east.
4 It's a city in the east of the country.
5 It's quite a big city, not far from Berlin.
6 It's a state in the west. It borders France and Luxembourg.
7 It's an industrial area in the west of Germany.
8 It's a town in the south-west of the country.

Rostock

Hamburg

Osnabrück

Berlin

Potsdam

Ruhr

Cologne

Langula

Frankfurt

Chemnitz

Saarland

Freiburg

Munich

B **Work in pairs. Cover 1–8 in exercise A. Use the map of Germany and take turns starting conversations like this:**

A: *Where are you from?*
B: *Germany.*
A: *Really? What part?*
B: *Rostock. Do you know it?*
A: *No, where is it?*
B: *It's a big port in the north-east on the Baltic coast.*

> **When we explain where places are, we also often draw (or pretend to draw) maps and talk at the same time.**
> ....
> *So say that's Venice, Treviso is just here to the north.*
> *So you've got Saudi Arabia here and the UAE up here and Oman goes down here to the right.*

C **Work in groups. Try to explain where the countries and cities below are. Use phrases from exercise A and pretend to draw maps as you explain in more detail.**

Countries	Cities
Slovenia	Beijing / Shanghai
Kazakhstan	New York / Boston
Venezuela	Rio de Janeiro / Brasilia
Vietnam	Paris / Lyon
Mali	Moscow / St Petersburg

D **Check the world map in File 6 on page 157 to see if you were right. Which group in the class knows the most about geography?**

VOCABULARY Cities and areas

A **Decide which word is the odd one out in each of the groups 1–10 and explain your decision.**
1 dry / climate / warm / cold / buildings
2 industrial / a forest / steel / factories / a car plant
3 green / parks / trees / dirty / countryside
4 churches / traffic / transport / pollution / metro
5 village / exciting / cinemas / bars / 24-hour culture
6 agriculture / fields / squares / farms / rural
7 coast / desert / fishing / port / ocean / beach
8 museum / old / historic / city wall / modern
9 crime / lovely / dangerous / murder / steal
10 river / bridge / financial / boat / bank

B **In groups, try to think of places that fit these descriptions. Discuss what you know about each place. Have you ever been to any of the places?**
 • A place on the coast with a warm climate where old people often retire.
 • An industrial city with a big steel factory or car plant.
 • A town or city with a good transport system.
 • A city which is quite dirty but that's surrounded by nice countryside.
 • A very exciting city with a 24-hour culture.
 • A rural area with a lot of farms and agriculture.
 • A town by the sea with a fishing industry.
 • A historic city which has a wall round part of it.
 • A place which is quite dangerous with a lot of crime.
 • A town with a river going through it.

C **Write three more descriptions of places in your country using words from exercise A. Can your partner guess the places?**

CONVERSATION PRACTICE

You're going to have conversations similar to the ones you heard in *Listening.*

A **EITHER choose a country from the world map on page 157 OR think about where you are really from. Then decide how to answer these questions:**
Where are you from?   *Where's that?*
Whereabouts (do you live)?   *Where's that?*
What's it like?

B **Have conversations with other students to find out where they are from and what it's like.**

SPEAKING

A Work in groups. Discuss these questions.
- Do you know anyone who has left home in the last year?
- Look at the pictures below. Do you know anyone who lives / has lived in places like this? When? Why? Do / Did they like it?
- What do you think is good / bad about living in each kind of place?
- Which do you think is the best place to move into when you leave home? Why?

LISTENING

You are going to hear a Chinese man, Guo, talking about leaving home.

A 🌀 6.2 Listen and decide what kind of place he's living in.

B Listen again and take notes on the good / bad things Guo mentions about the place he's living in. Compare what you heard with a partner.

C Can you complete these sentences that Guo said? Compare your ideas with the audioscript on page 167.
1 I .... speak English all the time.
2 I .... share the bathroom and kitchen.
3 I .... do whatever I want.
4 I .... come home late if I want to.
5 I .... be a good big brother and good son here.

LANGUAGE PATTERNS

Write the sentences in your language. Translate them back into English. Compare your English to the original.
I can do whatever I want – whenever I want.
It's a great shop. You can get whatever you want there.
It's your party. You can invite whoever you want.
Sit wherever you want.
Choose whichever one you want.

GRAMMAR *have to, don't have, can*

Use *have to* + verb to talk about things you feel are essential or necessary to do. *Have to* is also used to talk about rules.
I have to share a room with two other students!
Do you have to travel far to work?
I think *she has to pay* about 100 euros a week rent.

Use *don't have to* + verb to talk about things that are NOT necessary, but that you are free to do if you really want to.
You *don't have to tell* me if you don't want to.
He's so lucky! He *doesn't have to work* at all!

Use *can* + verb to show something is possible.
I can always talk to my flatmates if I have a problem.
Can you have friends to stay in your flat?

A Complete the sentences with the correct form of *have to, don't have to* or *can*.
1 My flat's quite close. We .... walk there in ten minutes.
2 Do you .... pay extra for the bills or are they included?
3 I .... pay my parents rent, but I do sometimes give them some money if I have some.
4 My parents are quite liberal. For example, friends .... stay at my house if they want to.
5 She's so lucky! She .... do any housework at all!
6 You .... cook for everyone in the flat, but if you want to sometimes, please do.
7 My parents are quite strict. I .... help with all the cooking and cleaning.
8 I'm close to my sister. I .... talk to her about anything.
9 My grandmother is ill and wants to live with my parents, so they .... find a bigger place.

▶ Need help? Read the grammar reference on page 145.

In normal speech, *have to* is usually pronounced /hæftə/ and *can* is pronounced /kən/.

a bedsit

a shared flat / house

a university hall of residence

staying with relatives

B 🔊 **6.3 Listen and repeat the sentences from exercise A.**

C Make a list of good things and bad things about where you live . Use *have to, don't have to* and *can*. For example:
It's great where I live. *I can play* football in the park.
It's great, because *I don't have to walk* far to school.

D Compare your ideas in groups. Who has the best life? Does anyone know a person outside the group who has a better life? Explain why, using *has to / doesn't have to / can*.

READING

You are going to read an article about things you should know before you leave home.

A What advice do you think the writer might give about the following subjects?
money   food   housework   flat-sharing   loneliness

B Which of the five subjects above do you think each of the words below is connected to? Why?

tools	fill your time	your weight
a pint of milk	argue	iron your clothes
frozen meals	a budget	your own company
a healthy bank balance		

C Read the article and find out which subjects the words connect to. What does the writer say about each thing?

D Work in pairs. Discuss these questions.
- Which piece of advice do you think is best? Why?
- Have you ever had any problems with any of the things mentioned? When? What happened?

FIVE THINGS YOU SHOULD KNOW BEFORE LEAVING HOME

1

MONEY DOESN'T GROW ON TREES

One the most depressing things you learn after leaving home is that everything costs money. You move out with a healthy bank balance, you buy a few bits of furniture and some new jeans and before you know it, the cash machine has eaten your card! Of course, banks will lend you as much money as you want, but remember – you don't have to borrow! Learning to manage a budget may be boring, but it's

2

YOU CANNOT LIVE ON BREAD ALONE

Although you may not miss your parents very much when you first leave home, you can bet you'll miss their cooking! Learning to cook well takes time, so start learning now. If you don't, you'll end up living on frozen meals and takeaway pizzas, and that'll add kilos to your weight and take pounds from your

3

MACHINES ARE YOUR FRIENDS

While you are still living at home, life is easy. You don't have to do the washing, iron your clothes, cook, shop, or fix things. Once you're on your own, though, knowing how to do simple things like setting a washing machine to the correct temperature or using basic tools can make a huge difference to your

4

FLAT-SHARING IS THE EASIEST WAY TO LOSE FRIENDS

Living with your best friends might sound like a really great idea, but trust me – it isn't! You'll argue about everything and nothing. You'll shout at each other about whose turn it is to clean the toilet and about who paid for the last pint of milk and before you know it, you'll be enemies rather

5

LIVING ON YOUR OWN CAN BE LONELY

Living away from home can be incredibly exciting. You can come and go whenever you want; you can eat whatever you want and wear what you want, but spending time on your own can be hard. You may want to fill your time with a social life, meeting people and going to parties, but sooner or later you have to learn how to enjoy your own company. You might just become the best friend you'll ever

VOCABULARY Staying with people

A Complete the sentences with the verbs in the box.

borrow	help	hang	leave	lend
lock	show	sit	take off	use

1 Do you want me to .... my shoes before I come in?
2 Can I .... an umbrella? They said it might rain later.
3 The food looks great! Where do you want me to ....?
4 You can just .... your bag and things in the corner there.
5 You can .... your coat on the back of the door there.
6 Could you .... me an alarm clock for the morning?
7 Make sure you .... the door if you come home late.
8 Let me .... you around the house.
9 Is it OK if I .... the computer while I'm here?
10 .... yourself to something to eat or drink.

B Which five sentences above do you think the guest says – and which five does the host say? Compare your ideas in pairs.

C Work with your partner. Can you think of two more things guests might say at someone's house? And two more things hosts might say?

SPEAKING

A Work in groups. Discuss these questions.

• When was the last time you went to someone's house for dinner? What was the occasion? What did you have?
• When was the last time you stayed at someone's house? How long did you stay? Where did you sleep?
• Which of the things below do you think it's normal to do when you visit – or stay in – someone's house?
  - take off your shoes before you go in
  - bring flowers and/or chocolate for the host(s)
  - bring a bottle of something for the hosts
  - offer to help with the cooking
  - do the washing-up after dinner
  - sleep on the sofa or the floor
  - ask for a spare set of keys
  - offer to pay something to help with food, etc.
• Have you stayed with a host family in another country? Has anyone else you know? Where was it? What was it like?

LISTENING

You are going to hear a student from Uzbekistan arriving at the home of his host family in London.

A ⏺6.4 Listen and take notes on what you learn about the host family and the house rules.

B Listen again and decide if 1–10 are true or false.

1 Maksim hangs his coat on the back of a chair.
2 He asks for a cup of tea.
3 His host family really like the present he's brought.
4 He's going to get a spare key from the family.
5 He has to be home by midnight.
6 Anyone who visits him has to leave before a certain time.
7 He's shocked to hear his host family are vegetarians.
8 He needs to borrow an alarm clock.
9 His host father offers to drive him to school in the morning.
10 He's not allowed to smoke in his room.

C Work in pairs. Discuss these questions.

• Would you like to stay in this house? Why? / Why not
• What is a good present from your country to give a host family?
• Do you know any vegetarians? Do you think they have a good diet? Why? / Why not?

DEVELOPING CONVERSATIONS
Asking for permission

Do you mind if I + verb is one way of asking for permission to do something. It means the same thing as *Is it OK if I* + verb. Look at the positive and negative ways to respond.

A: *Do you mind if I smoke?*
B: *No, of course not. Go ahead. / Well, actually, I'd rather you didn't.*

A: *Is it OK if I smoke?*
B: *Yes, of course. Go ahead. / Well, actually, I'd rather you didn't.*

A Match the questions 1–6 to the responses a–f.

1 Do you mind if I open the window?
2 Do you mind if I use your computer?
3 Do you mind if I borrow your phone for a minute?
4 Is it OK if I leave class early today?
5 Is it OK if I close the window?
6 Is it OK if I stay a few more days?

a No, of course not. It is quite hot, isn't it?
b I'd rather you didn't. My mother is visiting tomorrow, you see.
c No, of course not. One minute. I'll just log off.
d Yes, of course. It is quite cold, isn't it?
e Yes, of course. Just make sure you remember to do your homework.
f Well, actually, I'd rather you didn't. I don't have much credit.

B ⏺6.5 Listen to check your answers. Then practise asking and responding to the questions in exercise A with a partner.

C Work in pairs. Write three questions people might ask when staying in someone else's house. Use *Do you mind if I / Is it OK if I ...?*

GRAMMAR *will / won't*

> Use *will / won't* + verb for immediate responses to things – or to say decisions you make at the same time you're speaking.
> *I'll just go and get some water for you.*
> *I'll just have a quick coffee. I won't stay long.*
>
> ··
>
> To offer to do things for people, we often use *I'll* + verb (instead of *Do you want me to ...?*)
> *I'll help you with the cleaning, if you want / like.*
>
> ··
>
> To promise to do things – or to not do them – use *will / won't.*
> *I'll call you later tonight, OK?*
> *I won't forget, I promise. (= I will not forget)*

A Complete the sentences with '*ll* / won't and a suitable verb.

1 I'm not really sure what I'm doing tonight. I .... probably just .... at home and relax.

2 It's quite hard to explain where it is. I .... you a map, OK?

3 I can't talk now. I'm at work. I .... you later when I'm not as busy.

4 A: Have you got my laptop with you?
    B: I'm really sorry, but I totally forgot. It's still at home. I .... it tomorrow, I promise.

5 The flowers are lovely. Thank you. I .... just .... and put them in some water.

6 It's quite hard to explain how to get there. I .... you on this map. That'll be easier.

7 I'm just going to the shop. I .... out for long.

8 A: It's a secret. You're the only person that knows!
    B: Don't worry. I .... anyone!

▶ **Need help? Read the grammar reference on page 145.**

B Work in pairs. Decide what to say in response to each of the sentences below. Use *I'll* + if you like / want.

1 These bags are really heavy.
2 I'm catching the eight thirty flight tomorrow morning.
3 I don't have any money with me!
4 I'm really thirsty.
5 I'm completely lost. I'm looking for the station.
6 I've left my books upstairs – and I'm in a terrible rush.
7 Are you ready to order?
8 There's someone at the door.

C With the same partner, have three-line conversations using your ideas and the sentences in exercise B. For example:
A: *These bags are really heavy.*
B: *I'll carry one for you, if you want.*
A: *Well, if you don't mind. Thank you. It's very kind of you.*

> In normal speech, we use the weak form of will – *'ll* – when it appears before a verb. It is pronounced /əl/.

D ⏺ 6.6 Listen and repeat the sentences you hear.

SPEAKING

You are going to role-play a conversation between a foreign student and a British host.

A Work in pairs. Make a list of five things the host mother / father should tell the foreign student about the house rules, the area and the town / city.

B Decide which roles you are going to play. The foreign student should ask the three questions from exercise C of *Developing conversations*.

C Read the audioscript for the *Listening* on page 168. Underline any expressions or sentences you want to use.

D Now role-play the conversation. The host father / mother should begin by saying: *Hello there. Come in, come in.*

E When you have finished, change roles and start again.

07 MIND AND BODY

VOCABULARY Illnesses and health problems

A Match the illnesses and health problems in the box to whichever pictures you think each one connects to best.

a headache	hay fever	an upset stomach
the flu	an allergy	asthma
a sore throat	a nosebleed	a temperature

(a) an inhaler

(b) a cat

(c) flowers

(d) a thermometer

(e) some aspirin

(f) honey & lemon

(g) oysters

(h) a bed

(i) toilet paper

B Compare your answers with a partner. Discuss how you think the words in the box are connected to the pictures you chose.

C Work in pairs. Discuss these questions.
- Which of the illnesses / health problems in the box above do you think is the most / least serious? Why?
- Do you know anyone who suffers from hay fever, asthma or an allergy? How does it affect them?
- Can you remember the last time you had any of the other illnesses / health problems in the box?

D Decide whether the words in **bold** are adjectives, verbs or nouns. Then translate them into your language.

1 It happens every spring. It's horrible. My eyes **water** and I **sneeze** all the time.
2 I think it's because of something I ate. I was **sick** three times last night – and I still feel awful today.
3 If I eat any kind of chocolate, I get a horrible red **rash** all over my body.
4 I get out of breath very easily and I **cough** a lot at night.
5 I sometimes just suddenly get them. I don't know why. On bad days, they can **last** for up to 20 minutes!
6 I feel dreadful. I've got a temperature, my whole body **aches**, I've got a horrible cough and I've lost my **appetite**.
7 It hurts when I **swallow** – and I'm losing my voice as well.
8 It was 38 degrees the last time I checked. I feel hot and cold and I'm **sweating** a lot as well.
9 I've had it all morning. I can't **concentrate** on anything. I took some painkillers earlier, but they didn't work.

E Match each of 1–9 above to one of the illnesses / health problems from exercise A.

LISTENING

You are going to hear two conversations. In both, people talk about how they're feeling.

A 🔊 7.1 Listen and answer the questions about each conversation.
1 What problems do they have?
2 What extra information do you hear about the problems?
3 What advice are they given?
4 Do they take the advice?

GRAMMAR Giving advice
(*should, ought to, why don't you*)

> To give advice, we can use *should* + verb, *ought to* + verb or *why don't you* + verb. We use all three structures to say what we think the best thing to do is.
>
> ·······································
>
> *Maybe you should go* home and get some rest.
> *Maybe you ought to try* it.
> *Why don't you get* some sunglasses to protect your eyes a bit?

A **Complete the sentences with ONE word in each space.**

1 What a terrible thing for him to do! You .... leave him!
2 You .... to apologise to her and say you didn't mean it.
3 You .... book well in advance. .... don't you call them and see if they have any left?
4 I don't think we .... leave a tip.
5 It's a big decision. Why .... you think about it for a few days?
6 What .... we do about the car? We really .... to pay someone to look at it sometime soon.
7 Maybe he ought .... move back into his parents' house.
8 A: You .... to complain to your boss.
   B: Yes, I know I ...., but I'm worried I'll lose my job.
   A: If you feel like that, why don't .... just leave?

▶ Need help? Read the grammar reference on page 146.

B **The sentences in exercise A respond to different problems. What do you think the problem is in each situation?**

C **With a partner, decide what advice to give in each of the situations below.**

1 I'm really unfit.
2 I'm really tired. I'm not sleeping well at the moment.
3 I feel quite depressed for some reason.
4 My wrist really hurts.
5 I'm really worried about my exams.
6 My parents don't give me enough money.

DEVELOPING CONVERSATIONS
Common questions about illness

A **Match each of the questions to two possible answers.**

1 Are you OK?
2 Have you been to the doctor's about it?
3 Are you taking anything for it?

a Yes. The doctor gave me some tablets the other day.
b No, not really. I've got a terrible headache.
c No, not yet, but I've got an appointment this afternoon.
d No, not really. I'm just drinking lots of water. That's all.
e Yes, I went yesterday. He just told me to go home and take it easy.
f No, not really. I've got a bit of a cold.

B **Work in pairs. Think of two more possible answers to each of the three questions.**

CONVERSATION PRACTICE

You are going to role-play two conversations similar to those you heard in *Listening*.

A **Choose an illness or health problem. It could be something from *Vocabulary* or something else. Decide how serious it is, what the symptoms are, if you've been to the doctor's or taken anything for it, etc.**

B **Work in pairs. Decide who is going to play the ill person first. The other student should start the conversation by asking: *Are you OK?* Use as much language from these pages as possible.**

C **Change roles and have the second conversation.**

READING

You are going to read an article about mental health.

A Check you understand the words in **bold** in 1–4 below. Look up any words you don't know in the *Vocabulary Builder.*

1 What **mental illnesses** can you think of? Do you know what treatments can be used to deal with these illnesses?
2 Can you think of any diseases that can't be **cured**?
3 Have you heard of anyone who has **recovered** from a very serious disease?
4 Do you know anyone who has been successful after **overcoming** a difficulty such as:
   - being **blind** or having some other **disability**?
   - other people's **negative attitudes**?
   - growing up in a very poor home?

B Work in pairs. Discuss the questions above.

C Now read the first paragraph of the article and discuss with your partner the questions that the writer asks.

At least a quarter of us will suffer from a mental illness sometime during our lives. Some estimates in the United States put that figure at 50% of the population. Do you believe that? Does it sound like too many people?

D Read the second paragraph of the article. Does it change your opinion at all?

Well, now consider this statistic – 99.99% of us will suffer a physical illness sometime during our lives. Does that sound believable to you? Probably. There are very few people who go through life without getting a cold, a sore throat or an upset stomach, even if they don't suffer from something more serious. So why should mental illness be so different?

E Read the rest of the article and decide if these sentences are true or false.

1 Our idea of mental illness is wrong.
2 Many mental illnesses only last a short time.
3 People with serious mental health problems can never go back to work.
4 A lot of mental health problems aren't treated.
5 Men don't show emotions because of nature.
6 There's been no improvement in dealing with mental illness.
7 Better science is all we need to deal with mental illness.

NOT JUST ALL IN THE MIND

The problem is that when we think of mental health problems, we often think of the most serious **cases**: people hearing voices; people seeing things that aren't really there; mad people murdering other people. The reality is that very few mentally ill people are dangerous and a lot of mental problems are quite mild. They are similar to flu: you feel bad for a week or two and then you **recover**. However, in the same way that you may need medical attention to overcome flu, so doctors can help cure mild depression or someone's **anxiety** about eating, for example. In fact, people control or completely recover from many of the more serious mental health problems through drugs, therapy or other support. For example, the mathematician John Nash, whose experiences were shown in the film *A Beautiful Mind,* **overcame**

paranoid schizophrenia and went on to win a Nobel Prize.

Unfortunately, because of negative attitudes towards mental illnesses, many people don't ask for help and when they do, they often get an unwanted **reaction** such as 'Don't be silly!' or 'Cheer up! Don't be so sad.' For men, the problem may be even worse, because society expects them to be less emotional. For example, people say 'boys don't cry' and 'he's a *strong*, silent type.' Showing your emotions means you are seen as weak.

Dealing with mental health problems is always going to be difficult because it's hard to know what's happening in someone's head, but science is making **progress**. In fact, it's becoming clear that many mental illnesses have a physical / chemical cause in the brain and that early treatment is important. What we need to do now is to change our **attitudes**. We can begin by **recognising** that mental illness is a more natural part of life than we think.

F Use the correct form of the words in bold in the article to complete these sentences.

1 He had a bad accident, but luckily .... from his injuries.
2 I was really surprised by his .... when I told him I'd crashed his car. He was very calm!
3 He's got a mild .... of the flu.
4 Medicine has made a lot of .... in dealing with cancer.
5 Until he .... he has a problem, we can't do anything.
6 She's had to .... a lot of difficulties to get where she is.
7 He gets .... attacks every time he has to fly.
8 He said he cured himself just by keeping a positive ....

G Work in groups. Discuss these questions:
- Do you think attitudes towards mental illness should change? Why? / Why not?
- Do you think men are less emotional? Why? / Why not?
- Do you know any famous people who have had a mental illness?
- Have you seen *A Beautiful Mind*? Did you enjoy it?

vercoming mental illness

im Carrey, the Canadian actor, has suffered from epression.
eethoven and **van Gogh** both had manic epression. Some say it contributed to their genius.
he Russian dancer **Nijinski** was schizophrenic.
he actress **Kim Bassinger** suffered for years from anic attacks. 'It can hit at any time. You feel like ou are in an open field, and there's a tornado oming at you.'

VOCABULARY Forming words

> We often form adjectives by adding *–able* to verbs and *–al* to nouns. If a noun ends in 'e', we don't include it in the adjective.
> Does that seem *believable*?
> Society expects men to be less *emotional*.
> Mental illness is a more *natural* part of life than we think.
>
> Note that not all adjectives ending in *–able* or *–al* come from verbs or nouns. The 'ment' of *mental* is not a noun in English!

A Which adjectives in the box come from verbs or nouns?

affordable	comparable	advisable	inevitable
financial	chemical	central	physical

B Complete the sentences using adjectives made from the underlined nouns and verbs.

1 He works in the car <u>industry</u>.
   It's a very .... area. There are lots of factories there.
2 I really <u>enjoy</u> cycling and walking.
   We had a really .... day. It was lovely.
3 I play a lot of <u>music</u>.
   Do you play any kind of .... instrument?
4 I like finding out about different <u>cultures</u>.
   Out school organises a lot of .... events.
5 They've <u>cured</u> him of cancer.
   A lot of mental illnesses are .... now.
6 They don't <u>accept</u> credit cards, so we need to take cash.
   The conditions in the hospital aren't .... It's a dirty place.
7 I <u>rely</u> on my family to support me while I'm studying.
   He's a very .... worker.
8 I only wear a suit on special <u>occasions</u>.
   I get the .... headache, but generally I'm very healthy.

SPEAKING

A In the article you read, it said people – especially men – try not to show emotion in public. Do you agree? Discuss these questions in groups to discover your own attitudes.

1 Do you cry easily? Have you ever cried:
   - while watching a film?
   - when you won or lost a game?
   - when you saw some news on TV or in the paper?
   - because of something someone said to you?
2 What do you do if you're feeling upset?
3 What kind of things make you laugh?
4 Are you good at telling jokes?
5 Do you find this joke funny?

> **Patient:** Doctor, my wife thinks I'm mad because I like sausages.
> **Doctor:** That's stupid. There's nothing wrong with that. I love sausages too.
> **Patient:** Oh, that's great. You should see my collection. I've got hundreds of them in my living room.

VOCABULARY Parts of the body

A **Label the pictures with the words in the box.**

| chest | finger | lip | ear | face | feet | back | arm | leg | shoulder | hand | mouth | knee | stomach | eye | hair |

© JOHN PRITCHETT

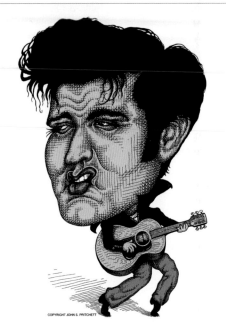

COPYRIGHT JOHN S. PRITCHETT

B **Complete each of the groups of collocations with a part of the body from exercise A.**

1 have a bad ~ / a pain in your lower ~ / stretch your ~
2 my ~ are wet / have big ~ / his ~ smell!
3 cut my bottom ~ / bite my ~ / ~-read / have thin ~s
4 straight ~ / long ~ / brush your ~ / have my ~ cut
5 a pretty ~ / a round ~ / a plain ~ / hit me in the ~
6 work on an empty ~ / have an upset ~ / take something to settle my ~

C **Work in pairs.**

Student A: imagine you are a doctor. Say the instructions below to your partner.
Student B: close your book. Listen and do what your partner tells you.

1 Stand up and then bend your knees.
2 Put your feet together.
3 Bend forwards and touch the floor with your hands.
4 Sit down and lift your leg straight.
5 Open your mouth and say 'Ahh'.
6 Take a deep breath so I can listen to your chest.
7 Turn your head so I can look in your ear.
8 Relax your face, shoulders and arms.
9 Raise your arm above your head.
10 Follow my finger with your eyes, but don't move your head.

LISTENING

A 🔊 **7.2 Listen to three short conversations and decide whether each one takes place:**

a at the dentist's.
b in a hospital.
c in a restaurant.
d in someone's house.
e in a chemist's.

B **Listen again and answer these questions.**
Conversation 1
1 What problem does she have?
2 What did she do to cure the problem?
Conversation 2
3 Which problem does the customer have: diarrhoea, indigestion or vomiting?
4 What instructions is she given?
Conversation 3
5 What two problems does the man have?
6 How did each one happen?

C **Check your answers in pairs. Then act or draw what happened in conversations 1 and 3.**

D **Work in groups. Discuss these questions.**
- What's your cure for hiccups? For indigestion?
- Do you ever ask pharmacists for advice? Are they helpful?
- Are prescriptions expensive where you live?
- What did you get last time you were in a chemist's?
- Are the hospitals good in your country?
- Have you ever been to hospital? Did you have to wait long? What was the service like?

GRAMMAR Imperatives

> Imperatives are used to give orders, instructions, advice encouragement, offers, etc. Use a verb with no subject.
> *Swallow the water slowly.*
>
> For negative imperatives, use *don't*.
> *Don't take more than four tablets in a day.*
>
> We often use imperatives with conditional *if*-clauses.
> *If they don't solve the problem, talk to your doctor.*

A Using the verbs in the box, write the imperatives people might say based on the warnings given with medication in 1–8.

drink	let	have	eat
put	stop	wash	leave

1 Don't exceed three doses in 24 hours.
.... any more today! That's the third one you've had.
2 Don't take on an empty stomach.
.... something first and then take them.
3 Keep refrigerated.
.... the bottle back in the fridge.
4 Complete the full course.
.... taking them. You have to finish the prescription.
5 For external use only.
.... it or eat it!
6 Avoid contact with eyes.
.... your hands after using it.
7 Store in a cool dry place.
.... it there in the sun. Put it in the cupboard.
8 May cause tiredness and drowsiness.
.... me drive in case you fall asleep!

B Work in pairs. Take turns saying an imperative ending to the conditional sentence starters. Continue until one person can't continue or you think your partner's ending doesn't make sense. Then play again using the next sentence starter. For example:

> **A**
> If you need any help, call me.

> **B**
> If you need any help, ask.

> **A**
> If you need any help, look on the Internet.

> **B**
> If you need any help, ...
> – I can't think! You win.

1 If you need any help, ...
2 If you've got a cold, ...
3 If you're feeling stressed, ...
4 If you see the teacher, ...
5 If the alarm rings, ...
6 If you can't sleep, ...

▶ Need help? Read the grammar reference on page 146.

Need help? Read the grammar reference on page 146.

LANGUAGE PATTERNS

Write the sentences in your language. Translate them back into English. Compare your English to the original.
I cut my head dancing with my son!
I cut my face shaving.
I once broke a toe playing football.
I hurt my back lifting some boxes.
I burnt my hand lighting the gas fire.

SPEAKING

You are going to tell someone about a scar you have. If you don't have one, use your imagination and invent one!

A Use the questions below to plan what you are going to say.
- When did it happen? How old were you?
- Where were you? What were you doing?
- Was anyone else with you?
- How did you get the scar?
- What did the other people do? Did anyone help you?
- Did you have to go to hospital or have stitches?
- Did you have to wait a long time to see a doctor?
- How long did it take for the cut to heal / for you to recover?

B Now tell your story to some other students.

"You're looking well."

In this unit, you learn how to:	Grammar	Reading
· talk about well-known buildings and places · ask for – and give – directions · ask questions in a more polite way · talk about different ways of travelling	· Articles (*a*, *an* and *the*) · Quantifiers with uncountable nouns **Vocabulary** · Places in town · Means of transport	· *The Two Travellers and the Farmer* **Listening** · Do you know if this is the right way? · The travel news

VOCABULARY Places in town

A **Find examples of each of the things in the box in the picture below.**

a crossing	a subway	a sports ground
a church	a police station	a town hall
a crossroads	traffic lights	a monument
a playground	a roundabout	a bridge

B **Which of the places in the box above:**
1 can you **turn left at**?
2 can you **go over**?
3 can you **take the kids to after school**?
4 can you **take the third exit on**?
5 can you **go through**?
6 can you **pray** in?
7 can you **report** a **crime** at?
8 does the **local council** hold meetings in?

C **Work in pairs. Discuss these questions.**
· What are the most famous landmarks and buildings where you live? Do you ever visit them?
· How would you give directions to each of these famous places?

LISTENING

You are going to hear a couple on holiday asking several different people for directions.

A 🔊 **8.1 Listen and answer these questions.**
1 Where are they trying to get to?
2 What three problems do they have?
3 What directions do they get from: the first man? the woman? the second man?

B **Choose the words that you heard. Then listen again to check your ideas.**
1 Do you know the *road / way* to the museum from here?
2 *It's / Is* better to get a bus.
3 Down this road. *Take / Turn* the second road on the right.
4 What bus *did he say / has he said* we should catch?
5 Is this the *correct / right* bus stop for the museum?
6 Do you know *where is the museum / where the museum is*?
7 Is it *near / near to* here?
8 You *got off / went off* at the wrong stop.
9 Just keep *going / go* ahead.
10 You can't *miss / lose* it.

C **Work in groups. Discuss the following.**
- Have you ever had any problems like the ones that the tourist had? When? What happened?
- Tell a partner about a time you got lost.

LANGUAGE PATTERNS

Write the sentences in your language. Translate them back into English. Compare your English to the original.
Do you know the way to the museum from here?
Do you know where the museum is?
Do you know if there's a swimming pool near here?
Do you know which bus I need to take?
Do you know where we're going?
Do you know what time the coach leaves?

DEVELOPING CONVERSATIONS
Giving directions

We often repeat similar phrases when we give directions. Keep a record and notice the prepositions used. For example.

cross *over* the street – go *along* the river
go *past* a monument – turn right *at* the crossroads
until you come *to* a church – go *through* the tunnel
directly *opposite* the town hall

A **Complete the directions with the prepositions in the box.**

at	along	on	opposite
over	past	to	through

You have to cross [1]........................... this big road here. There's a crossing over there that you can use or you can go [2].......................... the subway, under the road. Then you go [3].......................... the side of the park and [4].......................... a big statue and then you'll come [5].......................... some traffic lights. Turn left [6].......................... the lights and go straight on.. It's [7].......................... your right – directly [8].......................... a big bookshop. You can't miss it.

B **Draw a map that illustrates the directions given in exercise A. Then compare your map with a partner.**

C **Write a short email giving directions to your home from one of the following places:**
your school / workplace / nearest train station / bus stop

CONVERSATION PRACTICE

You are going to role-play conversations between a local person and someone who doesn't know the area.

A **Work in pairs.**
Student A: look at the map in File 4 on page 156.
Student B: look at the map in File 20 on page 160.
Take turns asking for directions. Use these structures:
Excuse me. Do you know if this is the right way for ....?
Excuse me. Do you know if there's a ... near here?
Do you know where ... is?

SPEAKING

A Read the quotes about travel below. Discuss with a partner whether you agree with each one or not. Explain why.

> It's better to travel than to arrive.

> If you go only once around the room, you are wiser than the person who stands still.

> When you travel, it's good to remember that a foreign country is not designed to make you comfortable. It is designed to make its own people comfortable.

> People travel to faraway places and then spend their time watching the kind of people they ignore at home!

> Travel makes wise people better and stupid people worse.

> The main reason why people are unhappy is because they are unable to stay quietly in their own room.

READING

You are going to read a folktale about travelling. The last paragraph is missing.

A Read the story. How do you think it will end?

B Now read the last paragraph in File 3 on page 156. Did you guess correctly?

C Decide which of the six quotes above best describes the message of the story. Compare your ideas with a partner.

D Work in pairs. Discuss which features of the story the adjectives in the box describe.

brief	keen	glad	disappointed
selfish	dusty	happy	hard-working

E Complete the sentences with the adjectives from the box above.

1 I'm not .... with what I've written. It could be better.
2 I'm .... that you're OK. I was worried about you.
3 My girlfriend's parents said they're very .... to meet me. I hope they won't be .... when they do!
4 I must admit, I'm a lot lazier than my brother. He's really .... and serious.
5 I know you're all busy, so let's try to keep this meeting as .... as possible.
6 He's so .... He only ever thinks of himself!
7 The room needs a good clean. It's very ....

The Two Travellers and the Farmer

One hot afternoon, a traveller was walking along a dusty country road when he suddenly noticed an old farmer working in the fields. Keen to rest his feet, the traveller stopped and called out to the farmer, who seemed happy enough to stop working and chat for a while. The farmer put down his tools, stretched his back and walked slowly over to the side of the road, where the two men sat down together and shared a glass of water.

After some brief introductions, the stranger asked, 'What kind of people live in the next town?'

'What were the people like where you've come from?' replied the farmer, answering one question with another.

'They were a bad bunch. They were all troublemakers - and very lazy too! They were the most selfish people in the world. I didn't trust any of them and I have to say, I'm glad I'm leaving them all behind.'

'Is that right?' replied the old farmer. 'Well, I'm afraid I've got some bad news for you. In the next town you come to, you'll find more of the same sort of people.'

Disappointed, the traveller continued on his way, while the farmer returned to his work.

A couple of weeks later, another stranger appeared, coming from the same direction. He also slowed down as he walked through the fields and shouted out to the farmer. The two men stopped to talk and after a few minutes, the second traveller said, 'Do you mind if I ask what kind of people live in the next town?'

'What were the people like where you've come from?' replied the farmer once again.

'They were the best people in the world. Hard-working, honest and friendly. I'm sorry I'm leaving them all behind.'

GRAMMAR Articles (a, an and the)

Use a / an to introduce something new. *A traveller* was walking along *a dusty country road* when he suddenly noticed *an old farmer* ...	**Use *the* when you think the listener knows the specific thing, because they can see or know there's only one or because it's already been mentioned.** ... *the traveller* stopped and called out to *the farmer*.	**Note that to talk about general things or a whole type / group, don't use any article:** ~~The~~ *Travel* makes ~~the~~ *wise people* better.

A Complete the sentences with *a*, *an* or *the*.

1 We rented ...... small flat near ...... city centre.

2 We missed ...... last train into ...... city, so we had to get ...... taxi to our hotel.

3 People in Gothenburg were really lovely. We made friends with ...... really nice Swedish couple.

4 When you get to Portobello Road, you'll see three houses: ...... orange one, ... blue one and ...... red one. We live in ...... blue one.

5 We stayed in ...... lovely hotel when we were in Greece. ...... food there was amazing. Most evenings, we ate in ...... hotel, but on ...... last evening, we went to ...... really nice restaurant nearby.

6 A: Is this ...... right way to ...... station?
   B: Not really. You need to go to ...... end of ...... road and turn left. Keep going until you get to ...... set of traffic lights. Turn right at ...... lights and ...... station's there.

B In 1–5, cross out *the* in the more general statements and leave it where it describes part of a type / group.

1 a I drink a lot of *the coffee*.
  b I can't drink *the coffee* they sell in the café round the corner.

2 a I really love *the dance music*.
  b I can't stand *the music* my parents listen to.

3 a *The food* my mum cooks is the best in the world!
  b I've never tried *the English food*.

4 a I always fall asleep on *the train journeys*.
  b *The train service* from my town to the capital is great.

5 a *The money* is the most important thing in life!
  b *The money* people make from most part-time jobs is awful!

C Which of the sentences in exercise B do you agree with? Tell a partner.

▶ Need help? Read the grammar reference on page 147.

PRONUNCIATION *the*

The is pronounced /ðə/ before a consonant and /ði/ before a vowel.

A Look at the places below. In pairs, decide where *the* is pronounced /ðə/ and where it is pronounced /ði/.

the Black Forest	the Alps	the Andes
the Great Wall	the Amazon	the Thames
the Mediterranean	the Nile	the Pyramids
the Indian Ocean	the Eiffel Tower	the Caribbean
the Great Barrier Reef	the equator	the Arctic
the Canary Islands	the Sahara	the Himalayas

B 🔊 8.2 Listen and check your ideas. Practise saying the places.

C Work in groups. Discuss these questions.
• Where are the places in exercise A? Are there any you don't know?
• What do you know about each place?
• Have you ever been to any of them? When? What were they like?

VOCABULARY Transport

A Match 1–10 with the forms of transport in the box.

bike	bus	coach	motorbike	taxi
boat	car	plane	foot	train

1 We **walked** all the way there.
2 A: How much did he **charge** you?
   B: Eleven dollars plus a **tip**. It wasn't too much, was it?
3 They stopped at **a service station** on the **motorway** for half an hour and let the **passengers** stretch their legs.
4 Our flight has been **delayed**, so we're going to **land** in Paris late. They said it'll be 10.30 local time.
5 I cycle to work. There's a good **cycle lane** that goes from my house, so I don't need to go on the roads.
6 They're planning to build a **high-speed rail line**, so the journey will be a lot shorter and almost as quick as by air.
7 We had to **drive** round a bit before we found somewhere to **park**.
8 You'll go past a row of shops and a mosque and you need to **get off** at the next **stop**. It's in front of a restaurant.
9 We spent a couple of days **sailing** down the coast. It was lovely to be out at sea.
10 A: Do you need a **licence** to **ride** one?
   B: Yes, you have to take a practical **test** of your riding skills, but it's quite easy – and shorter than a driving test.

B Work in pairs. Take turns to act or draw the words in bold above for your partner to guess.

C Think of places you have been to using six of the different forms of transport. Work in pairs. Have conversation like this:
   A: *We went to X last year.*
   B: *Oh really? How did you get there?*
   A: *Well, we drove to Y and then we sailed to the island by boat.*
   B: *How long did it take you?*
   A: *About six hours.*

LISTENING

You are going to hear the travel news in the middle of a radio programme. Next, they are going to interview a round-the-world sailor called Ellen McArthur.

A Before you listen, work in groups. Think of as many reasons as possible for the following to happen:
   • a flight is cancelled
   • a rail service is delayed
   • an underground station is closed
   • one lane of a motorway is shut
   • there's a traffic jam in a city
   • the police remove some cars

B 🔊 **8.3** Listen to the news and find out how many different pieces of travel information there are. How many give good travel news?

C Listen again and complete the table.

Place	Problem	Cause	Solution / advice
Airport	flight's delayed / cancelled		
A516		lorry crashed	
M6 motorway: junctions 5–6	diversion causing slow traffic.		take other routes
Northern Line	sections closed	repairs	
	closed		[none]
Wembley concert		no parking	
Central London			avoid driving

D Match the eight verbs with the nouns they went with in *Listening*. Then listen again and read the audioscript on page 169 to check your answers.

1	sail	a	its load
2	cause	b	a fallen tree
3	consult	c	the area
4	lost	d	complete chaos
5	clear up	e	round the globe
6	avoid	f	their airline's website
7	remove	g	their strike
8	end	h	the mess

E Work in groups. Tell each other about two situations in exercise A that you have experienced. Explain what happened.

GRAMMAR Quantifiers with uncountable nouns

> We use *many, much, a lot of, (a) few, (a) little, some, no* and *any* before a noun to show quantity. *Many* and *(a) few* are only used with plural countable nouns.
> *Many flights* are being delayed.
> Only *a few planes* can fly over France.
>
> *Much* and *(a) little* are only used with uncountable nouns.
> It doesn't sound like *much fun*.
> There's *little hope* of a deal yet.
>
> Don't use *no* or *some, few* or *(a) little* after a negative – use *any, much* or *many*.
> *There aren't any more problems* on the A6 now.
> *There's no parking* in or around the stadium.
> A demonstration is likely to cause *some traffic problems*.
> *Not much good news*, I'm afraid.
>
> We use *any* in positive sentences to mean 'it's not important which one or how little because it's true for all.'
> If you have *any questions* for her, ring *9837–3737*.
> Police will remove *any cars* parked in the area.

A Choose the correct word.

1 There aren't *no / any* buses today because of a strike.
2 There's not *much / many* traffic today. It's usually busier.
3 People shouldn't drink *some / any* alcohol at all if they're going to drive.
4 I've been sailing a *few / little* times.
5 I know taxi drivers have a bad reputation, but very *few / little* are actually dishonest.
6 The government's made very *little / few* progress in reducing pollution from transport.
7 Too *much / many* goods are transported by lorry.
8 There's so *much / many* bad news on TV that I've stopped watching it.
9 There are *some / any* cycle lanes where I live, but not *much / many*.
10 To get to the city centre, you can take *many / any* bus from the stop near my house. They all go there.

B In pairs, you are going to compete to 'win' each of the sentences below. Spend five minutes writing as many endings for each sentence as you can. Try to make the endings true, but if you can't, invent them.

1 I've got a lot of ....
2 I haven't got much ....
3 I haven't got many ....
4 I haven't got any ....
5 I don't like / know any ....
6 I like any ....

C Find out who 'wins' each sentence by seeing who has the most endings. If you don't believe something is true, ask questions to find out if your partner is lying.

▶ Need help? Read the grammar reference on page 147.

SPEAKING

A Work in groups. Discuss the questions below. Use vocabulary and grammar from these pages.

- What's the traffic like where you live? Is there much pollution? Could the situation be improved – how?
- What's the parking like where you live? Is it easy to park in the town centre? Does it cost anything?
- Are there plans for any high-speed rail lines where you live? Do you think they're a good idea? Why? / Why not?
- Are there any areas where you live where cars are banned? Do you agree with the policy? Why? / Why not?
- Is public transport reliable where you are? How could it be better?
- What are taxis like where you live? Do you ever take them? Do you give drivers tips?
- Is it safe to walk, cycle or ride a motorbike in your town? Why? / Why not?
- Are there any kinds of transport you've never used? Why not?
- Have you ever had any problems taking a plane or train? What happened?

LEARNER TRAINING

You can learn grammar in different ways. You can learn typical questions and phrases that use grammar (*How long have you been here?*; *Don't worry*); you can make lists of things you want to say with grammar (*I went to Paris last year*; *I have to get up at six*); you can do exercises to notice grammar and differences to your language: for example, you can translate sentences. Finally, you can learn rules and do exercises. *Outcomes* makes use of all these different ways:

- read the words for the unit in the Vocabulary Builder before class
- *Developing conversations* has lots of typical expressions and Grammar sections give natural examples. Learning these helps your speaking fluency

- the *Grammar* practice often asks for personal examples
- the *Language patterns* boxes help you to notice aspects of grammar around words
- the *Grammar reference* at the back of the book gives you examples, rules and exercises

GAME

Work in pairs. Student A use *only* the green squares; student B use *only* the yellow squares. Spend five minutes looking at your questions and revising the answers. Then take turns tossing a coin: heads = move one of your squares; tails = move two of your squares. When you land on a square, your partner looks at the relevant page in the book to check your answers, but *you don't*. If you are right, move forward one space (but don't answer the question until your next turn). If you aren't right, your partner tells you the right answer, and you miss a go. When you've finished, the game change colours and play again.

Start	**1** Vocabulary p. 36: say five of the questions in exercise B, using two words from the table for each	**2** Native Speaker English p. 37: if you can say what the *Native Speaker English* note was and give an example, throw again.	**3** Developing conversations p. 37: say six negative things using the three expressions.	**4** Grammar p. 37: your partner will say the th statements in exercis Ask them two differe questions for each us a future tense.
5 Miss a go!	**6** Native Speaker English p. 42: if you can say what the *Native Speaker English* note was and give an example, throw again.	**7** Vocabulary p. 46: say six of the sentences and questions from exercise A.	**8** Developing conversations p. 46: your partner will say the six questions in exercise A. Agree to four and disagree with two. Give reasons each time.	**9** Grammar p. 47: your partner will say the sentences in exercise B. You should respond with an offer or a promise.
10 Vocabulary p. 48: say two of the symptoms in exercise D for each of the following: allergy, sore throat, hay fever.	**11** Native Speaker English p. 49: if you can say what the *Native Speaker English* was and give an example, throw again	**12** Vocabulary p. 52: name 12 of the parts of the body in exercise A.	**13** Grammar p. 53: your partner will say six of the warnings on medication packets in exercise A. You should say the imperative.	**14** Miss a go
15 Vocabulary p. 54: say ten of the places in town in exercise A.	**16** Native Speaker English p. 58: if you can say what the *Native Speaker English* note was and give an example, throw again.	**17** Grammar p. 57: say two sentences (one with *the* and one without) for each of the following nouns: *coffee, music, food* and *money*.	**18** Vocabulary p. 58: say ten of the words in bold in exercise A and what kind of transport they're connected to.	**Finish**

For each of the activities below, work in groups of three. Use the *Vocabulary Builder* if you want to.

CONVERSATION PRACTICE

Choose one of the following *Conversation practice* activities.
Relax p. 37
Home p. 43
Mind and body p. 49
Getting there p. 55

Two of you should do the task. The third person should listen and then give a mark between 1 and 10 for the performance. Explain your decision. Then change roles.

ACT OR DRAW

One person should act or draw as many of these words as they can in three minutes. Their partners should try to guess the words. Do not speak while you are acting or drawing!

fishing	tools	a border	a nosebleed
trainers	cards	hang	a nightmare
swallow	kick	pray	city wall
a track	cross	cycle	a car plant
throw	glad	a rash	bend your knees
bounce	bridge	blind	out of breath

QUIZ

Answer as many of the questions as possible.
1 Say three activities that use **a net**.
2 Give an example of a score when it's a **draw**.
3 What happens if someone **cheats** in a game?
4 What might people want to **raise awareness** of? How do they do it?
5 Say four things you often find in a **rural** area.
6 What's a budget for? How do you **keep to** one?
7 When would you tell someone to **go ahead**?
8 What's the difference between **a host** and **a guest**?
9 What's the difference between a sneeze and **a cough**?
10 Is it a good thing if you **overcome** a problem?
11 What do people do if they **panic**?
12 Who gives you a **prescription** and what do you do with it?
13 Where would you **report** a crime?
14 Say two kinds of **lane**.
15 Why might there be **a traffic jam** on a road?

COLLOCATIONS

Take turns to read out collocation lists from units 5–8 of the *Vocabulary Builder*. Where there is a '~', say '*blah*' instead. Your partners should guess as many words as they can.

PRONUNCIATION
Words containing *o* or *u*

The letters *o* and *u* can be pronounced in lots of different ways. For example, golf /gɒlf/ and love /lʌv/ or upset /ʌpset/ and cure /kjʊə/. Learning some phonetic symbols can help you because then you can find the pronunciation in a dictionary.

A ● R 2.1 **Listen and repeat the sounds and words below.**

/ɒ/	golf	/ɜː/	work
/uː/	pool	/ʊ/	put
/ʌ/	lovely	/əʊ/	throw
/ə/	spectator	/aʊ/	out
/ɔː/	shorts	/ɔɪ/	boy

B **In each group below, four words have the same sound for the 'o' or 'u'. Find the word in each group that has a different sound.**
1 /ɒ/ concentrate / forest / cough /couple / foreign
2 /uː/ loser / remove / statue / mood / wood
3 /ʌ/ countryside / budget / brush / month / move
4 /ə/ season / recognise / swallow / contain / freedom
5 /ɔː/ forecast / score / court / factory / shortage
6 /ɜː/ burst / murder / worst / cause / survey
7 /ʊ/ put / flu / pull / full / wool
8 /əʊ/ mouth / boat / ocean / shoulder / progress
9 /aʊ/ doubt / launch / allow / town hall / ground
10 /ɔɪ/ noisy / annoy / voice / coincidence / avoid

C ● R 2.2 **Listen and check. You will hear the common sound first, then the four words with that sound and finally the word with the different sound.**

D ● R 2.3 **You are going to hear eight groups of words. Write them down. Then compare what you have written.**

LISTENING

A ⏺ R 2.4 **Listen to four people talking about things connected with travel. Match travel activities a–e to speakers 1–4. There is one activity you do not need.**

a ...... going somewhere by car
b ...... going somewhere by plane
c ...... walking somewhere
d ...... going places by bicycle
e ...... going somewhere by bus

B **Listen again and match items a–e to speakers 1–4. There is one item that you do not need.**

a slept too much
b was ill
c missed catching something
d borrowed something
e almost had an accident

[... / 8]

GRAMMAR

A **Find the eight mistakes in words in italics. Correct them.**

A: What are you doing on Saturday.
B: I'm not sure. ¹*I'm going to play* tennis with a friend in the morning. It depends if he's free. What about you?
B: We ²*will have* a barbecue. Would you like to come?
A: Yeah, why not? How do I get to your place?
B: Well you ³*don't have to* park round here, so don't drive. It's not that far to walk, but ⁴*the most easy* way for you is to take the 67 bus. It stops just outside my house and you ⁵*can get* it from the end of your road.
B: OK, great. ⁶*I'm bringing* you something for dessert, if you like.
A: Are you sure? You ⁷*don't have to.*
B: No, I'd like to.
A: OK. Thanks. That'd be great. ⁸*We're going to eat* about two o'clock.
B: Fine – ⁹*I'm seeing* you at around half one then.
A: Exactly.
B: Who else ¹⁰*is* there?
A: I'm not sure exactly, but I know Javed and Keira ¹¹*come* for sure, so you ¹²*won't be* on your own.
B: That's great.

[... / 12]

B **Complete the short description with the words in the box.**

a	the	few	some	lots	any	many	much

There isn't ¹......................... green space in my town – in fact there aren't ²......................... parks. Not one! There aren't ³......................... trees either! We only have a ⁴......................... playgrounds where kids can play, and two or three squares where people meet. One of the squares is at the end of my road. ⁵......................... of people go there because it's quite big and there are ⁶......................... shops and ⁷......................... café. I often go to ⁸......................... café to have a coffee in the morning.

[... / 8]

C **Complete the second sentence with the word in CAPITALS so that it has a similar meaning to the first one.**

1 Maybe you should rub some cream on that rash.
.... rub some cream on it?
DON'T
2 She scored the best marks in the class.
She's .... in the class.
INTELLIGENT
3 Please be quite.
Pease .... noise. **MAKE**
4 I really should do more exercise.
I really .... more exercise.
OUGHT
5 There aren't any parking spaces.
There .... parking spaces. **ARE**

[... / 5]

▶ **Find this difficult? Look back at the grammar reference, pages 144–147.**

PREPOSITIONS

Choose the correct preposition.

1 The quickest way to get to the station is to walk *through / for* the park.
2 There's a nice path *in / along* the banks of the river.
3 A: Is there a bank near hear?
   B: Yes, if you turn left *at / on* the lights you'll see one just next to a vegetable shop.
4 *At / on* average, I takes me an hour to get to work.
5 We're going *in / on* a trip to the mountains at the weekend.
6 She's going to stay at home. She's still recovering *from / of* her operation.
7 I really rely *for / on* my car to get around, so it's expensive with the price of petrol increasing.
8 It's a port *in / on* the south coast. There are some lovely beaches nearby too.

[... / 8]

LANGUAGE PATTERNS

Complete the sentences with one word in each gap.

1 More and .... people are deciding to move to the countryside.
2 Do .... you want.
3 You can sit .... you like.
4 I broke my leg .... football.
5 Do you know .... this is the way to the park?
6 Do you know where the nearest cash machine .... ?

[... / 6]

FORMING WORDS

Complete the sentences with the correct forms of the words in bold.

1 The virus only causes mild .... **ILL**
2 Our flat is very .... so I just get round on foot. **CENTRE**
3 Frankfurt is a major .... centre in Europe. **FINANCE**
4 I actually lost .... at one point. I thought I was going to die. **CONSCIOUS**
5 If you're taking these tablets, it's not .... to drive. **ADVISE**
6 He suffered from .... for years, but now he's completely recovered. **DEPRESSED**
7 When the ambulance arrived, she was given emergency .... **TREAT**
8 London has an economy which is .... in size to Norway's. **COMPARE**

[... / 8]

ADJECTIVES

Match the adjectives in the box with the groups of nouns.

| tiny | foreign | spare | dry |
| weak | right | brief | sore |

1 .... place / kitchen / minority
2 .... stop / bus / direction
3 .... throat / back / eye / point
4 .... meeting / visit / description
5 .... room / key / clothes / time
6 .... language / country / policy
7 .... signal / heart / light / leader
8 .... lips / hair / clothes / climate

[... / 8]

NOUNS

Complete the sentences with the nouns in the box.

| appointment | case | budget | motorway |
| pollution | back | line | progress |

1 The increase in traffic has caused a lot of .... The new law will try to reduce it.
2 We were making a lot of .... with the building, but the bad rain has stopped it.
3 We went over our .... last year, so this year we need to manage it better.
4 I have a bad .... I have to be careful when I stretch it.
5 It was a serious .... of flu. I had to go to hospital!
6 We had to come off the .... at an earlier exit because they were repairing two lanes.
7 I had an .... with the dentist, but it's been cancelled.
8 They're building a high-speed rail .... between here and the capital, and it'll reduce journey times by an hour.

[... / 8]

▶ **Find this difficult? Re-read units 5–8 in the *Vocabulary Builder* for more information on these words.**

VERBS

Choose the correct verb (a, b or c) below for each gap.

My brothers and I love sport. When we were young, we were really competitive. We spent hours throwing and ¹...... a ball or kicking a football against a wall. The first person to ²...... the ball or miss the wall lost the game. We played *Monopoly* every Sunday until our parents ³...... us from playing because my eldest brother often ⁴...... and the game nearly always ended in an argument. My cousins lived near us and they were keen cyclists. We often ⁵...... each other to a village a few miles away or we timed ourselves to see who got there the fastest. My cousin's record was 22 minutes, but my middle brother almost ⁶...... it one day. Unfortunately, he was ⁷...... by some cows that were ⁸...... the road from another field! The only thing we don't compete at is watching football! We all ⁹...... Liverpool and go to see their home games together.

1	a removing	b catching	c taking
2	a fall	b drop	c remove
3	a cancelled	b overcame	c banned
4	a trusted	b prevented	c cheated
5	a raced	b bet	c cycled
6	a won	b beat	c time
7	a reduced	b delayed	c avoided
8	a spreading	b riding	c crossing
9	a support	b attract	c recognise

[... / 9]

 [Total ... /80]

09 SCIENCE AND NATURE

In this unit, you learn how to:
- talk about the weather
- talk about animals and pets
- talk about scientists and research
- discuss and respond to news stories
- report what people said

Grammar
- The past perfect simple
- Reporting speech 1

Vocabulary
- Science and nature
- Animals

Reading
- Man's best friends
- The Milgram experiment

Listening
- Science and nature in the news
- The Milgram experiment

VOCABULARY Science and nature

A Put the words in the box into the list they are connected with.

a discovery	freezing	snow	a horse
experiments	mosquitoes	boiling	a bee
a storm	investigate	windy	rain
a rocket	nuclear	protect	extinct
a whale	pets	sunny	space

Science	The weather	Animals

B Work in groups. Tell each other about when you last experienced each of the different kinds of weather in exercise A. Say something about at least two of the following things in each case:
- how you felt about the weather
- what temperature it was
- how strong the wind was
- how long the storm / rain / snow, etc. lasted
- how much rain / snow fell
- if you suffered because of the sun / rain / heat / snow, etc.

C Complete the sentences with one word from exercise A in each space.
1 .... racing is cruel.
2 Launching a .... into space is a waste of money.
3 We should do more to protect animals like whales or they'll become ....
4 Scientists shouldn't conduct ....
   on animals.
5 They should build more ....
   power stations.
6 The government should spend more money on research to .... the causes of cancer.
7 Electricity is the greatest scientific .... ever.
8 .... are the most dangerous animals in the world because they spread so much disease.
9 Cats are the best kind of .... for children.

D Work in groups. Vote on whether or not you agree with each of the sentences. For example:
How many people think horse racing is cruel?

LISTENING

You are going to hear four short conversations about science and nature in the news.

A 🔊 9.1 **Listen and decide which conversation mentions:**
1 a discovery to help people?
2 a government policy to help the environment?
3 a problem with very negative effects?
4 a change in the weather?

B **Compare your ideas in pairs and discuss what happened in each conversation. Then listen again to check your ideas.**

LANGUAGE PATTERNS

Write the sentences in your language. Translate them back into English. Compare your English to the original.

They should do something – fund research or something.
We should go out – go to the beach or somewhere.
I can't remember who told me – Harry or someone.
I was bitten by a mosquito or something like that.
They live in Chicago or somewhere near there.
You should ask a friend or someone you trust.

DEVELOPING CONVERSATIONS
Responding to news and comments

We can comment on news we hadn't heard about by saying:
Really? That's bad news / nice / great / awful / interesting, etc.

We can agree with a comment or opinion by saying:
(Yes) I know. It's good news / really good / fantastic / terrible, etc.
We can agree to a suggestion by saying:
Good idea.
Absolutely / Definitely.

A **Look at the audioscript on page 170 and find examples of each kind of response. Then read all the conversations in pairs.**

B **Write a response to each of the sentences below.**
1 They've opened a new park near my house.
2 Really? That's awful.
3 We should have a party to celebrate.
4 That's fantastic news.
5 They should do something about it.
6 They're doing an experiment to investigate how the Big Bang worked.
7 It's going to be freezing tonight.
8 They should ban it.

C **In pairs, take turns saying 1–8 above. Your partner should say their own response.**

CONVERSATION PRACTICE

You are going to have conversations like the ones in *Listening*.

A **Student A: look at the news in File 11 on page 158. Student B: look at the news in File 13 on page 158.**

B **Now take turns starting conversations about your pieces of news. Use the plan below.**

Did you see / hear ...?	
	No.
It said / It's ...	
	Really? That's ...
I know. It's ...	
	(make a suggestion)
(agree)	

VOCABULARY Animals

A **Which of the animals in the box can you see in the pictures above?**

rat	dog	cow	shark	pigeon
lion	fly	sheep	rabbit	parrot

B **Decide if each animal in exercise A could be described as a wild animal, a farm animal, an insect or a pet?**

C **Work in pairs. Think of two more examples for each of the four categories in exercise B.**

D **Work in groups. Discuss these questions.**
- What pets do people you know have?
- Which of the animals in exercise A can help humans? How?

READING

You are going to read some short newspaper stories about animals helping humans in some way.

A **Read the stories on the oppsite page and match each to one of the headlines below. There is one you will not need to use.**

Barking witness   Wedding goes with a 'woof'
Jail bird   Milk of human kindness
Tips for birds   Dinner not well done
From zero to hero

B **Work in pairs. Discuss the following:**
- What do you think the headlines mean?
- One of the texts isn't true. Which one do you think is invented? Why? (Now look at File 9 on page 157 to check.)
- Explain why you think each story is nice, interesting, silly, surprising or boring.

C **In pairs, discuss what you think the words in bold in the stories mean. Check your ideas in the *Vocabulary Builder*.**

D **Work in groups. Discuss the questions.**
- What animals can you think of that have an amazing sense of smell / hearing / sight?
- Can you think of eight things dogs are often trained to do?
- How can pets boost your health?
- Which other animals are used to detect things?
- Have you heard of anyone being arrested recently? What are they suspected of?

GRAMMAR The past perfect simple

> The past perfect is *had / hadn't* + a past participle. We use it to emphasise that something happened before another past action.
> A Dorset couple *got married* yesterday.
> The dogs *had brought* the couple together.
>
> If we write the sentences in the order in which they really happened, we usually use the past simple.
> Three dogs *brought* a Dorset couple together.
> Yesterday, the couple *got* married.

A Match 1–8 with a–h to make complete sentences.

1 The ground was wet
2 We found a cat which had been abandoned
3 They took him to court
4 There was a long line of traffic
5 I had to wait outside home until my mum got back
6 I was very nervous
7 I was really shocked
8 My dog was going crazy when I got home

a because I'd forgotten my keys.
b because it had rained the night before.
c because I hadn't made a speech in public before.
d because there were roadworks.
e because he hadn't paid his bills.
f because I hadn't taken him for a walk all day.
g so we took it home and looked after it.
h when I saw the rat in the kitchen!

B Check your answers with a partner and discuss why the past simple or past perfect is used in a–h.

▶ Need help? Read the grammar reference on page 148.

C Write endings to 1–5 using the past perfect. Then compare what you've written.

1 I was hungry because ....
2 She was quite upset because ....
3 I was really tired ....
4 I was quite nervous because ....
5 Before I was 18, I'd never ....

D Work in groups. Discuss what you think happened before each of these events. Use the past perfect.

1 A pigeon was caught and arrested at a jail.
2 A woman's pet dog was found on a desert island.
3 A couple were saved by their pet rabbit.

E Find out what actually happened by reading File 7 on page 157.

SPEAKING

Work in pairs. Choose one of the following:

A Have you heard any other animal stories in the news recently? Tell a partner what happened.

B Do an Internet search for animal stories in the news and then tell your partner about the one you liked most. Who found the best story?

MAN'S BEST FRIENDS

1 A Dorset couple, Andrew and Harriet Athay, got married with their dogs acting as best man and maids of honour on the big day because they had brought the couple together. Andrew and Harriet met when they were walking their respective pets along a beach. They started chatting when the dogs were playing with each other.

2 A very rare shark, which has only been seen on 40 occasions, has been eaten by a Filipino fisherman. The megamouth shark died in a net after it had been caught by mistake. The World Wildlife Fund, which wants to protect the sharks from extinction, tried to persuade the fisherman to let scientists have the body, but the fisherman **insisted on** using it to prepare a traditional Filipino dish called *kinunot*.

3 A Japanese restaurant is employing two parrots as waiters. The parrots take drinks orders from customers and repeat them to a waiter at the bar, who then brings the drinks to the table. The parrots had previously lived in a **cage** in a corner of the restaurant. One day the owner, Mr Otusaka, heard the parrots copying his customers' requests and after that, he

4 Rats may have a bad reputation, but, says a spokesman for the charity HeroRats, they are saving hundreds of lives in Africa because of their incredible **sense of smell** and intelligence. The rats are trained to **detect** mines and bombs lying in the ground. Being so small, they don't cause the mines to explode when they stand on them. They can also detect some diseases in humans.

5 Researchers from Newcastle University have discovered that farmers who are friendly and talk to their cows can **boost** milk production. They found that cows that had been given names by their farmers produced over 300 litres more milk a year than those which hadn't been named.

6 A dog called Scooby has appeared in court in a murder case. The animal's owner had been found dead in her flat and the family had asked for an investigation. Scooby, who had been in the flat, was brought into court to see how he would react to the man **suspected of** the crime. It barked very loudly. The police now need to decide if there is enough evidence to take the case further.

READING

You are going to read about one of the most famous experiments of the 20th century.

A Complete the text with the words in the box.

button	list	participants	purpose	research	results

In 1961, a psychologist called Stanley Milgram conducted 40 experiments at Yale University. Each experiment involved three people: a 'scientist' in a white coat, and a 'learner' and a 'teacher'. The 'scientists' and the 'learners' were actors and knew the real aim of the [1]........................... . The 'teachers' were just normal people. Milgram told them that the [2].......................... of the experiments was to study memory and learning, but this wasn't true.

The 'teacher' was given a [3].......................... of pairs of words to teach the 'learner', who was in another room and was out of sight. The 'teacher' first read the whole list to the 'learner'. Then the 'teacher' repeated the first word of each pair and the 'learner' had to remember the other word in the pair. If they were wrong, the 'scientist' told the 'teacher' to press a [4].......................... to give the 'learner' an electric shock – and with every wrong answer, the shock got stronger. The experiments were stopped after the 'teacher' had given the maximum 450-volt shock three times.

Milgram observed all the experiments and recorded the point at which the [5].......................... refused to continue giving shocks. Before conducting his experiments, Milgram had asked his students what they expected the [6].......................... to be. They predicted that only 1.2% of the 'teachers' would give the maximum shock.

B Label the picture below and discuss the roles of each person in the experiment with a partner.

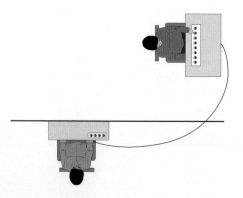

C Work in pairs. Discuss the following questions.

- Have you heard of this experiment – or any others like it – before? If yes, what did you hear?
- Would you participate in an experiment like this? Why? / Why not?
- What do you think happened during the experiment?
- What percentage of people do you think gave the maximum electric shock? Why?

LISTENING

You are going to listen to two radio extracts giving more details about the Milgram experiments.

A 🔊 9.2 Listen and see if your ideas about what happened during the experiment were correct or not.

B Listen again and decide if 1–6 are true or false.

1 The 'learners' didn't actually get electric shocks.
2 Some of the 'learners' had heart problems.
3 Some participants found the experiments funny.
4 After hearing the banging and screaming, several participants got very worried.
5 If they complained, the 'teachers' were told to carry on with the experiment.
6 A minority of people gave the maximum shock.

C The second radio extract describes the aim of the experiments. You will hear all the words below. In pairs, discuss how they might be connected to the experiments.

the Second World War	terrible crimes
cruel	people in authority
cause pain	kill someone

D 🔊 9.3 Now listen and check your ideas.

E Work in groups. Discuss how the words in exercise C are actually connected.

F In groups, discuss these questions.

- How do you feel about the experiment now? Do you agree with the findings?
- Do you think the results would be the same if the experiment was done today? Why? / Why not?
- What effects do you think the experiment had on the participants? Think about both the short-term and the long-term effects.

GRAMMAR Reporting speech 1

> We use lots of different verbs to report what people say.
> The most common are *say, tell* and *ask*. Look at some of the
> patterns used with each verb:
>
> *The 'scientist' said (that)* the experiment required them to
> continue. *He then said (that)* it was absolutely essential that
> they continued.
>
> *The 'scientist' told the 'teacher' to* give the 'learner' an electric
> shock.
> *Milgram told them (that)* the purpose of the experiments was
> to study memory and learning.
>
> *Many people asked to* stop the experiment.
> *The 'teachers' asked the 'scientist' if* he was sure.
>
> Note that other patterns are also possible with these verbs.

A Complete the sentences with past simple forms of *say, tell* or *ask*.

1 When I was younger, my dad often .... me to just do
   what I love doing – and that's what I've done!
2 I .... to see the manager, but they .... he
   wasn't available.
3 A: What .... you .... to your boss?
   B: I just .... him I didn't want to work for him any more.
4 My older sister once .... me to never date anyone more
   attractive than me!
5 Last year I .... my grandfather to .... me
   about his childhood. Some of the things he .... he'd
   seen were just unbelievable!
6 My last English teacher always .... I asked too many
   questions!
7 I .... if she wanted to leave a message, but she
   .... she'll call back tomorrow.
8 I once .... a friend when her baby was due – and then
   found out she wasn't actually pregnant!

▶ **Need help? Read the grammar reference on page 148.**

B Try to complete these sentences in interesting or funny ways. The sentences should be true for you.

1 When I was growing up, my parents often
   told me to ... .
2 My mum / dad once told me to never ... .
3 One of my teachers once said I ... .
4 My mum / dad / brother / sister once said
   she / he ... .
5 I'd like to ask my parents / grandparents .... .
6 Someone once asked me ... .

C Compare your sentences in groups. Who has the most interesting / the funniest?

SPEAKING

A Work in groups. Discuss these questions.

- Which science subjects do / did you study
  at school? Are / were you good at them?
- What are / were your science teachers like?
- What experiments were you asked to do
  at school? How did they work? What were
  they for?
- Have you ever taken part in any kind
  of research (scientific research, market
  research, etc.)? What did you do?
- Who are the most famous scientists from
  your country? Why? What do / did they do?
- Do you know anything about any of the
  scientists below? Where were they from?
  What did they do research on? What did
  they discover?

Archimedes	Galileo Galilei
Isaac Newton	Ivan Pavlov
Louis Pasteur	Marie Curie
Charles Darwin	Alexander Fleming
Guglielmo Marconi	Albert Einstein

10 EDUCATION

In this unit, you learn how to:
- describe your academic experiences
- talk about future plans
- respond with surprise to negative sentences
- explain what you use computers for
- talk about the school system in your country

Grammar
- First conditionals
- *had to / could*

Vocabulary
- School and university
- Computers and the Internet
- Students and teachers

Reading
- A web of lies?

Listening
- School and university
- School in two different countries

VOCABULARY School and university

A Put the sentences below into order, starting with the one that happens first.

1 I'm **leaving school** next month. ☐
2 I've just started doing **a Master's in** Law. ☐
3 He starts **primary school** this year. ☐
4 I've just **graduated** from university. ☐
5 I'm **taking a year out** before university. ☐
6 I'm **doing a PhD in** Maths at the moment. ☐
7 I've got **my finals** next term. ☐
8 She's just finished primary school. ☐
9 I'm in my third year at **secondary school**. ☐

NATIVE SPEAKER ENGLISH

graduate

In British English, you *graduate* when you finish university. In American English, you can *graduate from high school* as well as from university. In Britain, *high school* is called *secondary school* and *elementary school* is *primary school*.

B In pairs, discuss how old you think the people in each of the sentences in exercise A are. Explain your ideas.

C Work in groups. Discuss these questions.
- Do you know anyone who is at primary school / secondary school / university at the moment?
- What year are they in? Are they enjoying it?
- What are their plans for the future?
- Do you know anyone who's doing – or who has done – a Master's or a PhD? In what subject?

LISTENING

You are going to hear three conversations about school / university.

A ⏺ **10.1 Listen and answer the questions about each conversation.**

1 Is the second speaker studying at the moment?
2 How do they feel about their studies? Why?
3 What subjects do they mention? Why?
4 Do they mention any plans for the future?

B Work in pairs. Try to complete the questions below. Then listen again to check your answers.

Conversation 1
1 What .... favourite subjects?
2 How long .... left?
3 What're you going to do ....?

Conversation 2
4 What course ...., Pep?
5 What year ....?
6 Have you .... yet?

Conversation 3
7 Did you go ...., Dhanya?
8 What .... study?
9 And did .... it?

C Can you remember the answers to the questions above? Compare your ideas and then check the audioscript on page 171.

LANGUAGE PATTERNS

Write the sentences in your language. Translate them back into English. Compare your English to the original.
How long have you got left?
I've got two months left before my course ends.
They don't have any places left on the course.
I'll see if they have any left in the shop.

D Work in groups. Discuss these questions.
- Is it better to study what your parents want you to study or what you want to study? Why?
- What are the advantages and disadvantages of NOT going to university?

PRONUNCIATION School subjects

A 🔊 **10.2** Listen to how each of the school subjects in the box below is pronounced. Mark the stress in each one.

Geography	Economics	History	Biology
Mathematics	Chemistry	Physics	Latin
Sociology	PE	RE	IT

B **Listen again and repeat what you hear.**

C **Work in pairs. Discuss these questions.**
- Did you study all of the subjects above at some time?
- Which of the subjects above were / are you good at? Which were / are you bad at?
- Which are the most / least useful? Why?
- Any there any other subjects you study / studied at school or college / university not mentioned above?

DEVELOPING CONVERSATIONS *No?*

When someone tells us a negative sentence that surprises us, we often respond by asking *No?* We then expect the other person to explain what they mean.

A: *Dad doesn't want me to, though.*
B: *No?*
A: *No, he just wants me to stay in the system and go straight to university.*

A **In pairs, take turns asking *No?* in response to the sentences below – and offering explanations.**
1. I don't want to go university.
2. I'm not really enjoying the course.
3. I didn't really like PE when I was at school.
4. I haven't done my homework.
5. I didn't study for the test.
6. I don't want my son to study Fashion!

GRAMMAR First conditionals

Use first conditionals to talk about things that are likely to happen in the future. The *if*-clause describes a possible future situation. Use present tenses in this clause. The other clause describes the future result. We usually use *will / won't* + verb in this clause.

If I get the grades I want, *I'll* probably *do* a Master's.
You won't pass if you don't start working harder!
What *will you do if you don't get into* university?

A **Complete the sentences with the correct form of the verbs in brackets.**
1. My parents are going to pay for the course, and if I .... more money, I .... part-time. (need, work)
2. My parents have promised me that if I .... all my exams, they .... me a car! (pass, buy)
3. If I .... the score I need in the IELTS exam, I .... it in a couple of months. (not / get, retake)
4. If I .... the grades I want, I .... my first-choice university! (not / get, not / get into)
5. They .... your application if you .... the deadline. (not / consider, miss)
6. A: What .... you .... if you don't get a place on the course? (do)
   B: I'm not sure. I guess that if that ...., I .... probably just .... looking for a job. (happen, start)

▶ **Need help? Read the grammar reference on page 149.**

B **Work in pairs.**
Student A: you are an optimist.
Student B: you are a pessimist. Take turns completing each of the sentences below using *will / won't* + verb.
1. My dad said that if I do well in my exams this year, ...
2. If I study Physics at university, ...
3. If I have any problems with the course, ...
4. If my parents can't afford to support me while I'm studying, ...
5. If I fail my finals, ...
6. If I can't find a good job when I graduate, ...
7. If I spend a few months living in England, ...
8. If I do a PhD, ...

CONVERSATION PRACTICE

You are going to have similar conversations to the ones you heard in *Listening*.

A **Choose the questions from conversations 1–3 you want to ask other students – and decide how to answer the ones that apply to you.**

B **Now have conversations with some other students in the class.**

VOCABULARY Computers and the Internet

A Match the verbs with the best endings.

1	chat	a	chat rooms
2	listen	b	with friends on Messenger
3	visit	c	a blog
4	organise	d	to music
5	write	e	your finances

B Do the same.

6	play	f	for information
7	upload	g	clothes online
8	make	h	online games with people
9	buy	i	PowerPoint presentations
10	search	j	photos onto the Internet

C Work in pairs. Discuss which of the ten things above you do on your computer. Say as much about each activity as you can.

SPEAKING

A Work in groups. Discuss these questions.

- How many hours a day do you spend on the computer?
- Which websites do you visit the most? Why?
- Do / Did you use computers at school? In which classes? What do / did you use them for?
- What are some good / bad things about using computers for schoolwork?

READING

You are going to read an article about the Internet, students and school.

A Read the article. What good / bad things about the Internet does it mention?

A WEB OF LIES?

JANE WILSHERE EXPLORES THE EFFECT THAT THE WORLD WIDE WEB IS HAVING ON SCHOOL LIFE.

The incredible growth of the Internet over recent years has caused problems for parents and teachers. Parents worry about which sites their children spend time on, who they chat to online and the possible effects that computer games might have on them. For teachers, meanwhile, the main **worry** is the way the Internet makes cheating easier!

Schools and universities say there has been a huge **increase** in plagiarism – taking other people's words and ideas and pretending that they are your own. In the past, anyone who wanted to copy had to go to a library, find the right books, read through them, find the sections they needed and then physically write down the words they wanted to use. Nowadays, though, students can simply **copy** extracts from websites – while really desperate students sometimes copy whole essays! As if this wasn't bad enough, sites offering to actually do homework – at a price – have also started appearing.

Despite all this, we shouldn't assume that the Internet only brings problems. Indeed, you could say that for every problem the Internet creates, it also brings a solution. Parents can now use sophisticated controls to stop kids accessing sites that might do them **harm**, whilst new software helps teachers to detect copied work immediately. Many, of course, are already able to recognise when someone is cheating! 'Some students suddenly start using words they can't possibly understand like 'dialectical antagonism',' explains one teacher, 'or parts of their essays feel different. In fact, one of my students recently gave me an essay he'd copied from the Web and it even contained Web advertisements – AND the name of the original author!'

One of the hardest things for teachers today is deciding how to **mix** modern technology with traditional study skills – and how best to use the Web in class. As more and more schools install computers in every classroom, the role of the teacher is changing. Making sure students don't just copy things and do learn how to **quote** copied work properly is part of their job, but so is designing suitable projects.

My 13-year-old son is currently working on a project that involves listing all the trees in our town. Along with three other students, he has to **photograph** them, write about their characteristics, describe the fruit and flowers they produce and so on. This is all uploaded onto a website, and his group discusses their work on Messenger. Finally, they'll give a PowerPoint presentation about their ideas to the class. Instead of helping him **cheat**, the Web is actually helping him learn about school subjects, while also helping to develop his life skills and social skills!

B **Discuss these questions in pairs. Then read again and check your ideas.**
1 What is plagiarism – and how has the Internet affected it?
2 How does new software help parents?
3 How can teachers recognise plagiarism?
4 Why does the writer mention his son?
5 How is his son using computers at school?

C **Work in pairs. Discuss these questions.**
• Do you think parents and teachers are right to worry about how students use the Web? Why? / Why not?
• Was plagiarism a problem where you studied?
• Do you know how to quote – i.e. use other people's words and ideas in your writing – properly?
• What do you think of the project that the writer's son is working on? Why?

> Lots of words in English can be both verbs and nouns without changing their basic form. For example:
> I'll *email* you later.   (= verb)
> I need to send some *emails*.   (= noun)

D **Decide if the words in bold in the article are used as verbs or nouns. Compare your ideas with a partner and explain how you made your decisions.**

E **Complete the sentences using the correct form of the words in bold from the article.**
1 Can I make a .... of your notes from yesterday?
2 It's a famous .... from Shakespeare.
3 Don't .... about it! I'm sure it'll be fine.
4 I found one of my old school .... the other day. I look really funny in it.
5 There's a good .... of people in the class.
6 The number of students studying abroad .... a lot last year.
7 Do you think violent computer games can .... kids?
8 I'm not a ....! I didn't copy anything!

F **Work in pairs. Try to think of five more words that have the same basic form when used as verbs and nouns. The first pair to think of five wins!**

SPEAKING

A **The article talked about how the Internet helps students cheat when doing homework. Discuss these questions about cheating in groups.**
• How do people cheat in the areas of life below?
• Do you think it is acceptable to cheat in any of these situations? Why? / Why not?
• What do you think are suitable punishments for each different kind of cheating?

tests and exams	sport	cooking
job interviews	CVs	relationships
tax and personal finances	politics	game shows

LISTENING

You are going to hear an interview with an English girl, Rebecca, who has a Spanish mother and an English father. They moved to Spain when she was 11 (she is now 13) and she now goes to a Spanish school – and so does her younger brother.

A Before you listen, discuss in groups which of the following things you think are good about school in your country.
- the relationships between students
- the class sizes
- the amount of homework
- the subjects available
- the resources
- the textbooks
- the approach to teaching
- the parent-teacher relationship
- the school hours
- the holidays

B 10.3 Listen and find out which things in exercise A Rebecca talks about.

C Discuss in pairs whether you think these sentences are true or false. Listen again to check your ideas.
1 Rebecca and her brother made friends straight away.
2 She needed help with Spanish.
3 She had to do the last year of primary school in both England and Spain.
4 There are fewer years of secondary school in Spain.
5 In primary school, she had several different teachers in Spain, but not in England.
6 The approach of the teachers was different.
7 She didn't have to do much homework in England.
8 Her friends in England seem to like school more.
9 In both England and Spain, students sometimes have to repeat a year.

D 10.4 Now listen to Rebecca's father talking and answer the questions:
1 Which of the things in exercise A does he mention?
2 Is he positive or negative about them?

E Read the audioscript on page 172 to check your answers.

F Work in pairs. Discuss these questions.
- Which system sounds more like your country?
- Do you disagree with anything the father says? Why?
- What differences would you like to see in schools?
- Is / Was there anyone from another country in your class at school? What is / was their experience of school?

VOCABULARY Students and teachers

A Add the nouns below to the groups of words they go

assignment	class	school	subject
textbook	test	approach	course

with.
1 choose an optional ~ / study eight ~s / my favourite ~
2 do an ~ / set an ~ / hand in my ~ / mark some ~s
3 buy a ~ / read from the ~ / copy from the ~
4 have a ~ / study for a ~ / pass a ~ / set a ~
5 do a Maths ~ / design a ~ / fail the ~ / teach on a ~
6 give a ~ / go to ~ / pay attention in ~ / control the ~
7 leave ~ / the head of a ~ / enjoy ~ / go to a state ~
8 have a good ~ to learning / take a traditional ~ / change your ~

B Which of the collocations above apply to teachers and which to students?

GRAMMAR *had to / could*

> Use *had to* + verb to talk about things in the past that were necessary. Use *Did ... have to* in questions.
> *She had to do* the last year of primary school again.
> *Did you have to buy* the books?
>
> Use *didn't have to* + verb to talk about things in the past that were not necessary.
> *She didn't have to do* much homework in England.
>
> Use *could* + verb for things in the past that were possible – that you had a choice about. Use *couldn't* for things that were impossible.
> *We could wear* whatever we liked at school.
> *I couldn't hear* the teacher because everyone was talking.

A **Complete the sentences with *had to, did ... have to, didn't have to, could* or *couldn't*.**

1 I .... go out last night because I .... finish an essay for class.
2 I .... come to class last week. .... you .... do any homework?
3 At primary school, we .... do a spelling test once a week.
4 When I was at university, we .... go to all the lectures. A lot of them were optional.
5 In the past, everyone .... study Maths, Language and Literature, and French, but they were the only compulsory subjects. You .... choose the others. Now you don't really have any choice.
6 When I was at school, there were strict rules about dress. You .... wear a tie, a black jacket and black trousers, a blue jersey and grey socks. You .... wear any different colours or jewellery.

B **Choose two of the pairs below. Write what was different about the two things, using *had to, could,* etc. For example:**
primary and secondary school
When I was at primary school, I could go home for lunch, but at secondary school I had to stay at school.

- primary and secondary school
- secondary school and university
- school / university and work
- living with my parents and living on my own
- being single and being married

Note that if you talk about your experience now, you will need *have to, don't have to, can* or *can't*!

C **In pairs, tell your sentences to each other. Ask each other questions to find out more information.**

▶ **Need help? Read the grammar reference on page 149.**

SPEAKING

A Work in groups. Discuss the questionnaire about school below. Decide who was the best student.

SWOT OR NOT?

1 It was late and you had to do an assignment. Did you:
a do it quickly, although you knew it'd get a bad mark?
b search the Internet and copy some things?
c stay up all night to do it well?
d decide not to do it?

2 Most terms:
a I usually got OK grades.
b I usually failed at least one or two subjects.
c the only subject I passed was PE.
d I got top grades: As and Bs

3 When I was at school, I knew I wanted to:
a do a PhD at some point in the future.
b train to be a mechanic or something instead of be at school.
c go to university.
d leave as soon as possible and start work.

4 In class:
a I tried to pay attention all the time.
b I sometimes chatted or sent text messages.
c I often threw paper planes and disturbed the class.
d I always paid attention, answered questions and pointed it out if students were doing something wrong.

5 I never:
a skipped classes.
b cheated in a test.
c worried about what grades I got.
d did my homework.

6 I think computers are good to have in class because:
a the teacher can show you more interesting things.
b you can keep up with Messenger.
c you can play games.
d you can do more research on the topic while waiting for others to finish.

7 When I did my assignments:
a I often made lots of spelling mistakes.
b I did them on the computer.
c my writing was often difficult to read.
d I liked to do them neatly and sometimes design them - for example, with different colours.

8 The best part of school was:
a the lunch breaks.
b science lessons.
c doing things like plays and concerts.
d leaving.

B Do you know anyone who would answer the questions very differently to you? Tell a new partner.

11 PLACES TO STAY

In this unit, you learn how to:
- describe and get information about places to stay
- give bad news in a polite way
- talk about past habits
- explain and deal with problems in hotels

Grammar
- Second conditionals
- *used to*

Vocabulary
- Hotel problems

Reading
- Happy campers

Listening
- Phoning a hotel
- Calling room service

SPEAKING

A How important are the following things when you are deciding where to stay on holiday? Give each a mark from 0 (= not important at all) to 5 (= very important).

- low price
- comfort
- Wi-Fi or Internet access
- cooking facilities
- parking
- air conditioning
- views from the building
- a convenient location
- a good breakfast
- a babysitting service
- a swimming pool or gym
- organised activities or entertainment
- a good restaurant

B Where was the last hotel, apartment, hostel or camping site you stayed at? What facilities did it have? Would you recommend it? Why? / Why not?

LISTENING

You are going to hear a conversation between an English man, David, and a hotel receptionist.

A Before you listen, read the following and decide what questions you think David will ask about rooms, cars, facilities or services his colleague and family might need, etc.

> A Portuguese colleague of David's is going to do some work in Dublin between the 13th and 15th of August. He is taking his wife and three-year-old child with him. They are going to spend some more days afterwards driving round Ireland. He has found a hotel in central Dublin close to the office and has asked David to ring and find out some more information, because he doesn't speak much English.

B ◈ 11.1 Listen and take notes on the information David gets. Discuss in pairs what you think David's colleague will decide to do and why.

C Listen again and read the audioscript on page 172. Underline five words or expression that you think are useful to learn. Compare what you chose with a partner.

LANGUAGE PATTERNS

Write the sentences in your language. Translate them back into English. Compare your English to the original.

Let me just check our availability.
Let me just talk to my friends.
Let me see that for a second.
Let me have a go.
Let us think about it and we'll let you know.

DEVELOPING CONVERSATIONS
Giving bad news

> We often say *I'm afraid* to apologise for giving bad news.
> *I'm afraid we're fully booked that weekend.*
> ....
> To reply to questions, we use *I'm afraid so / I'm afraid not.*
> D: *So you have to pay, right?*
> R: *I'm afraid so* (= I'm sorry, but yes you do)
>
> D: *Can they do it through the hotel?*
> R: *I'm afraid not* (= I'm sorry, but they can't)

A Work in pairs. Take turns asking the questions 1–8. Your partner should reply with *I'm afraid so* or *I'm afraid not*.
1 Is Internet access free?
2 Do I need to pay a cancellation fee?
3 You haven't got a room at the back, away from the noise, have you?
4 Are you closing already?
5 Did it reject my credit card again?
6 Are there any tickets left for tonight's performance?
7 Is it going to rain again tomorrow?
8 Can't you do something about it?

B Work in groups. You have three minutes to write as many things as you can that a hotel employee might say to guests using *I'm afraid*. For example:
I'm afraid we're full.
I'm afraid the air conditioning is broken.

C Which group thought of the most sentences? Which group had the funniest ones?

PRONUNCIATION Spelling and numbers

A 🔊 11.2 Listen and repeat the vowel sounds.
/iː/
/eɪ/
/e/
/aɪ/
/əʊ/
/uː/
/aː/

B Work in pairs. Say the alphabet and put each letter against the correct vowel sound. For example:
a – /eɪ/, b – /iː/, c – /iː/, etc.

C 🔊 11.3 Listen to the receptionist taking David's credit card details. Complete the form below.

Name on the card:

Card number:

Security number:

Expiry date:

Contact number:

> When we say card or telephone numbers, we often say /əʊ/ instead of zero. We say individual numbers – two four three nine – and not twenty-four, thirty-nine, etc.

D Invent some card details. Then work in pairs. Take turns asking for and giving these details. Note down the details and then compare them with what your partner wrote.

CONVERSATION PRACTICE

You are going to have two similar conversations to the one you heard in *Listening.*

A **Student A:** read the role card in File 8 on page 157.
Student B: read the role card on in File 5 on page 156.
Write down the questions you want to ask.

B Take turns being hotel receptionists and role-play the conversations. The receptionist should give at least two pieces of bad news starting with *I'm afraid.*

VOCABULARY Hotel problems

A What problems are the people having in each of the pictures above?

B Complete the sentences with the pairs of words.

available + booking	fixed + low
bill + overcharged	main road + noisy
boiling + air conditioning	toiletries + room service
filthy + insects	wake-up call + missed

1 Our room was next to the .... so there was lots of traffic and it was really ....
2 I didn't get my .... and so I overslept and I .... my flight!
3 My room was absolutely .... – and there was no ....!
4 I couldn't understand why it was so expensive. Then I checked the .... and found they'd .... us by 100 euro!
5 The room was absolutely ....! There were .... all over the walls and the bathroom. It was disgusting.
6 There were no .... in my room. I tried ringing ...., but there was no answer.
7 They told me that the room wasn't .... and that they didn't have any record of my ....
8 The shower really wasn't designed for tall people. It was .... to the wall – and the water pressure was so .... that hardly any water came out!

C Work in pairs. Discuss these questions.
· Which of the problems above is the worst? Why?
· Can you think of three more problems people might have in hotels?

GRAMMAR Second conditionals

> We use second conditionals to talk about imaginary situations now or in the future. The *if*-clause describes an imaginary situation. We use past tenses in this clause. The other clause describes the imaginary result. We usually use *would / wouldn't* + verb in this clause.
>
> *They'd lose* their deposit *if they didn't come.*
> *If they wanted* to rent a car, *could they do* it from the hotel?
> And what *if they came* earlier? *Would that be* better?

A Complete the sentences with the correct form of the verbs in brackets.
1 The hotel was awful! I .... stay there again if you .... me! (not / stay, pay)
2 A: The Conrad's an amazing hotel. I .... there more often if I .... afford to! (stay, can)
   B: I know what you mean. I'm sure they .... more business if they .... so expensive! (do, not / be)
3 A: I .... you to a quieter room if we .... one, but I'm afraid we're fully booked. (move, have)
   B: That's just not good enough! Can I speak to the manager, please?
   A: I'm afraid she's not here, but if she ...., I know she .... you exactly the same thing. (be, tell)
4 A: Double rooms are 100 each per night.
   B: Wow! OK. .... it .... cheaper if we .... a twin room instead? (be, have)
   A: A little bit, yes. That .... 85 a night – and that .... actually .... to 70 a night if you .... for more than four nights. (be, drop, stay)

▶ Need help? Read the grammar reference on page 150.

B Work in pairs. Look at the eight problems in *Vocabulary*, exercise B. Discuss what you would do in each situation. Try to continue each conversation. For example:

A: *If my hotel room was next to a noisy main road, I'd just wear earplugs.*

B: *Really? I wouldn't. I'd ask to change rooms.*

A: *What if they wouldn't let you or if they didn't have any other rooms?*

C Write three questions for other students in the class. Start *What would you do if …* . Then ask and answer the questions in groups.

> We often give advice using the expression *If I were you, I'd …*
> ....
> *If I were you, I'd look for somewhere else to stay.*
> *If I were you, I'd just take a taxi from the airport to your hotel.*
> *I wouldn't worry about it if I were you.*

D With a partner, decide what advice to give in each of the situations below. Use *If I were you, I'd …* .

1 I can't really afford to stay anywhere nice.
2 They expect tips for almost everything. It's so annoying!
3 There's a building site next to the hotel.
4 I'm thinking of renting a car from the hotel.
5 My flight gets in at midnight and I'm not sure how I'm going to get to my hotel.
6 When I turn the air conditioning on, it's too noisy, but when I turn it off, it's too hot!

LISTENING

You are going to hear a conversation between a guest and a hotel receptionist.

A Before you listen, work in pairs. Look at the things below. Discuss how you think they might be connected to this conversation.

B 🔊 11.4 Listen and see if you were right.

NATIVE SPEAKER ENGLISH

One second / a minute

We often say *one / a second* or *one / a minute* when we want someone to wait for us to do something. *Second / minute* can also just mean a very short period of time.

That's it for now. Oh, wait. Just one second.
I'll send someone up with the flowers in a minute.
I'm nearly ready. Give me two seconds.
I just need to make a phone call. I won't be a minute.

C Put the sentences in the order you think they appeared in in the conversation. Then listen again to check your ideas.

a … I'm afraid that's just not possible.
b … We really didn't have much time to prepare them.
c … I'll see what I can do.
d … I'm calling on behalf of Lady Zaza.
e … I'll tell her, but she's not going to like it.
f … She has a really bad nut allergy.
g … There was no way we could stay in that last place.
h … I would if I could, but I'm afraid I can't.

D Which of the adjectives below do you think describe Lady Zaza? Compare your ideas in pairs. Explain your choices.

> selfish   tidy   ambitious   demanding   lazy

E Work in groups. Discuss these questions.

- Can you think of any other adjectives to describe Lady Zaza? Do you know anyone else with these characteristics?
- Have you ever heard of anyone else making similar demands? What did they ask for?
- Why do you think people make demands like this?
- Why do you think people agree to these demands? Would you?

a bunch of roses

chocolates

a light bulb

kittens

the gym

READING

You are going to read about people's experiences of camping.

A Before you read, work in groups and make a list of the good and bad things about camping.

B Work in two groups. Group A, read the texts about Andro and Falah below. Group B, read the texts about Sherise and Marcia in File 14 on page 158. Find the good points and bad points that the people mention.

C Work in pairs with someone from your group. Decide how the people you read about would answer these questions.
1 What's your name?
2 Where are you from? What part?
3 Do you like camping?
4 When did you first go camping? Why?
5 Where did you go?
6 What was it like?
7 What did you do while you were there?
8 Were there many facilities at the campsite?

SEARCH BLOG | FLAG BLOG | NEXT BLOG

Falah Khiladi, Jordan

I live and was brought up in Amman, the capital of Jordan, but I'm actually from a family of Bedouin. My grandfather used to follow the traditional nomadic life, moving from place to place. I'm a real city boy now and I would never give it up. However, I usually go camping in the desert once a year with my father. I really love it. You feel a peace you can never get in the city with its noise and pollution. You feel closer to nature and God in the desert, and you wouldn't believe how many stars you can see!

Andro Zelic, Croatia

We used to go to the same campsite every year when I was a kid. It's a place on the coast not far from Split. It was a different world to Zagreb. We always used to see the same people there. There was a gang of us that just ran around all day. We went to the beach, played table tennis or football, explored the campsite and played hide and seek: we just did whatever we liked and we never used to go to bed before one in the morning. I can afford to stay in hotels now with my family, but to be honest, we prefer to camp. Hotels have a cold atmosphere. They're less friendly and there's not the same freedom and, actually, there are often more facilities at campsites – especially for kids.

D Work in pairs with a partner from the other group. Interview each other about the people you read about. Use the questions from exercise C. Don't read from the texts. Which sounds like the best place to you?

E Match two items from the box to each person. Explain the connections to your partner.

a fire	cool down	hide and seek	an achievement
peace	comfort	a city boy	a cold atmosphere

F Work in groups. Discuss these questions.
- Are you a city person or do you prefer the country? Why?
- Do you prefer hotels or camping? Why?
- Have you ever stayed up late at night looking at the stars or sitting round a fire with friends? Where? When?
- What do you know about the Girl Guides / the Boy Scouts?

GRAMMAR *used to*

A Which of the sentences 1–5 from the texts describe:
- a habit in the past? ..., ..., ...
- a habit in the present? ...
- a single action / event in the past? ...

1 We used to go to the same campsite every year.
2 There was a gang of us that just ran around all day.
3 I usually go camping in the desert once a year.
4 We never used to go to bed before one.
5 We all jumped into the pool to cool down.

> We often use *(never) used to* + verb instead of the past simple to describe past habits or states – especially to talk about things that have changed since. *Used to* does not have a present form. For habits in the present, use the present simple + *usually / never*, etc.

B Complete the sentences using *used to, never used to* or *usually*.
1 We moved to Madrid this year. We .... live in quite a small place on the coast.
2 I .... go to the beach every day, but now I can't.
3 We .... go to the cinema because the nearest one was 60km away!
4 Although there weren't many facilities, we .... get bored, because we .... make our own entertainment at home.
5 Now that I'm in Madrid, we .... go out three or four nights a week.

C You can rewrite some of the following sentences using *(never) used to*. Decide which ones and rewrite them.
1 I didn't like camping, but I love it now.
2 I did rock climbing when I was younger, but then I stopped.
3 We usually camp, but we rented an apartment this year.
4 He's quite fit and healthy now, but he smoked quite heavily when he was younger.
5 I had really long hair when I was at college, but I had to cut it when I started at the bank.
6 It's become a very popular place to go. It wasn't very crowded before.
7 I went camping once and I never went again after that.
8 This is my first summer holiday. I didn't go away on holiday in the summer when I was younger, because my parents ran a hotel.

▶ Need help? Read the grammar reference on page 150.

D Discuss in pairs what you think happened to cause the changes in 1–8 above.

E Work in groups. Tell each other about:
- something you never used to like, but do now
- a habit you changed and why
- someone you know whose appearance has changed
- a place, activity or thing that used to be popular, but now isn't
- a place, activity or thing that never used to be popular and now is.

12 PHONE

VOCABULARY Using phones

A **Use the extra information in 1–9 to guess the meanings of the words in bold. Translate the sentences into your language. Then check in the *Vocabulary Builder*.**

1 My son never answers his mobile when I call. I always have to **text** him.
2 When I called, I was put **on hold** for about 20 minutes with this terrible music playing.
3 I tried calling six times, but the **line** was always **busy**.
4 We couldn't finish our conversation because we **got cut off**.
5 Matt! Can I **call** you **back**? I'm having dinner.
6 The **coverage** isn't very good here. You might have to go outside to make a call with your mobile.
7 Sorry, I can't hear you very well. It's a very poor **signal**.
8 The number I had was for the wrong person, but she was helpful and **put** me **through** to the right department.
9 We started to argue and I didn't want to hear any more, so I just **hung up**.

B **Work in groups. Discuss these questions.**
· Do you know anyone who never answers their phone?
· Do you text or phone more? Why?
· Do you know anywhere that often puts you on hold?
· Why might you get cut off during a phone call?
· Do you know anywhere with bad coverage?
· Have you ever hung up on anyone? Why?

LISTENING

You are going to hear two short telephone conversations.

A 🔊 **12.1 Listen and complete the messages written after each conversation.**

1 ....
called. Meet him at
2 .... - not
3 ....

Diane 4 ....
called. 5 .... *is*
fine. Phone her to sort out
6 ....
Mobile: 7 ....
Phone today - she's
8 .... *tomorrow.*

PRONUNCIATION Sentence stress

We usually only stress the key words in a sentence. Generally, these aren't grammar words like articles, auxiliary verbs, prepositions or pronouns.

No, he's <u>not</u> <u>up</u> yet. Is it <u>urgent</u>?
Just <u>tell</u> him we're <u>meeting</u> <u>earlier</u> – at <u>seven</u>, not <u>eight</u>.

A **Look at the conversations in the audioscript on page 173 and notice the stressed words.**

B **Practise reading the conversations in pairs.**

DEVELOPING CONVERSATIONS
Asking for people and explaining where they are

When we answer the phone, we often explain where people are.

Diane's out visiting a client. (= she went and will return today)
He's away on business. (= in a different place for some time)
It's her day off. (= she doesn't work today)
He's off sick. (= he's not at work because he's ill)

A **Complete the sentences with the prepositions in the box.**

away	from	in	of	off	out	up

1 A: Hello, is that Mary Williams?
   B: No, it's Jane. Mary's .... She's just gone to the shops. Is it urgent?

2 A: Hello, could I speak to Mr Haskell?
   B: I'm afraid he's .... He won't be back for a few days. Can I take a message?

3 A: Hello, could I speak to John Waterman?
   B: Of course. Hold the line. I'm afraid there's no answer. He must be .... a meeting.

4 A: Could I speak to Ken Paterson, please?
   B: Oh, you've just missed him. He's just walked out .... the door.

5 A: Hi. Frazer?
   B: No, it's actually Sylvia. I'm covering for Frazer. He's .... sick at the moment. How can I help?

6 A: Hi, is Jay there?
   B: Yes, but he's not .... yet. Shall I wake him?

7 A: Hi, is Greg there, please?
   B: No, sorry. He's working .... home today.

B **Read the conversations in pairs. Reply to the questions and continue each conversation for as long as you can. Take turns to start.**

GRAMMAR *Just, already, yet* and *still*

We often use *just*, *yet* and *already* with the present perfect. *Just* shows the action happened very recently.
You've just missed him. He's just walked out of the door.

..

***Already* shows something happened before – often sooner than expected.**
We don't need any help. We've already finished it.

..

***Yet* shows we expected – or continue to expect – something to happen. It's used in questions and negatives.**
He's not up yet. Shall I wake him?

..

***Still* shows an action continues unchanged. It's used more with the present simple / continuous than the present perfect.**
Ask him if he's still looking for a job.
Could you tell him I still don't know when I'll be there.

A **Choose the correct word.**

1 Could you tell him I've *already / yet* spoken to Brittany, so he doesn't have to email her now?

2 Could you tell him I'm *already / still* waiting for confirmation of the price, but I'll ring as soon as I get it?

3 Just tell him I haven't got the money *already / yet*, but I should have it by Friday.

4 Could you tell her we're going to be late? We've only *already / just* left the house!

5 Could you tell her we're *still / just* having terrible problems with our computers and apologise for the delay?

6 Could you find out if she has received the package *still / yet* and ask her to let me know if she has?

7 Could you let her know I've sold the car *already / just*, but if she's *still / yet* interested in the bike to call me?

8 Could you tell him I've *still / just* come back from holiday and I've only *just / yet* received his message, so I haven't done anything about it *still / yet*.

▶ **Need help? Read the grammar reference on page 151.**

CONVERSATION PRACTICE

You are going to have similar conversations to the one you heard in *Listening*.

A **Before you start, write two messages you want to leave for different people. One should be more formal / in a business situation, the other one should be for a friend.**

B **Work in pairs. Role-play four telephone conversations. Take turns to start. Follow the plan in File 19 on page 159.**

READING

You are going to read three short news stories about phones and emergencies.

> In newspaper stories, the first sentence usually summarises what happened. Understanding this can help you understand the whole story.

A Read the first sentence of each of the stories below. Work in pairs. Discuss your ideas about the answers to the questions. **DON'T read the full stories yet.**

1 A police force has launched a campaign against misuse of the emergency phone number.
  a What's the emergency number?
  b How are people misusing the number?
  c What things are part of their campaign?

2 A doctor in Australia has saved the life of a young boy using a domestic drill and a mobile phone.
  a What happened to the boy?
  b What did the doctor use the drill for – and why a 'domestic' one?
  c Why did he need the mobile phone?

3 A chef has saved his own life, thanks to the photo of a rare spider that he took with his mobile phone.
  a Where was the man?
  b What happened to him?
  c What was the spider like?
  d How did the photo save his life?

B Now read the news stories and answer the same questions. Then compare in pairs. How many did you guess correctly?

C In pairs, discuss what the words in bold in the stories mean. Then complete sentences 1–8 with the words.

1 He's received three .... for driving too fast.
2 He .... because of the heat, but he was OK in the end.
3 After my wallet was stolen, I .... it to the police, but they said they couldn't do anything about it.
4 He keeps phoning, ... me telling him to stop.
5 There are hundreds of .... of animals that are becoming extinct each year.
6 I phoned the main number and then I was .... to the correct department.
7 It was quite urgent, so we .... him to the hospital.
8 The bump was huge. I had to keep ice on it to reduce the ....

D Imagine you are one of the following characters:
- Doctor Carson
- Matthew Stevens
- someone who receives 999 calls.

In pairs, role-play a conversation where you talk about your experience. Start like this:
A: How was your day at work?
B: Quite strange, actually!
A: Really? What happened?

1

Every day, the police in northern England have to answer three hundred 999 calls, but a third of them are totally unnecessary. Last year, the calls that police received included someone wanting a ride home, a man complaining about his TV not working and two people who **reported** lost cats. A number were also from young children who had accidentally dialled 999.

The police are sending leaflets to houses to explain the problem and have introduced £80 **fines** for those making improper calls.

3

Nicolas Rossi, a 13-year-old boy from a remote town in Australia, fell off his bicycle and hit his head. Although Nicolas initially seemed fine, his mother, a nurse, noticed a **swelling** on his head. She **rushed** him to the nearest hospital, where the doctor realised the boy was in danger of dying if he didn't have an operation to reduce the pressure on his brain.

Unfortunately, Doctor Carson had never done the operation, which required him to make a hole in the boy's head, and only had a normal household drill. After cleaning the drill, he phoned a colleague in Melbourne, who explained where and how to make the hole.

The one-minute operation was successful and the boy was **transferred** by plane to a Melbourne hospital, where he has made a complete recovery. Carson described his actions as 'just part of the job'.

Matthew Stevens, 23, was bitten by one of the world's most poisonous spiders, the Brazilian wandering spider, in a pub in south-west England, while he was cleaning the kitchen. The spider probably came into Britain in a box of bananas.

After the incident, Mr Stevens took a photo of the 12-centimetre spider with his mobile phone, but then went home, **despite** his hand swelling 'like a balloon'. At home, he **collapsed** with breathing difficulties and had to be rushed to hospital. Fortunately, he was able to show the picture on his phone. The photo was sent to a university, where they identified the **species** of spider and a cure for the poison.

LANGUAGE PATTERNS

Write the sentences in your language. Translate them back into English. Compare your English to the original.
A 13-year-old boy from a remote town in Australia ...
The one-minute operation was successful.
I got a 40-euro fine for parking in the wrong place.
There's a 50-metre swimming pool next to the hotel.
It's a 12-hour flight.

VOCABULARY Forming negatives

We add un– to lots of adjectives and adverbs to mean *not*.
100 calls are totally unnecessary.

When words begin with *p*, we usually use im–
introduce fines for improper calls

There are other prefixes meaning not: *il–*, *in–*, *ir–*

A Write the opposites by adding or removing a prefix.
1. a wise decision
2. it's illegal
3. a fortunate result
4. very polite
5. a happy marriage
6. totally expected
7. a practical solution
8. very fair
9. a comfortable bed
10. an uncommon name
11. a patient customer
12. an inconvenient time
13. completely possible
14. a natural product
15. an irrational fear
16. a very unpleasant man

B Write five sentences using the words with prefixes.

SPEAKING

A Work in groups. Tell each other about:
- any stories you've heard that are similar to the ones you read
- a time you were really glad you had a mobile phone
- an unusual phone call you made or received.

SPEAKING

A Work in groups. Discuss these questions.
- Have you ever phoned any of the places / people below?
- Why? What did you say to them?
- Did you sort out the situation(s)?

a bank	an Internet provider
an embassy	a gas or electricity company
a landlord	the local council
a postal service	a mobile phone company

LISTENING

You are going to hear a woman calling World Mail. Jaslyn is expecting two packages. They were sent by registered post some time ago and she wants to find out where they are.

A ⦿ 12.2 Listen and decide which number she should press next. Compare your ideas with a partner. Explain your choice.

B ⦿ 12.3 Now listen to Jaslyn talking to a World Mail employee. Answer these questions.
1. When were the packages sent?
2. What's Jaslyn's address?
3. Where are the packages now?
4. What's going to happen to them?

C Ten days later, Jaslyn has still not received her packages. She decides to call again. In pairs, discuss what you think she will say – and how she will report her previous conversation with World Mail. Use the extract below to help you:

The last time I called, the man I spoke to said my packages ¹........................ England on June the 16th, I think, and ²........................ in Manchester. He said they ³........................ that week and promised me that they ⁴........................ with me by the end of that week.

D ⦿ 12.4 Listen and complete the extract above by adding the verbs in the correct tense.

E Work in pairs. Discuss these questions.
- What would you do next if you were in Jaslyn's situation? Why?
- Have you ever had any similar problems to Jaslyn's? When? What happened?
- How do you feel about the postal service in your country? Why?
- Are automated telephone systems common in your country? What kinds of companies use them?
- How do you feel about automated systems? Why?

GRAMMAR Reporting speech 2

> **To report things people said, we often move 'one tense back'.**
> Present simple / continuous →Past simple / continuous
> Present perfect →Past perfect
> Past simple →Past perfect
> *Will* →*Would*
> *Can* →*Could*
>
> **Time expressions often change as well. For example:**
> *This week* →*Last week / That week*
> *Today* →*Yesterday / That day*
>
> 'They *entered* England on June the 16th.'
> →The man I spoke to said my packages *had entered* England on June the 16th.
>
> 'They'*re going out* this week.'
> →He said they *were going out* that week.

A Complete each of the sentences that report direct speech.
1. 'We're installing a new computer system.'
   → I phoned last month and the man I spoke to told me you .... a new system. Why is your system still so slow?
2. 'We've tried to deliver the package twice this week.'
   → The man I spoke to on Friday said you .... to deliver my packages twice last week, but that's impossible! I was at home all last week.
3. 'According to our records, the package arrived in the country on May the 1st.'
   → The last time I called, I was told that the package .... already .... in the country – and now you're saying it hasn't!
4. 'Your letter will be with you by Friday at the latest.'
   → I called two weeks ago and was told that my letter .... with me within a couple of days, but I still haven't received it.
5. 'We can offer you a full refund for the lost item.'
   → Last time I called, the guy told me you .... me a full refund, and now you're saying there's nothing you can do!

▶ **Need help? Read the grammar reference on page 151.**

B Look at the extract from an email below. In pairs, decide the exact words of the five questions that Joe was asked in his interview.

I couldn't believe it! I thought the interview would be easy. I mean, how difficult can it be to deliver mail? They asked me all kinds of strange things, though. They asked me how well I knew the area, if I could work nights and what kind of exercise I usually did. Then they asked why they should give the job to someone who would probably leave in a few months! Unbelievable.

Finally, right at the end, they asked me if I had any questions and I said 'Yes. Have I got the job?' and they all just started laughing and said they'd let me know! It was awful.

Anyway, hope you're well.
Joe

C Work in groups. Discuss these questions.
- Do you think the questions Joe was asked were strange?
- Have you ever had a job or university interview?
- How did it go? What did they ask you?
- What advice would you give someone about interviews?

SPEAKING

You are going to role-play a conversation between Jim, a Canadian studying in the UK, and an employee. Jim saw the advert below and decided to use World Mail as his Internet provider.

NEW FROM WORLD MAIL
Home broadband could not get any easier!

- £5 per month
- Delivery and installation within three days
- 24-hour-a-day telephone help desk
- Free wireless box
- Unlimited downloads
- No fixed minimum term for new customers

A 🔊 12.5 Listen to a message Jim left on a friend's answering machine. Note down the problems he describes.

B Work in pairs. Role-play the telephone conversation between Jim and a World Mail employee.
Student A: you work for World Mail. Decide how you are going to explain the problems – and what you can offer Jim to make him happy.
Student B: you are Jim. You're very unhappy about the service you're getting from World Mail – especially because it is different to what the advert promised. Decide what you want to complain about. These structures might help you:

The advert said ..., but actually ...
To begin with, I was told ...., but now you're telling me ...

C Role-play the conversation. Then change roles and start again.

NATIVE SPEAKER ENGLISH

drives me mad
We often say something *drives us mad* if it makes us really angry or annoys us.

I always just get this automated system, which drives me mad!
I get lots of sales calls. They really drive me mad.
People talking loudly on their mobiles really drives me mad.
She spends six hours a day on the phone. It drives me mad!

LEARNER TRAINING

If you want to get better at listening to English, it helps if you understand the different reasons why listening can be difficult. Sometimes it's hard to understand things because you don't know the words you're hearing. This is a language problem. At other times, you might find it difficult to understand things when you hear them, but when you see them in written form, you understand them OK. This is a listening problem. There are several ways to deal with these problems.

- Learn groups of words together – collocations, expressions, etc. *Outcomes* is full of examples.
- Practise saying individual sounds, but also practise saying – and listening to – how words are linked together in normal speech. The *Pronunciation* sections help with this.
- Read and listen to the audio at the same time to see what's a language problem and what's a listening problem.
- Replay listenings from the Workbook. Listen until you understand everything.

GAME

Work in pairs. Student A use *only* the green squares; student B use *only* the yellow squares. Spend five minutes looking at your questions and revising the answers. Then take turns tossing a coin: heads = move one of your squares; tails = move two of your squares. When you land on a square, your partner looks at the relevant page in the book to check your answers, but *you don't*. If you are right, move forward one space (but don't answer the question until your next turn). If you aren't right, your partner tells you the right answer, and you miss a go. When you've finished the game, change colours and play again.

Start	1	2	3	4
	Vocabulary p. 64: say four words connected with science and four connected with the weather.	*Vocabulary* p. 66: say eight different animals – and whether they are wild animals, farm animals, insects or pets.	*Native Speaker English* p. 66: if you can say what the *Native Speaker English* note was and give an example, throw again.	*Grammar* p. 67: say three different possi endings to this sente *I was really upset bed ...* . Use the past perf

5	6	7	8	9
Vocabulary p. 70: say six things that people do before doing a PhD.	*Native Speaker English* p. 70: if you can say what the *Native Speaker English* note was and give an example, throw again.	**Miss a go!**	*Pronunciation* p. 71: say six school subjects – with the correct stress.	*Grammar* p. 75: talk about an old school job. Say five things y had to do – and thre things you could do.

10	11	12	13	14
Miss a go!	*Developing conversations* p. 77: your partner will read 1–8. Respond with either *I'm afraid so* or *I'm afraid not*.	*Grammar* p. 78: your partner will read the eight problems in *Vocabulary*, exercise B. Say what you would do in each situation.	*Native Speaker English* p. 79: if you can say what the *Native Speaker English* note was and give an example, throw again.	*Grammar* p. 81: say six things you used t do when you were o holiday.

15	16	17	18	Finish
Developing conversations p. 83: say six reasons why people can't come to the phone.	*Grammar* p. 83: give four reasons why someone isn't in the office at the moment using *just, yet, already* or *still*.	*Vocabulary* p. 85: your partner will say ten of the adjectives from exercise A. Say the opposites.	*Native Speaker English* p. 87: if you can say what the *Native Speaker English* note was and give an example, throw again.	

For each of the activities below, work in groups of three. Use the *Vocabulary Builder* if you want to.

CONVERSATION PRACTICE

Choose one of the following *Conversation practice* activities.
Science and nature p. 65
School and university p. 71
Places to stay p. 77
Phone p. 83

Two of you should do the task. The third person should listen and then give a mark between 1 and 10 for the performance. Explain your decision. Then change roles.

ACT OR DRAW

One person should act or draw as many of these words as they can in three minutes. Their partners should try to guess the words. Do not speak while you are acting or drawing!

a whale	an operation	a view	poisonous
a storm	punishment	hand in	a brain
a play	a light bulb	a tie	a wedding
a cage	a mechanic	filthy	shocked
a tent	babysitting	hang up	a campsite
upset	jewellery	a refund	text

QUIZ

Answer as many of the questions as possible.
1 What's the opposite of **boiling**?
2 Say two things that are **extinct**.
3 Say three things you can be **suspected of**.
4 What kind of things do **cruel** people do?
5 When might you **make a speech**?
6 What kind of things do you study in **RE**, **IT** and **PE**?
7 If your tutors are **supportive**, is it good or bad? Why?
8 What's the opposite of an **optional** assignment?
9 What happens if someone **overcharges** you?
10 Say two different kinds of **toiletries**.
11 Where do you find an **expiry date**?
12 Say three things you can get **bitten** by.
13 When might you need to **apologise**?
14 Give an example of an **irrational fear**.
15 Say three different times when you might have to **sign a contract**.

COLLOCATIONS

Take turns to read out collocation lists from units 9–12 of the *Vocabulary Builder*. Where there is a '~', say *'blah'* instead. Your partners should guess as many words as they can.

PRONUNCIATION Words containing *e* or *i*

The letters e and i can be pronounced in lots of different ways. For example, retake /riːteɪk/ and pet /pet/ or windy /wɪndi/ and mines /maɪnz/. Learning some phonetic symbols can help you because then you can find the pronunciation in a dictionary.

A ☻ R 3.1 **Listen and repeat the sounds and words below.**
/e/   pet
/iː/   retake, mosquito
/ə/   fisherman, authority
/ɪ/   rocket, windy
/ɜː/   term, first
/aɪə/   environment
/eɪ/   jail

B **Work in pairs. Decide if the underlined sounds in each pair of words are the same or different. Use the phonetic symbols in exercise A to help you.**
1 canc<u>e</u>r / disc<u>o</u>v<u>e</u>ry
2 conv<u>e</u>nient / inv<u>e</u>stigate
3 syst<u>e</u>m / rock<u>e</u>t
4 flow<u>e</u>rs / bunch<u>e</u>s
5 heat<u>ed</u> / train<u>ed</u>
6 b<u>ee</u> / r<u>ea</u>son
7 <u>e</u>xtracts / <u>e</u>ffects
8 f<u>i</u>nals / pr<u>i</u>mary
9 redel<u>i</u>very / <u>i</u>tem
10 s<u>i</u>ght / w<u>i</u>tness
11 b<u>i</u>ology / meanwh<u>i</u>le
12 <u>i</u>ntroduce / <u>i</u>dentified
13 r<u>e</u>covery / <u>i</u>mproper
14 assignm<u>e</u>nt / respons<u>i</u>ble

C ☻ R 3.2 **Listen and check your ideas.**

D ☻ R 3.3 **You are going to hear eight groups of words. Write them down. Then compare what you have written.**

LISTENING

A ♫ **R 3.4 Listen to four people talking about things they do at work. Match jobs a–e to speakers 1–4. There is one job you do not need.**

a ...... a tour operator
b ...... a help-desk support worker
c ...... a teacher
d ...... a politician
e ...... a scientist

B Listen again and match items a–e to speakers 1–4. There is one item that you do not need. Which speaker:

a ...... describes a lucky accident?
b ...... recently visited an airport?
c ...... mentions the disadvantages of a job?
d ...... deals with the financial side of a job?
e ...... was involved with research in the countryside?

[... / 8]

GRAMMAR

A Put the verbs in brackets into the correct tense.

1 My cat was really hungry when I got home because I
.... to leave any food for her. (forget)
2 I .... you later this afternoon if I have time.
(call)
3 I .... already .... this film twice.
(see)
4 I'm not really sure. I .... yet. (not / decide)
5 He said he .... me last week, but he didn't.
(email)
6 I .... about it if I were you. (not / worry)
7 .... it still .... outside? (rain)
8 He's not here at the moment. He .... just
.... to the bank. (go)

[... / 8]

B Complete the sentences with one word in each gap.

1 Sorry I couldn't come last night. I .... to
work late.
2 He .... me if I wanted to go out with him.
3 I ordered it a month ago, but I'm ....
waiting for it.
4 I just couldn't believe it! I .... never seen
anything like it before.
5 I'd help you if I ...., but I'm afraid I can't.
6 Have you decided what you want ....?
7 I've .... come back from holiday, actually. I
arrived back at nine this morning.
8 I .... do it later this afternoon, if I don't
forget.

[... / 8]

C Find the four mistakes and correct them.

1 If I would have enough money, I would buy one.
2 In my last job, we could to start work any time
between seven and ten.
3 I was lucky at my secondary school because we
hadn't to wear uniforms.
4 He told me he's going to go to Spain next month.
5 I never used to like spicy food, but now I love it.
6 Maria asked me to say you she's going to be late.

[... / 6]

LANGUAGE PATTERNS

Complete the sentences with one word in each gap.

1 You should talk to your parents – or ....
you're close to – about the problem.
2 .... me just check with my boss.
3 London to Tokyo is a 12-.......................... flight.
4 I think her name is Dezeree, or .... like that.
5 You've got ten minutes .... before the end
of the exam.
6 I get a 15-.......................... coffee break at 11.

[... / 6]

▶ **Find this difficult? Look back at the grammar reference, pages 148–151.**

PREPOSITIONS

Choose the correct preposition.

1 I'm sorry. I'm afraid she's *away / off* sick today.
2 Have you heard the forecast *for / about* the
weekend?
3 You can't always protect kids *from / with* harm.
4 I'm not very good *in / at* Physics.
5 It can be really hard to say no to people *from / in*
authority.
6 I'm just going to put you *on / in* hold for a minute.
7 I'd like to do a Master's *in / about* Law.
8 There has been a huge increase *of / in* plagiarism
over the last few years.
9 I work *in / from* home two days a week.

[... / 9]

FORMING WORDS

Complete the sentences with the correct forms of the words in bold.

1 Passing all my exams was a real ....
   achieve
2 I can't hear you very well. The .... here isn't very good. **cover**
3 The course was a bit too .... for me. **theory**
4 We'll email you .... of your booking.
   confirm
5 Electricity is one of the greatest ....
   discoveries of all time. **science**
6 Will I need to make a .... when I make the booking? **pay**
7 Many of the .... later complained about the way the experiments had been conducted.
   participate
8 I'm afraid you have to pay a .... fee of 100 pounds. **cancel**
9 I'm not very good at organising my ....
   financial
10 We're hoping to publish the .... of our research sometime next year. **find**

[... / 10]

ADJECTIVES

Complete the sentences with the adjectives in the box.

| suitable | first-choice | desperate | urgent |
| ordinary | long-term | demanding | remote |

1 I've got a six-month-old daughter. She's lovely, but very ....
2 Hull wasn't my .... university, but I'm still enjoying my course here.
3 I don't really have any .... plans. I just live life day by day.
4 He comes from a .... part of the Philippines.
5 The film is not really .... for anyone under 18.
6 I can lend you some money if you're really ....
7 It's OK. It's not .... Just tell her I called and I'll phone back later.
8 He's very rich. I don't think he really understands how most .... people live.

[... / 8]

NOUNS

Match the nouns to the words they go with.

| fine | challenge | delivery | resources |
| uniform | environment | location | homework |

1 do my ~ / hand in my ~ / mark some ~
2 protect the ~ / damage the ~ / bad for the ~
3 a convenient ~ / a secret ~ / be in a perfect ~
4 financial ~ / have good ~ / a lack of ~
5 a school ~ / wear a ~ / men in ~
6 a big ~ / face a serious ~ / an exciting new ~
7 special ~ / sent by recorded ~ / next-day ~
8 introduce a ~ / get an 80-pound ~ / pay a ~

[... / 8]

▶ **Find this difficult? Re-read units 9–12 in the *Vocabulary Builder* for more information on collocation.**

VERBS

Choose the correct verb (a, b or c) below for each gap.

Police are [1]...... the death of three cyclists on one of the city's busiest roads last week. The head of the police force has [2]...... claims that too little is being done to [3]...... cyclists and has promised that all witnesses will be [4]...... in the next few days.

Meanwhile, cyclists have [5]...... a new campaign designed to [6]...... more people to start cycling to work or school. They are asking the city council to [7]...... more cycle lanes and introduce a new tax on cars that enter the city centre. 'We believe this would [8]...... the amount of traffic in town, which would then [9]...... the number of people who are happy to cycle,' a spokesman said.

1	a searching	b detecting	c investigating
2	a rejected	b received	c refunded
3	a access	b protect	c predict
4	a asked	b questioned	c investigated
5	a launched	b appeared	c aimed
6	a insist	b persuade	c let
7	a buy	b pay	c fund
8	a drop	b beat	c reduce
9	a boost	b emphasise	c grow

[... / 9]

[Total ... /80]

13 CULTURE

In this unit you learn how to:
- describe different kinds of films
- explain what you have heard about things
- talk about feelings
- talk about your favourite things

Grammar
- -ed / -ing adjectives
- The present perfect continuous

Vocabulary
- Films
- Music, art and books
- Compound nouns

Reading
- Welcome to Nollywood!

Listening
- Deciding what to go and see at the cinema
- My favourite

SPEAKING

A Work in groups. Discuss these questions.
- What was the last film you saw?
- Did you see it at the cinema or on DVD?
- What kind of film was it?
- Who was in it?
- What was it like?

VOCABULARY Films

A Work in pairs. Think of an example of each of the kinds of film below. Can you think of any different kinds of film?

a horror movie	a war movie
a science-fiction film	a thriller
a martial arts movie	an action movie
a historical drama	a musical
a romantic comedy	a comedy

B Discuss which of the kinds of films above might:
- have amazing special effects
- have a happy ending
- have complicated plots
- have car chases and explosions
- have amazing costumes
- be set in space
- be really scary
- be quite violent
- be quite predictable
- be really boring.

LISTENING

You are going to hear two friends deciding which film to go and see.

A 🔊 13.1 Listen and answer the questions.
1 What do you hear about these three films?

Dust and Heat	The Redeadening	It's a Love–Hate Thing

2 Which film do they decide to go and see in the end?
3 Where's it on?
4 What time does it start?

NATIVE SPEAKER ENGLISH

on
When an activity is happening, we often say that it's *on*.

What's on at the cinema tonight?
What else is on?
What time is that programme on?
There's a great exhibition on at the moment.

DEVELOPING CONVERSATIONS
supposed to

When we talk about something we know about, but don't have experience of, we often use *be supposed to* + verb to say what we have heard or what we know about it.

It's a new horror movie. It's supposed to be really scary.
It's supposed to have great special effects.

A Match 1–6 with a–f to make complete sentences.

1 I've never been to Hawaii,
2 I haven't seen *Mad Dog 3*,
3 I've never tried Indonesian food,
4 I've never heard The Boredoms,
5 I've never seen him play tennis,
6 I haven't been to the new shopping centre yet,

a but he's supposed to be really good at it.
b but it's supposed to be a violent film.
c but they're supposed to be quite strange.
d but it's supposed to be a beautiful place.
e but it's supposed to have a great selection of stuff.
f but it's supposed to be quite spicy.

B Think of one example of each of the following things – and think of what each one is supposed to be like.

• a very famous film that you've never seen
• a new film that you haven't seen yet
• a famous book you've never read
• a group, singer or CD you haven't heard
• a country you've never been to
• a kind of food you've never tried

C Work in pairs. Share your ideas.

GRAMMAR -ed / -ing adjectives

> There is a small group of adjectives that can end in either –*ed* or –*ing*. When they end in –*ed*, they describe people's feelings. When they end in –*ing*, they describe the thing or person that causes the feeling.
>
> *I got a bit bored with it after a while.*
> *What a boring lecture!*

A Complete the pairs of sentences with the correct adjectives.

1 tired / tiring
  a Let's just watch a DVD. I'm too .... to go out.
  b The film was in English – with no subtitles – so I found it quite .... to watch.
2 surprised / surprising
  a The ending was really ....
  b I'm not .... you didn't like it.
3 excited / exciting
  a I'm quite .... about the new Collocini film.
  b The car chase was really ....
4 bored / boring
  a It sounds a bit .... to me.
  b I got really .... about halfway through.
5 interested / interesting
  a I just wasn't really .... in any of the characters.
  b Isn't there anything more .... on?

▶ Need help? Read the grammar reference on page 152.

B Choose two of the things below. Tell your partner as much about them as you can.

• something you're quite excited about
• something you're really interested in
• something you found really surprising
• a tiring day you had
• an annoying person – or someone who has an annoying habit

CONVERSATION PRACTICE

You are going to have conversations like the one you heard in Listening.

A Think of three films you would like to see. They can be new films or old films. Note down what you know about each film. Think about:

• what it's called
• who directed it
• who's in it
• what kind of film it is
• what it's supposed to be like

B Work in pairs. Role-play the conversation using the three films you thought of. Decide which of the three films you want to go and see, where it's on and what time to meet. Then change roles and start again. Begin like this:

A: So what're you doing this afternoon? Have you got any plans?
B: I'm thinking of going to see a film. Would you like to come?
A: Maybe. What's on?
B: Well, there's a film called ...

VOCABULARY Music, art and books

A Put the words in the box into the list they are connected with.

| portrait | photographer | sculpture | album | exhibition | concert | singer | voice | composer | rehearse |
| landscape | instrument | publish | painting | auction | author | novel | crime | biography | comedy |

Music	Art	Books

B Work in groups. Discuss these questions about your favourites. Use some of the expressions below.
- Do you like art / reading / listening to music?
- Who's your favourite singer / composer / artist / author?
- What's your favourite song / album / piece of music / work of art / book? Why?

She's got an amazing voice / technique / style.

I'm a big fan of ... .

I don't really have a favourite, but I like ... .

I don't know why I like it so much. I just do.

It's a song / painting / novel by ... .

I think my all-time favourite is ... .

It changes. I've been reading / listening to ... a lot recently.

It's just really exciting / sad / beautiful, etc.

LISTENING

You're going to hear four people talking about their favourites.
1 Peter, UK, 27
2 Gustavo, Venezuela, 18
3 Zelda, Germany, 20
4 Mary, Ireland, 19

A 🔊 13.2 Listen and find out about who / what is their favourite. Match each person to one of the pictures below.

B Work in pairs. Discuss which person:
a has been a bit disappointed with something. Why?
b escaped problems when they were a kid. How?
c has been studying a language. Why?
d has changed their tastes recently. How? Why?

C Listen again and complete the following sentences.
1a I first heard her in 2003 when she won the Eurovision Song Contest and I .... ever since then.
1b In fact, I've been learning Turkish .... years.
2a I've been playing the trumpet .... now.
2b We've been .... *The Rite of Spring* .... for a concert.
3a For the last few weeks, they .... a drama series on TV.
3b There's less suspense because I .... the books!
4a I've known I wanted to be an artist ....
4b I .... more of a painter, especially people-portraits.

GRAMMAR The present perfect continuous

> **The present perfect continuous is *have / has* + *been* + *-ing*.**
> **Use it with *for* and *since* to talk about an activity that started in the past and is unfinished. Don't use the present continuous.**
> ~~*I'm living*~~ *I've been living here for ten years now.*
> *How long ~~are you playing~~ have you been playing the trumpet?*
> ....
> ***For* is used to say the amount or period of time:**
> *for six years, for ten minutes, for a while.*
> ....
> ***Since* shows when something started:**
> *since 2003, since I was 10, since yesterday, since then.*
> ....
> **Use the present perfect simple with *be, believe, hate, like, know, have* or if the verb is in the passive form.**
> *He's only known her since Christmas.*
> *It's been shown on TV for the last few weeks.*

A Write *how long* questions to ask about sentences 1–8. Use the verbs in brackets in the present perfect continuous or simple. For example:

1 I'm a member of a gym. (go there)
   How long have you been going there?
2 They have their dance class on Tuesdays. (do)
3 She speaks English well. (learn)
4 I'm a drummer in a band. (play)
5 I'm running in a marathon next week. (train)
6 Peter's my oldest friend. (know)
7 Franco is Violetta's boyfriend. (go out)
8 It's our wedding anniversary today. (be married)

B Work in pairs. Take turns asking the *how long* questions you wrote.
   Student A: reply using *for.*
   Student B: reply using *since.*

C Change partners. In pairs, ask each other the questions below. If your partner answers positively, ask a follow-up *how long* question. Your partner answers. For example:
   A: *Do you belong to any clubs?*
   B: *Yes, I'm in the Boy Scouts.*
   A: *Really? How long have you been going there?*
   B: *Since I was ten.*
   • Do you belong to any clubs?
   • Do you go to any classes outside school or work?
   • What languages do you know?
   • Do you play any musical instruments?
   • Who's your oldest friend?
   • Are you married – or do you have a girlfriend / boyfriend?

> **We use the present perfect continuous to focus on the activity – and to talk about how long.**
> *I've been learning Turkish for the last two years.* (=and I am still learning Turkish)
> ....
> **We use the present perfect simple to focus on finished actions in the time up till now – and to talk about how many.**
> *I've learnt 20 new words in the last two weeks.* (=that is the total for the last two weeks.)

C Choose the correct form.

1 *El Sistema* is a social programme in Venezuela. It aims to help children from poor backgrounds avoid problems like crime and drug addiction by teaching classical music. It has been running [1]*for / since* over 30 years and it [2]*has been producing / has produced* several international stars, including the conductor Gustavo Dudamel. He [3]*is conducting / has been conducting* the National Youth Orchestra for the last ten years. Since 2007, Scotland [4]*has been having / has had* a similar scheme and many other countries are also considering adopting the idea.

2 Henning Mankell [5]*has been writing / is writing* since the late 1960s. He [6]*has started / started* by writing plays, but then became internationally famous through his crime novels. He [7]*has been winning / has won* several awards for his books. In 1985, he founded a theatre in Mozambique and [8]*for / since* then, he's been working there part-time.

3 I've always [9]*loved / been loving* the Eurovision Song Contest. It's great. I've been watching it [10]*for / since* I was eight, when a rock band from Finland won. Apparently, it [11]*has been being shown / has been shown* on TV every year since 1956 and is one of the longest-running TV programmes in the world. Abba and Celine Dion were both past winners.

▶ **Need help? Read the grammar reference on page 152.**

SPEAKING

A In pairs, choose one set of questions and discuss them.

1 Have you heard of *El Sistema* before? Do you think it would be good in your country? What entertainment is there for young people where you live? What do you think is the best way to help kids avoid drugs and crime?

OR

2 Do you watch the Eurovision Song Contest or any other similar competitions? Why? / Why not? What do you think is the longest-running TV show in your country? Why is it so popular? Do you watch it? Why? / Why not? What competitions has you country won? How did you feel about it? Did you do anything to celebrate?

SPEAKING

A **Work in groups. Discuss these questions.**
- Does your country have a big film industry?
- Do most locally made films show at the cinema or do they go straight to video / DVD?
- What kind of films are most popular in your country?
- Why do you think this is?
- What are the most important local films from recent years?
- Who is the most famous director from your country?
- Do you know how many films he / she has made?
- Do you like his / her work? Why? / Why not?
- Is there any censorship of films? In what way?

READING

You are going to read an article about the film industry in Nigeria.

A **Before you read, discuss with a partner anything you know / have heard about Nigeria – and its film industry.**

B **Read the article and discuss in pairs how the writer, Femi Abulu, might answer the questions from *Speaking*. What else do you learn about Nigeria?**

C **Match the verbs with the words they are used with in the article.**

1	generate	a	tensions
2	represent	b	current issues
3	specialise	c	crazy
4	become	d	a common, neutral language
5	deal with	e	around £160 million a year
6	cause	f	civil war
7	experience	g	in action movies
8	go	h	involved with a religious cult

D **Compare your ideas with a partner. Can you remember who or what does / did each of the things in exercise C? Read the article again to check your ideas.**

E **Work in pairs. Discuss these questions.**
- What similarities / differences are there between the Nigerian film industry and the film industry in your country?
- Would you like to watch any of the Nollywood films? Why?/ Why not?
- Do you agree that 'films are about escaping from the problems of everyday life'? Why? / Why not?

LANGUAGE PATTERNS

Write the sentences in your language. Translate them back into English. Compare your English to the original.
Some dramas deal with current issues such as AIDS, corruption and women's rights.
He's starred in films such as *Frogs*, *Blue River* and *Hulk*.
The course covers areas such as music, theatre, TV and film.
Korean films such as *Old Boy* were big hits in Europe.

VOCABULARY Compound nouns

Compound nouns are made of two or more words that combine to make a single meaning. Some compound nouns are written as one word (*witchcraft*), some are joined with a hyphen (*my mother-in-law*) and some are written as two words (*the film industry*).

A **Look back at the article and find eight compound nouns. Compare what you found with a partner. Do you have the same words?**

B ⏺ 13.3 **Listen to how these compound nouns are pronounced. Where is the main stress – on the first or second word?**

business opportunity	sunglasses
security system	cash machine
social life	swimming pool
heart disease	tennis court
marketing manager	traffic lights

C **Listen again and repeat the words.**

D **Spend two minutes memorising the compound nouns above. Then work in pairs.**
Student A: close your book.
Student B: explain the compound nouns. See how many your partner can guess.

E **Work in groups. Make one extra compound noun from each of the 10 in exercise B. Use the first or the second noun of each to form your new words. The first group to think of 12 new connected nouns wins. For example:**
the film *industry* → the fashion *industry*
OR
the *film* industry → a *film* star

SPEAKING

The article said that some films are banned in Nigeria because they cause tensions between different groups in society.

A **Work in groups. Discuss these questions.**
- Can you think of any other reasons for banning films?
- Do you know of any banned films?
- Can you think of any reasons – funny or serious – why some people might think the things below should be banned?
- Do you agree with any of these reasons?

reality TV	advertising	homework
boxing	mobile phones	fast food
golf	shopping centres	smoking

come to Nollywood!

lu introduces the weird and wonderful world of Nigerian cinema.

It might surprise you to learn that the third biggest film industry in the world – behind the United States and India – is based in Nigeria. Producing over 500 films a year, the industry generates around £160 million a year. The majority of films are made on budgets of between £10,000 and £20,000, and take an average of just ten days to complete. Compare this to the £65 million and year-long filming period needed to make the average Hollywood movie! However, while they may be cheap to produce, Nigerian films obviously still make good money.

They are not designed for the cinema. Instead, they are filmed on video cameras and copied directly onto video cassettes or DVDs, which are then sold at street stalls and tiny shops not just in Nigeria, but right across Africa. Most films are recorded in English, as it represents a common, neutral language in a country of 150 million people, where over 230 different languages are spoken.

While Hollywood specialises in action movies and the Indian Bollywood studios produce amazing musicals, Nollywood – as the Nigerian film industry is known – is the home of voodoo horror movies: films about witchcraft and black magic.

It all began in 1992, with *Living in Bondage*, a terrible tale about a man who becomes involved with a religious cult that promises incredible wealth if he kills his wife. Since then, these kinds of movies have become increasingly popular, with Nigeria's most famous director, Chico Ejiro, being at the centre of the boom. Ejiro has directed over 80 movies, and despite the poor sound quality and predictable endings, his films are much loved.

Not all Nollywood films are horror movies, though. Gangster movies are also popular, as are success stories. Some dramas deal with current issues such as AIDS, corruption and women's rights. However, certain subjects are generally avoided and films are occasionally banned because they may cause tensions in a country with people from so many different backgrounds and which has experienced civil war.

In the end, the films about witches are popular for much the same reasons as *Harry Potter* or *Lord of the Rings*, even if they don't have quite the same special effects or amazing costumes. They are fantasies where the bad people are punished and the good people rewarded: the cheating husband loses his physical powers, or an evil love rival goes crazy, or the poor man becomes rich. Films are generally about escaping from the problems of everyday life and in a tough society like Nigeria this becomes even more important!

Glossary

voodoo: voodoo is an ancient religion still practised in some parts of Haiti and West Africa. Followers believe in magic and pray to spirits – beings that cannot be seen.

witchcraft: witchcraft is the use of magic to harm or help other people.

black magic: black magic is a type of magic where evil spirits are used to do harmful things.

14 THINGS

In this unit you learn how to:
- describe things / people / places that you don't know the names of
- talk about common household objects
- explain where things are
- discuss the environment and environmental issues

Grammar
- Relative clauses
- *must / mustn't*

Vocabulary
- Things in the house
- Containers
- Verbs with two objects

Reading
- Rubbish food

Listening
- Things we need to buy
- Receiving presents

GRAMMAR Relative clauses

A **Work in pairs. How many of the questions below can you answer?**

What do you call …
1 … the news about the weather that tells you if it will be hot, cold or rainy tomorrow?
2 … something fixed to a wall which you put books and things like that on?
3 … the thing in the kitchen that you can pull open and keep things like knives and forks in?
4 … the money which you borrow from a bank to buy a house?
5 … a person that has to leave their country because of war or because of their political beliefs?
6 … a person who lives next-door to you, or upstairs or downstairs from you?
7 … someone who sees a crime – or an accident?
8 … the place where you play football?
9 … the place in a school or university where you can read or borrow books?
10 … the place where you play tennis?

B **Now match the words in the box to the questions in exercise A.**

a shelf	a neighbour	a drawer	a pitch
a forecast	a refugee	a library	a court
a mortgage	a witness		

We use relative clauses to add information about what a thing, person or place is or does. We use *which / that* for things, *who / that* for people and *where* for places.

A net is the thing *which / that* separates one half of a tennis court from the other.
A pilot is someone *who / that* is trained to fly planes.
A car plant is a kind of factory *where* cars are produced.

C **Complete the sentences by adding *which, who* or *where*.**
1 A tent is the thing .... you sleep in when you go camping.
2 A conductor is a person .... tells an orchestra how to play.
3 A building site is the place .... a new building is being constructed.
4 The equator is a line .... goes round the middle of the earth.
5 Your colleagues are the people .... work with you.
6 A mosque is a building .... you go and pray if you're Muslim.
7 A drill is a kind of tool .... you make holes with.
8 A gallery is a building .... you can see art exhibitions.
9 A client is someone .... pays for the professional services of a person like a lawyer.

▶ **Need help? Read the grammar reference on page 153.**

D **Write definitions of the words in the box using *which / that, who / that* and *where*.**

a cancellation fee	a sink	a landlord
a babysitter	a town hall	an embassy

E **Work in groups. Tell each other about:**
- a thing which is really important to you. Explain why.
- a person who has influenced you. Explain how.
- a place where you were very happy. Explain why.

LISTENING

You are going to hear three new flatmates planning a shopping trip.

A 🔊 **14.1 Listen and decide which of the objects in the pictures opposite they are going to buy – and why they want them. What is each of these things called?**

B **Describe the other things in the pictures.**

VOCABULARY Things in the house

A Which of the rooms and places below do you have where you live? Compare your answers with a partner.

a kitchen	a bathroom	a bedroom
a living room	a garage	a spare room
an office	a garden	a dining room

B Which of the objects in the box can you see in the pictures below?

a mop and bucket	a towel	a pan
a hammer and nails	a hairdryer	a duvet
a needle and thread	a cloth	a stapler
a vacuum cleaner	a plaster	an iron
a bin a desk	a torch	a rubber

C Where in your house would you put each of the objects below? Discuss your decisions with a partner.

D Complete the sentences below with the correct words from exercise B.

1 Have you got .... I could borrow? I'd like to have a shower.
2 Have you got ....? I'd like to clean the table.
3 Have you got ....? I've just cut myself.
4 Have you got ....? I'll make us some soup.
5 Have you got ....? I need to go out into the garden and it's really dark out there.
6 Have you got ....? I need to put a button back on my shirt.
7 Have you got ....? I've just spilt water all over the kitchen floor.
8 Have you got ....? I've just spilt some sugar.

DEVELOPING CONVERSATIONS
Explaining where things are

> We often give two descriptions of where things are: one general, one more specific. Keep a record and notice the prepositions used. For example: *It's in the kitchen, in the cupboard under the sink.*

A Choose the correct prepositions.

1 There's one *at / in* the bathroom, *on / at* the shelf..
2 There's one *under / down* the sink in the kitchen.
3 There's one *on / at* the desk in my study.
4 There's one *at / on* the side – next to the sink.
5 There's one *at / in* the corner of the garage.
6 There's one *in / at* the cupboard *down / under* the stairs.
7 There's one *in / at* a drawer in the kitchen, the one *up / above* the fridge.
8 There's one in the garage, in a box *at / by* the door.

B Work in pairs. Take turns asking the questions in *Vocabulary*, exercise D. Give answers that are true for you. Use prepositional phrases from above. For example:

A: *Have you got a towel I could borrow? I'd like to have a shower.*
B: *Yes, there are some on a shelf in the bathroom, on the left when you go in.*

CONVERSATION PRACTICE

You are going to have a similar conversation to the one in *Listening*.

A Work in pairs. Imagine you are going on a picnic. Look at the pictures of the things you want to take.
Student A: look at File 15 on page 159.
Student B: look at File 1 on page 156.

B Discuss what you want to take. Explain what the objects are. Make sure your partner understands what you mean. Then decide where to go – and how to get there.

VOCABULARY Containers

A Label the pictures of each family's weekly shopping with the words in the box.

a can of cola	f box of cereal
b packet of biscuits	g sack of rice
c carton of milk	h pot of yoghurt
d jar of honey	i bar of chocolate
e tin of tomatoes	j tray of meat

B Work in pairs. Say which of the containers are usually made of metal, glass, plastic, cardboard or cloth.

C Work in pairs. Discuss these questions.
- Which family do you think spends the most?
- Which family has the healthiest diet?
- Which of the families do you think causes the most damage to the environment? Why?
- How does your family's weekly food shop compare to these families?

READING

You are going to read an article about supermarket shopping and the environment.

A Before you read, discuss the following in groups.
1 Does your family shop at a supermarket? Which one? Why?
2 Make a list of issues you think the article might mention.

B Read the article and find four things you shouldn't buy – and explain why.

C Discuss in pairs whether you think these sentences are true or false.
1 100% efficiency is impossible.
2 The writer lives in New Zealand.
3 The writer doesn't recycle anything.
4 Producing aluminium is very inefficient.
5 Plastic bottles reduce transport costs.
6 Tap water is better for the environment than bottled.
7 The author eats a lot of meat.
8 Eating a lot of cheese is bad for the environment.
9 The sausages which were found were 30 years old.

NATIVE SPEAKER ENGLISH

loads

We often say *loads* instead of *lots* or *a lot*.

There's loads of waste.
There were loads of people at the party.
He earns loads in that job!
I've got loads of work to do.

RUBBISH FOOD

There are laws of nature that we can't ignore, like gravity and waste. We know what goes up must come down and, similarly, we can't avoid the fact that everything we produce and consume leads to waste. In the case of my supermarket shopping, there's loads of waste. Professor Liam Taylor, an expert on the environment, is trying to convince me I could waste less.

From my shopping basket, he picks up a polystyrene tray of six New Zealand kiwi fruits covered in clear plastic. 'These probably caused three tons of carbon dioxide by being flown twelve thousand miles. To make things worse, this kind of plastic is almost impossible to recycle. What's wrong with local apples?'

'Nothing', I weakly reply, 'I just prefer kiwis.'

'Hmm. Well, if you must have them, eat Italian ones – and buy them with no packaging.'

He looks at the bottles of water and cans of cola. Before he can say anything, I say, 'I'm always careful to recycle those.'

'Well, that's good, but the aluminium in those cans is bad. They must mine

D Work in groups. Discuss these questions.
- Which of the families in *Vocabulary* do you now think causes the most damage to the environment? Why?
- Which things that the professor suggests do you do?
- Is there anything in the text you don't believe? Why?
- Do you recycle any of the containers in *Vocabulary*?

E Read the fact file together in pairs and discuss:
- if you find any of the facts surprising
- what your country does to encourage reducing, reusing and recycling.

- Every American produces an average of 2 kg. of rubbish a day.
- It costs around $100 per tonne to dispose of rubbish and $1000 a tonne to get rid of chemicals such as paint.
- In comparison, steel costs $200 per tonne to produce.
- The UK buries over 90% of its waste, Denmark under 10%.
- The airports in New York are built on top of rubbish.
- The Swiss have the best record for recycling.
- Switzerland charges people for throwing away rubbish. People mustn't leave rubbish outside without a sticker on the bag to show they have paid their tax.
- 3% of electricity in Switzerland is made from burning waste.
- Recycling is good, but it's better to reduce or reuse.

GRAMMAR *Must / mustn't*

Must shows something essential to do because of a law or an order – or because you think it's essential.
I must take out the rubbish before I forget.
You can also use *have to* in these examples.

Mustn't shows it is essential not to do something.
People mustn't leave rubbish outside without a sticker on the bag to show they have paid their tax.

You can't use *don't have to* instead of *mustn't*. *Don't have to* means it's not necessary to do something.

A Choose the correct form.
1. The new law means companies *must / mustn't* reduce waste by 10%.
2. The new law says you *must / mustn't* smoke anywhere in or around public buildings.
3. You *must / mustn't* throw chemicals away with the normal rubbish. It's against the law.
4. I *must / mustn't* repair my car. It's dangerous to drive.
5. I *must / mustn't* remember to call Frank and tell him the meeting's cancelled.
6. I *don't have to / mustn't* forget to pay my gas bill.
7. We *don't have to / mustn't* pay tax on rubbish.
8. If you *must / mustn't* have soft drinks, buy them in plastic bottles.

B Write four laws using *must / mustn't* to improve the environment or reduce waste.

▶ Need help? Read the grammar reference on page 153.

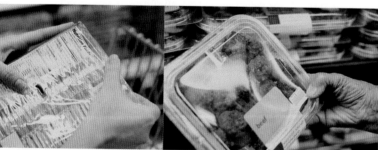

four tonnes of rock to get one tonne of aluminium, and the transport costs of the cans and glass bottles are higher as they are heavier than plastic. Anyway, what's wrong with having tap water? It's much more efficient.'

'I … er … prefer … .' The professor's look stops me from finishing the sentence!

'If you must have soft drinks, buy them in recyclable plastic bottles and get the largest size, because they use less plastic than lots of small bottles. The same is true of those small boxes of cereal.'

The next problem is the amount of meat I've bought. He tells me the chicken is OK, but generally meat is bad for the environment. 'Firstly, cows and sheep produce a lot of natural gas which causes global warming. Secondly, they're an inefficient way to get food energy. Better to be vegetarian, especially if the vegetables are locally grown and you don't eat too many dairy products.'

I am becoming depressed as all my favourite things get

crossed off my shopping list. 'What about those cakes?' I say. 'They were made in the supermarket bakery and the packaging is biodegradable.'

He laughs. 'Well, I guess the cake is OK, but forget about biodegradable!' Apparently, a team of archaeologists recently investigated sites where rubbish had been buried. They found newspapers that were thirty years old, and which you could still read, next to perfectly preserved sausages!

I feel slightly sick and very, very guilty.

Glossary

biodegradable: if something is biodegradable it means that it can be naturally changed by bacteria and can safely become part of earth or water.

SPEAKING

A **Work in groups. Discuss these questions.**
- What was the last present you received? What was the occasion? Were you happy with it?
- What's the best present you've ever received / given? What was so good about it?
- Have you ever received any strange or bad presents? Who from? What was wrong with them?

LISTENING

You are going to hear four people talk about presents they have received.

A **🔊 14.2 Listen and answer the questions about each speaker.**
1 What presents did they get?
2 What was the occasion?
3 Were they happy with the presents when they got them? Why? / Why not?

B **In pairs, discuss what you remember about how these words were used by each speaker. For example:**
clues: Her sister sent her an email with clues about the present.

1 clues	link	click
2 close	petrol	weight
3 message	attractive	broke up
4 taxi	polite	papers

C **Listen again and read the audioscript on page 176 to check your ideas.**

LANGUAGE PATTERNS

Write the sentences in your language. Translate them back into English. Compare your English to the original.
She's really good with computers.
I'm not very good with money.
She's amazing with children.
He's very good at Physics and Chemistry.
She's great at painting and drawing.
I'm not very good at swimming.

D **Work in pairs. Discuss these questions.**
- Which of the presents mentioned do you think is the best / worst? Why?
- Why do you think the third speaker's ex-boyfriend gave her an iron? What would you do if something similar happened to you?

VOCABULARY Verbs with two objects

Certain verbs are often followed by two objects. The first object is usually a person – or a group of people; the second object is usually a thing.
My big sister *bought me my own website*.
She *sent me an email* with the link in it.
He *gave me an iron* for my birthday!

If we want to put the thing first, then the person / people is / are added in a phrase that begins with *for* or *to* .
My big sister bought *a website for me*.
She sent *an email to me* with the link in it.

A **Complete the sentences with the verbs and the second objects in the box.**

ask + a personal question	make + a cup of tea
buy + a car	pour + a drink
cook + dinner	read + a bedtime story
give + something special	send + a card
lend + some money	tell + a secret

1 Do you mind if I .... you ....? How much did you pay for it?
2 Sorry about that. I couldn't talk earlier. I had to .... my kids .... before they went to sleep.
3 I can't believe it! My dad has promised to .... my brother .... when he graduates! He doesn't even have a licence yet!
4 I'm going to .... my flatmates .... tonight. I'm doing a traditional dish from my country.
5 I've left my wallet at home. Can you .... me ....? I'll pay you back tomorrow, I promise.
6 Sorry. I didn't realise your glass was empty. Let me .... you ....
7 Could you .... me ....? The kettle's over there. I'm sorry to ask, but I'm really busy!
8 It's my mum's 60th birthday next month and I want to .... her .... Do you have any ideas?
9 If I .... you ...., do you promise not to tell anyone else?
10 My parents don't really give me presents any more, but they usually .... me .... for my birthday.

B **Work in pairs. Discuss these questions.**
- Do you ever cook dinner for people? When was the last time? What did you cook? What was it like?
- When was the last time someone cooked you dinner? What was it like?
- Do you ever send cards / eCards to people? Why?
- Who was the last person you lent money to? Have they paid you back?
- Who do you usually tell your secrets to? Why?

SPEAKING

A Work in groups. Decide what is the best present to get in each of the situations below. Explain your ideas.

- It's your grandparents' golden wedding anniversary. They've been married for 50 years.
- Your cousin turns 13 next week and you want to buy her something special.
- Some friends of yours – or of your family – have just had their first baby.
- It's Valentine's Day next week and you want to get your boyfriend / girlfriend something romantic.
- You've been invited to someone's house for dinner and you want to take something for them.
- Someone where you work is retiring next month.
- Some friends have moved in to a new house and have invited you to a party there.
- Your English course is ending soon and you want to buy your teacher something.

15 MONEY

VOCABULARY
The economy and quality of life

A Translate the words in **bold** in exercise B into your language.

B Work in pairs. Decide if each item 1–8 shows that:
a   the economy is doing well.
b   the economy is doing badly.

1   **Inflation** is quite low. Prices don't change much.
2   There's a lot of **unemployment**. Around 15% of the working population don't have a job.
3   Our **currency** is very **strong**, so it's cheap for us to travel abroad.
4   The **cost of living** is very **high**. A lot of people can't afford basic things.
5   Unemployment has **gone up** a lot over the past year.
6   Our currency is really **weak** at the moment. It's very expensive to import things from abroad.
7   The **average salary** is quite high. I think it's about $35,000 a year.

C Work in groups. Discuss the following questions.
1   How do the following things affect your quality of life? For example: *I think if you have a close, strong family, you have a good quality of life.*

job security	time off	pace of life	crime
cost of living	climate	transport	family

2   Are there any other factors that you think are important for a good quality of life?
3   Which things do you think are most important? Why?

LISTENING

You are going to listen to two people, Aidan and Laima, speaking in a foreign country, Freedonia. Laima is on holiday and Aidan works in a school there.

A 🔊 15.1 Listen and find out:
1   what the quality of Aidan's life in Freedonia is like
2   how well the economy is doing
3   why he wants to leave.

B Listen again and choose the words you hear.
1   The economy's doing quite badly *at the / in this* moment.
2   I'm actually going back to Canada *in / for* a few months.
3   Unemployment has gone up quite a lot over the *last few months / rest of the month*.
4   I could get paid a lot more *back home / in Canada*.
5   Eating out is *twice / half* the price in my country.
6   That's true, but it used to be cheaper *in / at* the past.
7   Anyway, *in / at* the end, I miss my family and friends.
8   I don't mind the cold weather so much. You get used to it after a *time / while*.

C Work in pairs. Discuss these questions:
·   From what you heard, do you think Aidan is making the right decision? Why? / Why not?
·   Apart from family and friends, what *would / do* you miss if you *lived / live* abroad?
·   Which of the things below are unusual for you? Could you get used to those different things?

freezing weather	very spicy food
boiling weather	only two weeks off a year
wet weather	driving on the left
vegetarian food	working long hours

GRAMMAR Time phrases and tense

Some time phrases commonly go with particular tenses. For example:

currently	The present continuous
over the last two years in the last few months since last month / year	The present perfect simple
in a few days in two weeks' time over the next few weeks	Futures (e.g. *be going to* and *will*)
in the past when I was younger when I was at school	*used to* (+ verb)

A **Use the verbs in brackets with the present continuous, the present perfect, *be going to* or *used to*. Pay attention to the time phrases.**

1 At the moment, the economy .... quite well. (do)
2 Unemployment .... over the last few months. (fall)
3 The cost of living .... a lot in the last five years. (go up)
4 Eating out .... a lot cheaper when I was a kid. (be)
5 There .... an election in four months' time. (be)
6 The government .... currently .... popularity. (lose)
7 According to the government, inflation .... over the next few months. (fall)
8 Crime .... less of a problem when I was younger. (be)
9 Our currency .... stronger at the moment. (get)
10 We .... more job security in the past. (have)

B **Work in groups. Discuss which of the ten sentences above are true for your country. Explain your ideas.**

▶ **Need help? Read the grammar reference on page 154.**

DEVELOPING CONVERSATIONS
Comparing prices

We often compare prices in different places and times:
Eating out is twice the price in my country.
Milk is much more expensive than it used to be.

We often give an example:
You can get a three-course meal for about $6 here. A meal costs $20 back home.
You can't get a litre for less than a euro now and it used to be only 70 cents.

A **Give examples of the cost of the things in 1–8, using the words in the box and a price.**

can	pair	suit	laptop
kilo	litre	packet	digital camera

1 Clothes are much cheaper there than elsewhere. You can get a designer .... for ....
2 The crisps in here are four times more expensive than they are in the shops. A .... costs ....
3 Soft drinks there are four times the price they are here. You can't get a .... for less than ....
4 Computers are much cheaper than they used to be. You can get a .... now for ....
5 Petrol is a lot cheaper there. A ....
6 Shoes are much more expensive there. You can't get a ....
7 Electronic goods are much cheaper there. You can get a good ....
8 Rice is much more expensive than it used to be. You can't get a ....

B **Work in pairs. Take turns starting conversations. Use your ideas from exercise A to respond. For example:**
A: Clothes are much cheaper there than elsewhere.
B: I know. You can get a designer suit for about €200.

C **Work in groups. Tell each other about very expensive / cheap places you know and give examples. Are there any things that have risen or fallen in price over the last few years?**

CONVERSATION PRACTICE

You are going to have similar conversations to the one you heard in *Listening.*

A **Student A:** talk about your own country. Talk about what the economy and quality of life are like.
Student B: read the role card in File 17 on page 159.

B **Now change roles.**
Student A: read the role card in File 10 on page 158.
Student B: talk about the country you are really from.

You are going to read a short story about a woman going to the reading of her father's will. A *will* is a legal document where a person writes down what should be done with their possessions after they die.

A **Before you read, discuss these questions in groups.**
- Why is it important to have a will?
- When do you think is a good time to write one?
- Do you have anything special you'd leave to someone?
- What surprises can happen when a will is read?
- Have you heard of any stories in the news about wills?

B **Now read the story and find out why the author was surprised.**

C **Work in pairs. Discuss the following:**
1 Explain the different sayings the author's family had.
2 What things do you think the daughters liked when they were young, and what didn't they like? Why?
3 How do you think the parents became rich?
4 Why do you think they didn't tell their daughters?
5 How do you think the daughters felt about it when they found out?

WILL POWER

None of us had any idea what was going to happen when we arrived at the lawyer's office. Dad had died two months earlier in his bed in the same two-bedroom house where we'd grown up. Apart from the house, we didn't expect Dad to leave anything of value. I mean, for years after my mum died, he'd gone to a neighbour's house to watch TV. I offered to buy him a TV once, but he just said, 'Never buy what you can borrow!' That was typical of him. I guess he liked his neighbour's company as well.

My mum had never worked and Dad was an insurance salesman. We assumed he wasn't successful because we were never bought toys and we wore second-hand clothes. We just thought he couldn't afford these things. Dad used to find bits of wood and turn them into toy boats and dolls. Mum taught us to make and repair clothes, which we used to do together at night. They had funny little sayings that they'd repeat whenever we complained about things: 'Money's silver, but a needle and thread is gold!' 'Early to bed, early to rise, makes a man healthy, wealthy and wise'; 'Never buy what you can borrow, never throw away what you can repair.' We used to laugh at them, and sometimes invented are own silly sayings: 'A fool spends what the wise man saves'; 'A glass of water is worth all the tea in China.' We laughed, but having so little money was often annoying. I think we were the only family in our school without a TV; we never drank soft drinks, and sharing a room with two big sisters for sixteen years was difficult.

So we walked into the lawyer's office and sat down. We were serious, but not sad any more. Dad had had a good life. The lawyer started reading; I was hardly paying attention, really, but then the numbers seemed to continue without end. 'Wait, I'm sorry,' I said. 'How much did you say he had?' The lawyer smiled, 'Yes, I imagine it does need repeating. Two million, seven hundred and eighty-one thousand, six hundred and fifty three pounds and eighteen pence.'

We didn't know what to say! Nearly three million pounds! How? Why? We had so many questions, so many feelings.

LISTENING

You are going to listen to the rest of the story.

A 🔊 **15.2 Check you understand 1–6 below. Then listen and decide if the sentences are true or false.**

1 Her father had won the money.
2 He bought shares in a company that doubled in value.
3 The daughters didn't receive all of the money.
4 She's still angry about the situation.
5 The money will help other people.
6 She's planning to spend the money on a holiday.

B **Work in pairs. Discuss these questions.**

- How would you feel if you were in this situation?
- Do you agree that the parents did a fantastic thing? Would you do it? Why? / Why not?
- What would you do if you had a quarter of a million pounds now?

VOCABULARY Money verbs

A **Look at the story again and at the audioscript on page 177 and find as many words as you can that are connected to money. Compare your ideas with a partner.**

B **Complete the conversations with the correct form of the verbs in the box.**

borrow	buy	earn	give	invest
leave	owe	save	win	worth

1 A: Sorry, can I .... two euros? I don't have enough.
   B: Of course. Just take it. I .... you three euros, anyway.
2 A: I'm thinking of going to see the new opera.
   B: .... your money! It's not very good and the tickets cost a lot.
3 A: Hey, I've .... ten euros on the lottery!
   B: Wow! Ten euros. What are you going to do with it? .... it in shares? Buy a boat?
   A: There's no need to be sarcastic. I was going to .... you a coffee actually, but maybe I won't now.
4 A: Would you like to .... money to a children's charity each month?
   B: I'm sorry. I can't afford to. I don't .... much in my job.
   A: It doesn't have to be much. Every little helps.
   B: I'm sorry. Not today I'm in a hurry.
5 A: That's a nice painting. It looks quite old. Is it .... much?
   B: I don't know. My granddad .... it to me when he died. I don't know how valuable it is, but I'd never sell it.

C **Work in pairs. Answer the questions about the word *pay*.**

1 What different ways can you **pay for** something?
2 What kinds of **bills** do people have to **pay**?
3 When do you have to **pay** a bank / someone **back**?
4 How and when do people **get paid**?
5 When do you have to **pay interest**?
6 Who do you **pay to do** something?
7 Where do people have to **pay attention**?

PRONUNCIATION Numbers

A **How do you say these numbers from the story?**

B 🔊 **15.3 Listen and check.**

£2,000,000	653	£4.12	¼
781,000	1965	2.7	

C 🔊 **15.4 Listen and write down the numbers you hear in 1–8.**

1 The minimum wage at that time was .... an hour.
2 Inflation fell to .... last month.
3 The government is going to invest .... in schools.
4 .... of the population own a car.
5 The new factory will create .... jobs.
6 The house cost ....
7 We borrowed .... from the bank.
8 We'll finally pay back the mortgage in ....

SPEAKING

A **Work in groups. Discuss these questions.**

- Are you good at saving money? Is there anything you're saving for at the moment?
- What do you spend most of your money on?
- What are good things to invest money in? Have you ever invested in shares? Were they successful?
- In which jobs do you think people earn too much money? In which jobs do they earn too little? Why?
- Do you know anyone who's won any money? How?
- Have you ever lost money? How?
- Have you ever been left anything (e.g. in a will)? What?
- What charities have you given money to? What do they do?
- Would you consider borrowing money from a friend? In what situations? If not, why not?
- Does anyone owe you anything (money / a meal / a favour, etc.)? Why?

LISTENING

You are going to hear four conversations about money problems.

A **Work in groups. Discuss these questions.**
- What kind of money problems might the people in the pictures below have?
- What's the best way to deal with each of the possible problems?
- Which problem do you think is the worst? Why?
- Have you ever any had any similar problems? When? What happened?

B 🔊 15.5 **Listen and match each conversation to one of the pictures below.**
- What problems are mentioned in each?
- How are the problems dealt with?

C **Work in pairs. Try to complete the sentences. Then listen again to check your answers.**

Conversation 1
1 I'll get this. It's my ....
2 What's ....?
3 I've just realised I .... my wallet in my other jacket.

Conversation 2
4 It's hard to find things like that in this ....
5 Look – there's a .... here.
6 The best price I can .... is 150.

Conversation 3
7 .... have just gone up.
8 I haven't .... to save much yet.
9 Maybe we can .... some money from the bank.

Conversation 4
10 Your card was cancelled because of some .... activity.
11 We .... that your card was copied sometime last month.
12 Everything is covered by your ....

NATIVE SPEAKER ENGLISH

What's up?
We often use *up* to mean *wrong*.

A: Oh no!
B: What's up?
A: I've just realised I left my wallet in my other jacket.

What's up with you today? Why are you in such a bad mood?
There's something up with that cash machine. It's not working.
I think something is up with my car. It's making a funny noise.

D **Work in pairs. Discuss these questions.**
- Who do you think should pay on dates: the man, the woman or both? Why?
- Do you like vintage clothes? Why? / Why not?
- Are you good at negotiating good prices in markets?
- How much money do you think parents should give their children? Until what age?
- Have you heard any stories about credit cards being copied – or about any similar crimes?
- Have you managed to do anything difficult this year?

LANGUAGE PATTERNS

Write the sentences in your language. Translate them back into English. Compare your English to the original.
I haven't managed to save much yet!
How did they manage to do that?
I managed to borrow €1000 and my dad lent me the rest.
The best price I can manage is 150.
It's OK, thanks. I can manage.

GRAMMAR Present tenses in future time clauses

> We use present tenses to talk about the future in clauses with *when, as soon as, before, after* and *until*. We often use *will, won't, can, be going to* or imperatives in the other main clause.
>
> ....
>
> *I'll pay you back as soon as I get paid.*
> *You pay half back when you have the money, OK?*
> *You'll receive your new PIN number after you get the card.*

A Choose the correct form.

1 I'm going to try and find a part-time job when *I'm / I'll be* at university.
2 What *do you do / are you going to do* after you graduate?
3 Call me as soon as you *arrive / will arrive*, OK?
4 *I'm going to move / I move* back home before the recession here gets worse.
5 You'll just have to save until *you / you'll* have enough money!
6 The software is really good. It'll really speed things up, but it might take some time before *you get / you'll get* used to using it.
7 *I'll / I pay* you back when I get paid, OK?
8 Can you two please finish arguing about the bill after *I / I'll* leave?
9 *We'll / We* support you until you graduate. After that, though, you'll have to start looking after yourself!
10 I'm waiting for confirmation of the dates, but *I call / I'll call* you as soon as I hear anything.

▶ **Need help? Read the grammar reference on page 154.**

B Complete the sentences below using your own ideas. Then work with a partner and compare what you have written.

1 When I get home today, I'm going to ... .
2 As soon as I have enough money, I'm going to ... .
3 After this course ends, I'll probably ... .
4 Before I get too old, I'd really like to ... .
5 I'm going to carry on studying English until ... .

VOCABULARY Dealing with banks

A Match the verbs in the box to the pairs of collocations they go with.

cancel	change	charge	make
open	pay	take out	transfer

1 ~ a savings account / ~ a joint account with my partner
2 ~ a mortgage / ~ a loan
3 ~ a complaint / ~ a payment
4 ~ money / ~ my PIN number
5 ~ £1000 from my current account to my savings account / ~ money to my son in Thailand
6 ~ money into my account / ~ bills by direct debit
7 ~ my credit card / ~ a cheque
8 ~ 5% interest / ~ me 30 euros

B Try to remember the collocations in 1–8 above. Test each other in pairs.
Student A: read out the eight verbs.
Student B: close your book. Try to remember the pairs of collocations.

C Work in pairs. Discuss these questions.
- Why do you think people / banks do the things in exercise A?
- Which of these things have you done? When?

SPEAKING

A Work in pairs. Choose two of the following situations to role-play. Decide which roles you are going to play. Spend a few minutes preparing what to say. Use the audioscript on page 177 to help you if you need to. Then have the conversation.

1 Two friends are having lunch in a café. They try to decide how they are going to pay. One person realises he doesn't have any money. They work out what to do about it.
2 One person wants to buy a second-hand car. The seller asks a very high price. The buyer tries to negotiate a better price. The buyer points out problems with the car. They try to reach a deal.
3 A teenager wants her dad to buy her a new laptop. The father is worried about how much it will cost and how he will pay for it. He suggests alternative ideas. They try to reach a deal.
4 A customer is phoning a bank to find out why their credit card was rejected in a shop. The bank employee explains the situation and tells the customer what will happen next.

16 DATES AND HISTORY

SPEAKING

A **Work in groups. Discuss these questions.**
- Why do the events below usually happen?
- Where do they usually happen?
- What kinds of things usually happen at each one?
- Which do you think are the best / worst to go to? Why?

a birthday party	a leaving party	a dinner party
an office party	an end-of-term party	a house-warming
a surprise party	a launch party	a wedding reception

VOCABULARY Describing parties

A **Use the extra information in 1–10 to guess the meanings of the words in bold. Translate the sentences into your language. Then check in the *Vocabulary Builder*.**
1 Everyone was great – really **warm** and friendly.
2 It was nice – not too loud. Just good **background** music.
3 It used to be a factory, but they **converted** it a few years ago.
4 Not very friendly, actually. They seemed a bit **cold and distant**.
5 It was nice. They had a **buffet** and everyone helped themselves.
6 Well, the first DJ was great, but the second guy completely **cleared** the dance floor.
7 It was fantastic. It's an amazing **venue** for a party.
8 It was great to begin with, but then there was a big argument and that **ruined** the rest of the evening.
9 Oh, it was OK. They just put a few **bowls** of olives and crisps and things on the tables.
10 It was great. I thought the organisation of the whole event was very **impressive**. They did a brilliant job.

B **Match each of the questions below to two sentences from exercise A.**
1 What was the party like?
2 What was the place like?
3 What was the food like?
4 What was the music like?
5 What were the people like?

C **Work in pairs. Think of one more way of answering each of the questions above.**

LISTENING

You are going to hear three conversations about parties.

A 🔊 **16.1 Listen and answer the questions about each conversation.**
1 What kind of party was it?
2 Whose party was it?
3 Where was it?
4 What was it like?

B **Which conversations did you hear each of the adjectives below in? Can you remember what each adjective described? Compare your ideas in pairs. Listen again to check.**

spicy	easy to talk to	traditional
modern	gorgeous	grilled
lovely	impressive	full

C **Work in pairs. Discuss these questions.**
- What's the best kind of wedding / reception to have? Why? How much do you think it's right to spend?
- Are there are any converted buildings in your area / town? Would they be good places to live / have a party?
- Do you prefer dinner parties or eating out? Why?

NATIVE SPEAKER ENGLISH

round

We often use *round* when we talk about visiting people's homes.

I just felt like inviting some friends round.
My parents are coming round tonight.
I'm going round to my brother's tonight.
We're having a few people round on Friday.

DEVELOPING CONVERSATIONS
Linked questions

> When we ask for descriptions of things, we often ask one question followed by another. The first question is more general, the second contains our ideas about the answer. The second question is normally the one that is answered.
>
> A: So what did you do last night? Anything interesting?
> B: Yeah, I had a little dinner party at my place.
>
> A: So how did it go? Was it good?
> B: Yeah, it was lovely. It was really nice to see everyone.

A Match the general questions in 1–8 with the linked questions in a–h.

1 How was Michelle?
2 What was the weather like?
3 What time did the party go on till?
4 How did you feel when you found out?
5 Where did you have the party?
6 Who was there?
7 What's their new house like?
8 How was the launch party?

a Was it a bit of a shock?
b Anywhere nice?
c Was it late?
d Did everything go according to plan?
e Was she OK?
f Was it nice and hot?
g Is it big?
h Anyone I know?

B Work in pairs. Write positive and negative answers for each pair of linked questions in exercise A. For example:
A: How was Michelle? Was she OK?
B: Yeah, she was great. It was really good to see her again.
  or
B: No, not really. She'd just broken up with her boyfriend.

C Write linked questions to ask other students about:
• what they did last night
• their last holiday
• their house / flat
• their parents – or brothers and sisters.

D Ask your questions to some other students in the class.

CONVERSATION PRACTICE

You are going to have similar conversations to the ones you heard in *Listening*.

A Think of three parties or celebrations you have been to in the last five years – or invent three. Think about the following questions:
• What kind of parties were they?
• What was the occasion for each?
• Where were they?
• What was the place like?
• Was there any food / music? If yes, what was it like?
• What were the other guests like?
• What time did the party go on till?

B Pretend the parties / celebrations happened last night. Have conversations with other students. Start like this:
A: So what did you do last night? Anything interesting?
B: Yeah, I did, actually. I went to … .

VOCABULARY Historical events

A Complete the fact file about Britain with the correct form of the words in the box.

end	become	be defeated	invade	gain
join	rule	be founded	be crowned	

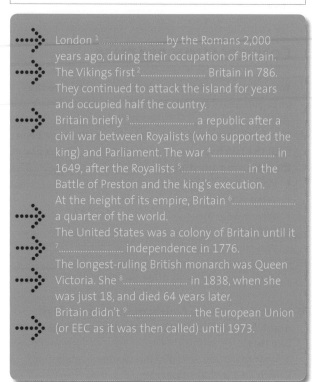

London ¹.......................... by the Romans 2,000 years ago, during their occupation of Britain.
The Vikings first ².......................... Britain in 786. They continued to attack the island for years and occupied half the country.
Britain briefly ³.......................... a republic after a civil war between Royalists (who supported the king) and Parliament. The war ⁴.......................... in 1649, after the Royalists ⁵.......................... in the Battle of Preston and the king's execution.
At the height of its empire, Britain ⁶.......................... a quarter of the world.
The United States was a colony of Britain until it ⁷.......................... independence in 1776.
The longest-ruling British monarch was Queen Victoria. She ⁸.......................... in 1838, when she was just 18, and died 64 years later.
Britain didn't ⁹.......................... the European Union (or EEC as it was then called) until 1973.

B Find the nouns in the fact file which mean:
1 a war between two groups in the same country
2 the time a foreign power lives in and controls a country
3 the act of killing someone for doing something wrong
4 a short fight which is part of a longer war
5 a royal leader such as a king or queen
6 a large group of countries controlled by another country.

READING

You are going to read an article from a newspaper series called *Around the world in 300 words*.

A Read the introduction and discuss the questions in pairs.
1 Do you know anything about the country? What?
2 Why do you think UK people don't know much about it?

Ask most people on the streets of the UK what they know about Kazakhstan and the only thing they can say is 'We played them at football.' Ask where it is, and they may mention it's near Russia, but that's all. Yet Kazakhstan is huge – the 9th largest country in the world and the size of Western Europe. We think it's time people got to know it better. Oh, and yes, it is near Russia – they share a border of 6,846 kilometres!

B Read the article and answer these questions.
1 How many years have people lived there?
2 How has the Kazakh lifestyle changed?
3 When did the country finally become independent?
4 What's the main industry?
5 What's the most interesting information for you?
6 If you know the country or know about it, is there anything important that isn't mentioned? Would you change anything in the text?

C Discuss your answers in groups.

Around the wor

KAZAKHSTAN

People have lived in the region since the Stone Age. The society was nomadic – Kazakh comes from a word meaning 'free spirit' – with different groups living off seasonal agriculture and animals such as goats, sheep and horses, that fed on the steppe grassland. For many centuries, the Silk Road trade route went through the region, which led to the founding of cities such as Talaz, now 2,000 years old.

Islam was introduced by the Arabs in the 8th century, and Genghis Kahn's Mongol army invaded in 1219. Over the next 200 years, a distinct Kazakh language, culture and economy emerged, although still based on nomadic life.

Population: 16.4 million.
Capital: Astana (changed from Almaty in 1997).
Place to visit: The Charyn Canyon.
Big building: The Pyramid of Peace, Astana. The cultural centre aims to bring together all the great religions.
Special day: 22nd March. *Nauriz* celebrates Spring, friendship and unity. It was banned during Soviet rule.
Firsts: The horse was first tamed in this region. The oldest and largest space launch site in the world is Baikonur Cosmodrome. It is leased to Russia.

GRAMMAR Prepositions and nouns / –ing forms

> Prepositions go before nouns. If we need a verb to follow a preposition, we use an *–ing* form to make the verb into a noun.
> *After gaining* independence in 1991, Kazakhstan's economy grew rapidly.
>
> ....
>
> Some verbs are followed by particular prepositions.
> Economic changes ... *resulted in* hunger and tension.
> It eventually *led to* fighting in 1916, followed by civil war.

300 words...

This traditional lifestyle changed during the 1800s, when the country was occupied by Russia. The political and economic changes and a population growth caused by people settling in the region resulted in hunger and tension. It eventually led to fighting in 1916, followed by a civil war.

In 1920, Kazakhstan became part of the communist Soviet Union. Over the following decade, the last Kazakh nomads were forced to live on farms or work in industry. Other people within the Soviet Union, including Germans, Ukrainians and Koreans, were also sent to work there.

After gaining independence in 1991, Kazakhstan's economy grew rapidly. It's now the 11th largest producer of oil and gas as well as exporting many other natural resources. *Next week Kenya*

A Match the verbs to the prepositions with nouns or prepositions + –ing forms.

1	lead	a	from the Stone Age
2	result	b	on support from the king
3	depend	c	of corruption
4	date	d	to a revolution
5	be accused	e	in people leaving the country
6	be opposed	f	for joining NATO
7	be caused	g	to joining NATO
8	be involved	h	people from playing music
9	ban	i	in the independence movement
10	vote	j	by economic problems

▶ **Need help? Read the grammar reference on page 155.**

B Write five true sentences about events or people in history, using verbs and prepositions from exercise A.

PRONUNCIATION Dates

> We write dates as *22nd March* or *the 8th century*. We say them as *the twenty-second of March / March the twenty-second* or *the eighth century*. We say years as two groups, so 1219 is said as *twelve nineteen*.

A ◐ 16.2 Listen and write down the dates you hear.

B Discuss which dates in exercise A go with the following.
1 the end of the Second World War
2 the Middle Ages
3 Christmas Eve
4 America declared independence
5 the deaths of both Shakespeare and Cervantes
6 Yuri Gagarin became the first man in space
7 the anniversary of the fall of the Berlin Wall
8 the Aztecs ruled in what is now Mexico

SPEAKING

Work in groups. Choose one of the following:

A How much do you know about politics and history? Can you think of:
- two countries that have had civil wars.
- two countries that have been invaded. Who invaded them?
- two organisations in which countries work together. When were the organisations founded?
- two countries which have executed a leader.
- two countries that've gained independence from Britain.
- two countries that've become democracies in the last 20 years.

B Do you know the dates these events happened and / or what led to them? What were the results?

C What should go in *Around the world in 300 words* for your country? What are the most important events? What places would you mention? Why? What would go under the headings *Place to visit, Big building, Special day and Firsts*?

Speaking

A Work in groups. Tell each other:
1 your birthday
2 the last day of term or of your English course
3 the next public holiday
4 a date you always remember for personal reasons
5 a date with national or global significance.

Listening

You are going to hear five people talk about special days.

A 🔊 16.3 Listen and take notes on what special days each person mentions – and why each day was special.

B There are three words missing from each of the sentences below. Can you remember the missing words? Compare your ideas with a partner.

1a As a black man, I was treated like a ....
1b I'll remember the day he was elected for as long ....
2a My great-grandmother on .... was Ukrainian.
2b I felt .... with the place.
3a It's .... of the day Princess Diana died.
3b Her death in 1997 was ....
4a I climbed Mount Kinabalu in Malaysia, one of the highest mountains ....
4b We .... just as the sun was coming up.
5a I had a special operation on my stomach to stop ....
5b Thanks to my surgeon, I've been given .... in life.

LANGUAGE PATTERNS

Write the sentences in your language. Translate them back into English. Compare your English to the original.
We reached the peak just as the sun was coming up.
I finally got to the cinema just as the film was ending.
It started raining just as we were leaving the house.
She was leaving just as we were arriving.
Just as I decided to start talking to her, her mobile rang!

C Listen again and check your ideas.

D Work in pairs. Discuss these questions.
• Which of the five days mentioned do you think is the most / least special? Why?
• Do you know where your mother's and father's sides of the family come from originally?
• Do you remember where you were when you heard about the death of someone famous?
• Do you think having an operation to stop you gaining weight is a good idea? Why? / Why not?

GRAMMAR Verb patterns
(-ing and to -infinitives)

When some verbs are followed by others, the second verb is in the *-ing* or the *to*-infinitive form. There are no rules for this. Learn which verbs have which patterns.

We *started climbing* at midnight
I *wanted to come*, but I couldn't *afford to buy* a ticket.

A Complete these sentences from *Listening* by putting the verbs from the box into the correct form.

become	gain	go	help	sit	travel

1 There were places I was never allowed ....
2 The fact that Barack Obama, a man of colour, managed .... President of the United States was truly remarkable.
3 My mum and I decided .... on a trip to the village that she came from.
4 Diana loved .... people.
5 I spent six months .... round South-east Asia.
6 I had a special operation on my stomach to stop me .... weight.

B Look at the audioscript on page 178 to check your ideas.

C Choose the correct form.
1 I'll never forget *seeing / to see* my baby son for the first time. It was an incredible experience.
2 My sister offered *taking / to take* me shopping for my birthday last year.
3 After failing five times, I finally managed *passing / to pass* my driving test this year!
4 I'll always remember *feeling / to feel* really, really excited as the plane was landing in New York.
5 January the 1st 2005 is an important day for me. That's the day I stopped *eating / to eat* meat.
6 I can still remember the day I decided *becoming / to become* an architect. That was a big day for me.
7 I'll never forget the night my boyfriend asked me *marrying / to marry* him.
8 The day I moved into my own flat was really special. I hated *sharing / to share* a house, so it was a huge relief!
9 I finished *watching / to watch* the last series of *Friends* last month. That was a big day! I'd like *watching / to watch* all the DVDs again, but my wife doesn't want to!
10 I didn't feel like *going / to go* to the party, but a friend persuaded me *going / to go* with her and I'm glad I did.

▶ Need help? Read the grammar reference on page 155.

D Work in pairs. Tell your partner about:
• something you'll never forget seeing or doing
• something you finally managed to do – after trying and failing for a long time
• something important you decided to do
• something you'd really like to do in the future
• something you hate doing.

Speaking

A **Think of two special days that you have good memories of. Think about the following questions.**
- Where were you on these special days?
- Who were you with?
- What happened?
- How did you feel?
- Why were these days so special?

B **Tell some other students about your special days. Who do you think had the most special experience? Why?**

LEARNER TRAINING

There are two different ways to practise your writing. The first is to write stories, emails or conversations that use new language you've learnt. This will help you remember what you've studied. The second way is to write emails, letters, essays, etc. for particular purposes. To do this, you need to study examples of the kinds of writing you want to do, and see how grammar and vocabulary work in them. You can then write similar pieces yourself, using what you've learnt.

- Each level of *Outcomes* contains eight two-page lessons on different kinds of writing. You will learn how to write for social, professional and academic purposes.
- In each lesson, try to re-use some of the language you study. This will help you write more fluently.

- You can also write stories or conversations after you finish each unit in this book. If you do this, use as much new language from the unit as possible.
- If possible, ask your teacher to check and correct any writing you do. Keep a note of any common mistakes.

GAME

Work in pairs. Student A use *only* the green squares; student B use *only* the yellow squares. Spend five minutes looking at your questions and revising the answers. Then take turns tossing a coin: heads = move one of your squares; tails = move two of your squares. When you land on a square, your partner looks at the relevant page in the book to check your answers, but *you don't*. If you are right, move forward one space (but don't answer the question until your next turn). If you aren't right, your partner tells you the right answer, and you miss a go. When you've finished the game, change colours and play again.

Start

1
Native Speaker English p. 92: if you can say what the *Native Speaker English* note was and give an example, throw again.

2
Developing conversations p. 92: talk about four things you know about, but don't have experience of, using *supposed to*.

3
Vocabulary p. 94: say five words connected to music, five words connected to art and four words connected to books.

4
Grammar p. 95: you partner will read sentences 2–8 from exercise A. Ask *how* questions about eac one. .

5
Vocabulary p. 99: say eight things from exercise B – and where you might keep each one.

6
Vocabulary p. 100: say eight different kinds of container – and what might be inside each one.

7
Miss a go!

8
Native Speaker English p. 100: if you can say what the *Native Speaker English* note was and give an example, throw again.

9
Grammar p. 101: sa four things people *must / mustn't* do if they want to impro the environment.

10
Miss a go!

11
Vocabulary p. 104: say five true things about your country using vocabulary from exercise B.

12
Grammar p. 105: your partner will say eight time phrases from the explanation box. Make sentences in the correct tenses using each one.

13
Native Speaker English p. 108: if you can say what the *Native Speaker English* note was and give an example, throw again.

14
Vocabulary p. 109: y partner will say the pairs of collocations exercise B. Say the v that go with each p

15
Native Speaker English p. 110: if you can say what the *Native Speasker English* note was and give an example, throw again.

16
Developing Conversations p. 111: your partner will read out 1–8 from exercise A. Say the linked questions.

17
Vocabulary p. 112: your partner will read the six definitions in exercise B. Say the correct words.

18
Grammar p. 114: your partner will read 1–10 from exercise C. Say whether the *–ing* form or the *to*-infinitive is correct in each.

Finish

For each of the activities below, work in groups of three. Use the *Vocabulary Builder* if you want to.

CONVERSATION PRACTICE

Choose one of the following *Conversation practice* activities.
Culture p. 93
Things p. 99
Money p. 105
Dates and history p. 111

Two of you should do the task. The third person should listen and then give a mark between 1 and 10 for the performance. Explain your decision. Then change roles.

ACT OR DRAW

One person should act or draw as many of these words as they can in three minutes. Their partners should try to guess the words. Do not speak while you are acting or drawing!

spill	a portrait	martial arts	a buffet
crisps	gorgeous	a car chase	sculpture
a will	a plaster	PIN number	be crowned
a mop	a bill	a conductor	a funeral
a shelf	a bowl	negotiate	packaging
pour	a wallet	a surgeon	an auction

QUIZ

Answer as many of the questions as possible.
1   Say the names of three films that have **amazing special effects**.
2   What's the difference between **an exhibition** and **a gallery**?
3   Give two examples of **censorship**.
4   Give two examples of **corruption**.
5   Why do people **take out mortgages**?
6   Say three reasons why people become **refugees**.
7   When do you need a **towel?**
8   What do **archaeologists** do?
9   Say two things that happen during **a recession**.
10 Why do people **take out loans**?
11 What kind of things might be **covered by insurance**?
12 Why might there be **an election**?
13 What could **ruin** your holiday?
14 What's the difference between **invading** a country and **occupying** a country?
15 If people are **nomadic**, where do they live?

COLLOCATIONS

Take turns to read out collocation lists from units 13–16 of the *Vocabulary Builder*. Where there is a '~', say 'blah' instead. Your partner should guess as many words as they can. s

PRONUNCIATION
Phonetic symbols

Learning how to pronounce new words in English can be hard. The spelling does not always help you. Learning phonetic symbols does help because then you can check the pronunciation in a dictionary. Remember that there is a full list of all the phonetic symbols in the *Vocabulary Builder*.

A   Match 1–10 to a–j.

1	/riːdʒən /	a	shame
2	/wɪəd/	b	publish
3	/eksɪkjuːʃn/	c	monarch
4	/vɔɪs/	d	diabetes
5	/mɒnək/	e	charity
6	/ʃeɪm/	f	execution
7	/ʃeəz/	g	region
8	/daɪəbiːtiːz/	h	weird
9	/tʃærəti/	i	shares
10	/pʌblɪʃ/	j	voice

B   🔊 R 4.1 Listen and check your answers. Practise saying 1–10.

C   Write the words shown in phonetic script below.
1   /rɪhɜːs/
2   /tekniːk/
3   /weləʊ/
4   /fɔːkɑːst/
5   /aɪən/
6   /duːveɪ/
7   /vedʒəteəriən/
8   /eksɪkjuːʃn/
9   /sɪvl wɔː/
10 /vækjʊəm kliːnə/

D   🔊 R 4.2 Listen and check your answers. Practise saying 1–10.

LISTENING

A **R 4.3** **Listen to four different radio extracts. Match extracts a–e to speakers 1–4. There is one extract that you do not need.**

a ...... an advertisement for a charity
b ...... an election advertisement
c ...... international news
d ...... a government statement
e ...... an advertisement for a new play

B **Listen again and match items a–e to speakers 1–4. There is one item that you do not need. Which speaker:**

a ...... discusses a possible change?
b ...... mentions a depressing contrast?
c ...... explains a decision?
d ...... talks about murder?
e ...... promises a surprise?

[... / 8]

GRAMMAR

A **Put the verbs in brackets into the correct tense.**

1 My parents have promised to support me until I .... (graduate)
2 I .... the cello when I was younger, but I stopped when I was about 16. (play)
3 I .... currently .... a new place to live. (look for)
4 How long .... you two .... each other? (know)
5 Phone me as soon as you .... anything. (hear)
6 I .... Spanish for the last two years now. (learn)

[... / 6]

B **Complete the sentences with one word in each gap.**

1 Why should I tell you who I voted ....?
2 I really .... remember to phone my mum later on.
3 I was accused .... plagiarism.
4 I can't do this now. I'm too .... I need to sleep.
5 That's the place .... I had my first job.
6 I'm going to buy a car in a couple of weeks' ....

[... / 6]

C **Rewrite the second sentence using the world in bold so that it has a similar meaning to the first sentence.**

1 The film started quite well, but it soon got boring.
   I .... the film after a while. **got**
2 I first met him when I was at university.
   We .... since we were at university. **other**
3 I'm 34 now and I started playing when I was 14.
   I've been playing .... now. **twenty**
4 A sitar is a type of Indian musical instrument.
   A sitar is a type of musical instrument .... India. **comes**
5 It is essential that you remember these numbers.
   Whatever you do, you .... these numbers. **forget**
6 Inflation has gone up a lot recently.
   Inflation has gone up a lot .... **few**
7 The idea doesn't have much support.
   A lot of people .... the idea. **opposed**
8 Her behaviour really worries me.
   I .... her behaviour. **worried**

[... / 8]

▶ **Find this difficult? Look back at the grammar reference pages 152–155**

LANGUAGE PATTERNS

Complete the sentences with one word in each gap.

1 We got to the station .... as the train was leaving!
2 I was good .... Maths when I was at school.
3 I failed my driving test five times, but finally .... to pass last year!
4 The exhibition features many important artists .... as Monet, Van Gogh and Renoir.
5 He's not very good .... money.
6 Two hundred is the best price I can ....

[... / 6]

PREPOSITIONS

Choose the correct preposition.

1 Prices have doubled *over / since* the last few years.
2 We've invested most of our savings *on / in* property.
3 The play was so boring that we left halfway *of / through* it.
4 I've just spilt coffee all *over / across* your carpet!
5 It's a song *by / of* The Clash.
6 It's in a box *down / under* the shelf in the garage.
7 The film is set *at / in* Cambodia.
8 The delay was caused *from / by* computer problems.
9 She was left a house *from / in* her father's will.
10 They've banned people *from / against* giving their kids strange names!

[... / 10]

FORMING WORDS

Complete the sentences with the correct forms of the words in **bold**.

1 She was the first woman to ever be .... prime minister. **election**
2 Everyone was really warm and .... **welcome**
3 The decision to go to war had a terrible effect on the government's .... **popular**
4 I wasn't invited to the wedding, but I went to the .... in the evening. **receive**
5 It was hard to find food during the .... **occupy**
6 She spends most of her money on expensive .... clothes. **design**
7 I felt a real .... with her the first time we met! **connect**
8 There's no plot! It's all car chases and .... **explode**
9 .... is much worse in the countryside than in the cities. **employ**
10 The first half of the film was really good, but the ending was just so ....! **predict**

[... / 10]

ADJECTIVES

Match the adjectives in the box with the groups of nouns.

dairy	high	social	violent
distinct	silly	strong	vintage

1 .... wine / cars / clothes
2 .... movie / crime / behaviour
3 .... issues / life / skills
4 .... thing to say / thing to do / mistake
5 .... unemployment / inflation / cost of living
6 .... culture / groups / identity
7 .... farmer / products / allergy
8 .... currency / family / wind

[... / 8]

NOUNS

Complete the sentences with the nouns in the box.

attention	condition	interest	scheme
border	diet	rival	significance

1 I bought it second-hand, but it was in good ....
2 Our company is starting to become a serious .... to many of the bigger companies.
3 At the time, I didn't really understand the .... of the event, but now I can see how important it was.
4 Sorry. What did you say? I wasn't paying ....
5 The council is planning to introduce a new ...., which will hopefully solve the parking problem.
6 I wanted to borrow some money from my uncle, but he wanted me to pay .... on the loan!
7 The people in that region have a very healthy ....
8 I'm from Lille. It's in the north-east of France, close to the .... with Belgium.

[... / 8]

▶ **Find this difficult? Re-read units 13–16 in the *Vocabulary Builder* for more information on collocation.**

VERBS

Choose the correct verb (a, b or c) below for each gap.

The British film, *A Night in Leeds*, has ¹...... as a possible winner during the awards season. ²...... by Anna Walker, the film ³...... Nick Barrett as a mad scientist who wants to ⁴...... an old spaceship before aliens invade Earth. Much of the action involves Barrett trying to ⁵...... politicians and bankers to ⁶...... in his scheme – before it is too late!

The film was ⁷...... on a tiny budget and was ⁸...... in just a month. On its release, it ⁹...... less than the £50,000 it had cost to make. However, its popularity has slowly grown and it was recently ¹⁰...... one of the most unusual films of the last ten years. Many writers now believe it may well win the Best Independent Film award for 2010.

1 a come   b made   c emerged
2 a directed   b represented   c adopted
3 a acts   b stars   c shows
4 a defeat   b repair   c win
5 a convince   b support   c declare
6 a lend   b borrow   c invest
7 a defeated   b shown   c made
8 a published   b completed   c composed
9 a generated   b owed   c consumed
10 a elected   b chosen   c voted

[... / 10]

 [Total ... /80]

SPEAKING

A Work in groups. Discuss these questions.
- Do you ever chat online or use social networking sites?
- Which sites do you use most? Why?
- Do you have online friends?
- What are some differences between your relationship with your face-to-face friends and your online friends?

WRITING

A Read the advertisement below. Would you like to try this company? Why? / Why not?

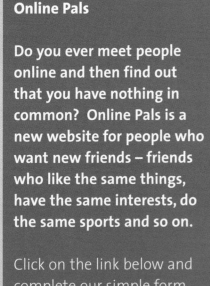

Online Pals

Do you ever meet people online and then find out that you have nothing in common? Online Pals is a new website for people who want new friends – friends who like the same things, have the same interests, do the same sports and so on.

Click on the link below and complete our simple form. You can then be sure that your new friends will have a lot in common with you.

PERSONAL PROFILE FORM

B Rita has decided to try this new service. Read the form she has completed and decide if you'd like to have Rita as an online friend. Why? / Why not?

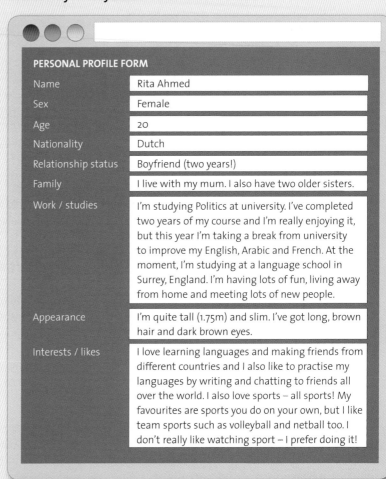

PERSONAL PROFILE FORM

Name	Rita Ahmed
Sex	Female
Age	20
Nationality	Dutch
Relationship status	Boyfriend (two years!)
Family	I live with my mum. I also have two older sisters.
Work / studies	I'm studying Politics at university. I've completed two years of my course and I'm really enjoying it, but this year I'm taking a break from university to improve my English, Arabic and French. At the moment, I'm studying at a language school in Surrey, England. I'm having lots of fun, living away from home and meeting lots of new people.
Appearance	I'm quite tall (1.75m) and slim. I've got long, brown hair and dark brown eyes.
Interests / likes	I love learning languages and making friends from different countries and I also like to practise my languages by writing and chatting to friends all over the world. I also love sports – all sports! My favourites are sports you do on your own, but I like team sports such as volleyball and netball too. I don't really like watching sport – I prefer doing it!

VOCABULARY Describing people

A Add the words in the box to the table below.

medium-height	curly	short	well-built
overweight	tall	straight	long
medium-length	slim	thin	blonde

Hair	Height	Body shape

B Work in pairs. Using the words above, take turns to describe other students in your class. Guess who your partner means.

GRAMMAR Adjectives

Position of adjectives
Adjectives describe nouns. They can come directly before nouns.
We both have *brown* hair.

Adjectives can also come after nouns when the verb is *be, get, become, seem, look, sound, taste, smell* or *feel*.
Your friend *seems* a bit sad.

Form of adjectives
Adjectives do not have plural forms in English.
She has *brown* eyes.
NOT ~~She has browns eyes.~~

Groups of adjectives
We often use two or three adjectives together. They are usually separated by commas.
I have *long, black* hair.

If you use two or three adjectives and one is a colour adjective, put the colour adjective last.
She has *short, brown* hair.
NOT ~~She has brown, short hair.~~

A **Find the five mistakes and correct them.**
1 His hair very long.
2 Is he OK? He sad looks.
3 She's got blonde, long hair.
4 He's a bit overweight and he's got very short hair.
5 That smells amazing!
6 I think I'm quite friendly and easy to talk to.
7 He's got big and blue eyes.
8 I've got eyes brown.

B **How would you describe yourself? Tell a partner. Does you partner agree with your description?**

KEY WORDS FOR WRITING *but, and, also, too*

Use *and* or *but* to join two ideas in a sentence.

Use *and* to link two similar ideas.
I love learning languages *and* making friends.

Use *but* to contrast two different ideas or to introduce some surprising information.
I like doing sport, *but* I don't like watching it on TV.

Use *also* to give extra information.
... and I *also* like to practise my languages.

Too* means the same as *also*, but usually comes at the end of a clause or sentence.
... but I like team sports *too*.

A **Complete sentences 1–5 using *but, and, also* or *too*.**
1 I've lived here for five years, ... I still can't really speak the language very well.
2 She has green eyes .... fair hair.
3 He has short, black hair .... blue eyes. He's very good-looking, ... I don't like his personality.
4 I'm very active. I love doing sport, ... I .... really like reading.
5 My favourite subject at school is Biology, but I quite like French and Maths ....

B **Complete sentences 1–5 with information about yourself. Then explain what your sentences to a partner.**
1 I like ...., but I don't like ....
2 At the weekend, I .... and I also .... a lot.
3 My favourite food is ...., but I ....
4 I love ...., but I like .... too.
5 I've been to .... and ...., but I haven't been to ....

PRACTICE

Write a personal profile for yourself. Use the headings in Rita's form on the opposite page.

A **Make notes on what you want to include under each heading.**

B **Write your profile. It should be between 120 and 150 words.**

SPEAKING

Work in pairs. Discuss these questions.
- Are you working or studying at the moment?
- Do you like what you do? Why? / Why not?
- What would be your dream job? Why?

VOCABULARY Talking about jobs

A **Complete the sentences with the words in the box.**

lonely	brilliant	satisfying	well-paid
tiring	boring	part-time	technical

1 My job's very .... I work very long hours and I work shifts, too.
2 My job's very .... The money's good.
3 My job's ....! I meet lots of people, the hours are good and I make very good money too.
4 My job's a bit .... I only make appointments – and coffee!
5 My job's very .... I sort out problems and help a lot of people.
6 My job's quite .... I install computer systems.
7 My job can be quite .... sometimes. I don't mind the travelling, but I don't see my family very often.
8 I'm studying Design at college, so I can only do a .... job.

B **Compare your answers with a partner. Do you know anyone with jobs like those described in exercise A?**

WRITING

You are going to read a text by Marta, the woman in the picture below. She describes how she feels about her job.

A **Look at the picture of Marta. Discuss with a partner how she feels about her job – and why she might feel like this.**

B **Check that you understand the five words in bold. Then read Marta's text and answer these questions.**
- Did she mention any of the problems you thought of?
- What other reasons for her feelings about work did you find?

> Most people think my job's very interesting, but I don't really like it very much. Why?
> ¹... work on my own most of the time. It's a lonely job, because I don't have much contact with other people. ²...
> so much **pressure** in my job that I can never **relax** and ³..., because I often have to work very long hours to finish an **experiment**.
>
> ⁴... always get **impatient** if experiments take too long so it's very **stressful** and ⁵..., I really hate sitting in one place all day long. I'd really like a job where I could move about more and get a bit of exercise and a job that is a bit easier.

C **Complete the gaps in the text with the expressions below.**
Thirdly, my bosses
finally,
Firstly, I have to
what's more, it's tiring
Secondly, there's

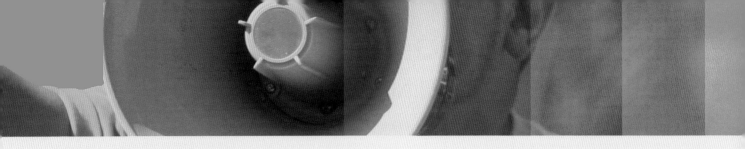

KEY WORDS FOR WRITING Sequencers

To add ideas when you write an essay, use these sequencers (adverbs of sequence): *firstly* (for the first idea), *secondly* (for the second idea), *thirdly* (for the third idea), etc., and *finally* for the last idea.

You can also use *what´s more* and *in addition* to add ideas.

Sequencers are followed by a comma and then a clause:
Firstly, I have to work on my own most of the time.

A Look at the picture of Luc. Discuss with a partner how he feels about his job – and think of four reasons why he might feel like this.

B Use your ideas to complete Luc's text.

I love my job! Why? Well, firstly, I like
¹...
Secondly, I enjoy ²...............................
Thirdly, I really love ³.............................
What's more ⁴.....................................
And finally, ⁵.....................................

PRACTICE

You are going to write a similar text about your work or studies. Describe how you feel about your job or studies. If you prefer to imagine a different job or course of study, write about that.

A Before you start writing, decide whether *you love, like, don't really like* or *hate* your job or studies. Think of as many reasons as possible.

B Work with a new partner. Talk about what you do. Your partner should ask you questions. This will give you more ideas for your text.

C Write a rough plan for your text using these notes as a guide.
I'm a / I study … . I … my job / studies. Why?
Firstly,…
Secondly, …
Thirdly, …
Finally, …

Try to use the expression *What's more / In addition* in your writing.

D Now write about 100–150 words about your job or studies.

SPEAKING

A **Work in pairs. Discuss these questions.**
- What's your favourite town / city? Why?
- Which cities would you most like to visit? Why?
- Have you ever visited any cities that you didn't like? What was wrong with them?

VOCABULARY Describing places

A **Match sentences 1–6 with sentences a–f.**
1 It's really green.
2 The climate's very hot and humid.
3 You find lots of modern buildings too, now.
4 It can be a bit noisy.
5 It's a very lively place.
6 The lake is a bit polluted.

a Plants grows really fast there.
b There are lots of parks and public gardens.
c Nobody swims there.
d There's a lot of traffic.
e The city is changing fast.
f There are lots of cafés and restaurants..

B **Complete sentences 1–6 with words from exercise A.**
1 I love visiting cities with lots of .... architecture. I find it fascinating.
2 The climate's so hot and .... in Jakarta that I usually have three or four showers a day.
3 It's a really .... city. There's always something happening!
4 The air is sometimes so .... here that the TV stations tell us not to go outside.
5 Just close the window if it gets too ....
6 I live in a city, but I love nature. That's why I like living somewhere with lots of .... areas.

WRITING

A **A student of English wrote a short description of her hometown for her blog. Match the headings a–d to paragraphs 1–4.**
a ... Things to see
b ... What people like to do
c ... Nature
d ... Where I'm from

www.myhometown.blogspot.co.vn

 1 Hanoi is a big city in the north of the country. I've lived there all my life, so I know it very well.

 2 It's a beautiful city. It's really green. There are lots of parks, and you find trees and flowers everywhere. The climate is very hot and humid, so everything grows really fast.

 3 The centre is very old and it has lots of historic buildings, but now you find lots of modern buildings, too, because the centre is changing fast. The city's very famous for the lake in the centre, called *Hoan Kiem*. It's a bit polluted, so nobody swims there, but it's nice to look at!

 4 It always feels very lively. People spend a lot of time outside, talking to neighbours, eating, studying or just going around town. However, it can be a bit noisy at times, because so many people ride around on motorcycles.

B **Work in pairs. Discuss these questions.**
- Does the description make you want to visit Hanoi? Why? / Why not?
- In what ways in your hometown / city similar to Hanoi?
- In what ways is it different?

KEY WORDS FOR WRITING *because, so*

We use *because* and *so* to join two parts of a sentence. Use *because* to talk about why something happens.
It can be a bit noisy at times, *because* so many people ride around on motorcycles.

Use *so* to talk about the result of something.
The lake is polluted, *so* nobody swims there.

A Complete the sentences by adding *because* or *so*.

1 That part of the city is new .... you don't see any old buildings there.
2 People don't go out between 12 and 3 .... it's very hot.
3 The city was really polluted .... I moved to the country.
4 Lots of tourists visit the museum .... it's home to a lot of wonderful art.
5 I moved to the coast .... I love walking on the beach and looking at the sea.
6 I love my hometown .... there are lots of parks, trees and lakes.

B Look at these sentences with *because* and *so*. They both give the same information.

1 I don't go out at night, because the city can be dangerous.
2 The city can be dangerous, so I don't go out at night.

Now use the information in sentences a to write sentences b. If sentence a uses *because*, use *so* in sentence b. If sentence a uses *so*, use *because* in sentence b.

1a I love living here, because it's very green and quiet.
1b ....
2a We're surrounded by lots of factories, so the area is really polluted.
2b ....
3a I love living in the city, because it's always very lively.
3b ....
4a I love history, so when I travel, I usually visit all the old buildings.
4b ....
5a We're going to move, because we think country life is better for children.
5b ....
6a The city's my home, so I love it here.
6b ....

GRAMMAR Modifiers

We use modifiers before adjectives to make them stronger or weaker. To make an adjective stronger, use *really* or *very*. To make it weaker, use *a bit*.
New York is a *really / very* busy city so it's *a bit* difficult to find a taxi at times.
Shanghai can be *a bit* noisy, but it's *really / very* lively.

When an adjective is already 'extreme', you can add *really*, but *not very*.
The weather is *really* (NOT ~~very~~) excellent / fantastic / incredible / wonderful / freezing.

A Add an appropriate modifier in each gap. Use the information in the second sentence to help you.

1 The river's .... polluted. It will take years to clean.
2 The service at this restaurant is .... wonderful. The people who work here are so helpful.
3 The roads can be .... dangerous. You sometimes have to drive quite carefully, especially after it rains.
4 The room can be .... noisy at times. It's not too bad, but sometimes I have to close the window because of the traffic.
5 The country has a .... amazing education system. Every child can read and write by the age of six.
6 The sea there is always .... cold. People never swim there.

B Think of places you know that sentences 1-5 describe. Add *very*, *really* or *a bit* to the sentences. Then tell your partner about each place.

1 It's a .... fantastic place.
2 It's .... dirty.
3 The buildings are .... old.
4 The beaches are .... polluted.
5 It's .... noisy at night.

PRACTICE

Write 150 words about your favourite town / city.

A Spend five minutes planning what to write. Think about the features of the place you want to describe. Write a list of the main adjectives that you'd like to use.

B Work in pairs and discuss your ideas. Tell your partner why you chose each adjective.

C Plan the paragraphs you are going to write. Use the paragraph topics from the blog spot as a guide or decide on other topics. Then write your article. Try to use some modifiers.

SPEAKING

A **All the pictures below are from the same meeting. Work in pairs. Discuss these questions.**
- What do you think is happening each photo?
- What do you think the people are talking about?
- What is their relationship with the others at the meeting?

WRITING

You are going to read an email about a meeting.

A **Complete the email with the words in the box.**

begin	break	continue	is	feedback
gives	go	meet	present	starts

To   tom.petersen@futuresforward.org

From   olga.williams@futuresforward.org

Subject   Sales meeting in Oslo

Dear Olga,

I look forward to seeing you at the Sales Managers' meeting in Oslo on Friday 13th July.

The meeting ¹.......................... at the Clarion Hotel. All managers ².......................... at 9.30 in the hotel lobby.

The meeting ³.......................... with coffee and a short welcome from Liv Applund, International Sales Director.

At 10.00, we ⁴.......................... to the conference room on the first floor. Each national manager then ⁵.......................... a presentation on this year's main challenges and results. The presentations ⁶.......................... until lunchtime.

Lunch is from 12.30 to 1.30 in the hotel restaurant

At 1.30, we divide into small groups and ⁷.......................... our brainstorming session. The topic is: *Sales strategy for next year.*

At 3.00, groups ⁸.......................... their ideas. We then ⁹.......................... on the presentations until 4.30, when we ¹⁰.......................... for coffee.

The final session begins at 5.00, when Liv Applund answers any questions and concludes the meeting.

Let me know if you have any questions.

All the best, Tom

GRAMMAR
Present simple for timetables

A Look at the email again. Underline all the examples of verbs in the present simple.

B Choose the correct answer, a, b or c. In the email, the present simple is used to talk about:
a possible future events
b events that happen all the time or regularly
c definite future events

> We can use the present simple to talk about definite future plans or events, especially when referring to timetables or schedules.
> ....
> We *start* with coffee at 9.30.
> The train *leaves* at 4.45.
> What time *does* the meeting *finish*?

C Complete the sentences below by putting the verbs in brackets into the present simple.
1 When .... the next sales meeting? (be)
2 My flight .... at 13.30. (leave)
3 I .... land in Oslo until 2 in the morning. (not / land)
4 What time .... your train ....? (arrive)
5 We .... for lunch at 1. (break)
6 The lunch break .... from 1.30 to 2.45. (last)
7 Remember – we .... until 11 tomorrow. (not / start)
8 When .... the meeting ....? (end)

KEY WORDS FOR WRITING
Time expressions

> We use *then* and *after that* to show that one action follows another. They mean the same thing.
> At 9.30, we go to the conference room on the first floor. Each national manager *then* gives a presentation.
> ....
> To show the point in time when something will finish, we use *until*.
> The presentations continue *until* lunchtime.
> She's in Britain *until* December.

A Complete the sentences with *then / after that* or *until*.
1 The hotel restaurant doesn't open .... 6.
2 The presentations finish at 1. ...., there's an hour break for lunch.
3 We start at 10 with a brainstorming session, which continues .... 12.
4 I have a meeting .... 12.45 but .... I'll call you back.
5 I'm afraid you have to wait here .... the room is ready.
6 The president gives her welcome speech at 9 and .... we divide into groups.
7 We don't break for coffee .... 4.30, I'm afraid.
8 The restaurant is booked for 8. We'll probably finish around 10 and maybe .... we can find a quiet place to discuss Asia.

PRACTICE

A You are going to write an email about a meeting at work, school or college. Work in pairs. Write a schedule for the meeting.

B Now work on your own. Write an email to the people who are coming to the meeting. Use the present simple.

C When you finish, check your work carefully and give it to your partner. Check each other's emails and make any changes or corrections you think are necessary.

SPEAKING

Work in groups. Discuss the following:
- What is your favourite restaurant? Why?
- Describe the best restaurant you've ever been to.
- Describe the worst restaurant you've ever been to.

WRITING

Read this email about a visit to a restaurant and find out:
- what good things happened.
- what bad things happened.

To	stevieg@shotmail.com
Subject	Re: A disastrous dinner!

Hi Stevie!

Just thought I'd write to let you know how my first few days at university are going. I haven't done much work yet, but I have met some very nice people. One guy, Scott, invited me out for dinner last night. ¹It was so funny!

²He took me to a very special fish restaurant, but, unfortunately, **when** we got there, ³it was very crowded. I said I didn't mind waiting, so we sat in the bar. **While** we were waiting for a table, we had a great chat. Scott's from California and he told me a lot about his life there. In fact, **during** the two-hour wait, he told me ALL about ⁴it!

We finally got a table, and ordered our food. When it came, Scott's dish was OK, but ⁵mine was awful. I complained, and, luckily, they changed it really quickly. The new ⁶one was really nice. Unfortunately, **during** the rest of the meal, the musical "entertainment" was playing right next to us, so we couldn't really continue our conversation without shouting. We decided not to have a dessert and left.

When ⁷they brought the bill, though, we noticed they'd charged us for all the dishes – including the ⁸one I'd sent back! Obviously, after that kind of service, we didn't leave a tip!

Anyway, I'll let you know how it goes with Scott!

Take care!

Kaori

KEY WORDS FOR WRITING
when, while and *during*

> *While, during* and *when* show how two or more actions relate to each other in time.
>
> *While* and *during* introduce a continuing action or a period of time in which another action happens.
> *While* we were waiting for a table, we had a great chat.
> ... *during* the two-hour wait, he told me ALL about it!
>
> *When* introduces a finished action.
> *When* we got there, it was very crowded
> *When* they brought the bill, we noticed they'd charged us for all the dishes.
>
> You can use *when* instead of *while* for continuous actions, but *while* is more common.

A Look at the examples above and in the email and complete the rules with *while*, *during* and *when*.
1. .... is followed by a noun.
2. .... is followed by a clause with past continuous.
3. .... is followed by a clause with past simple.

B Choose the correct word in italics.
1. I fell in love with Bob *during / while* our last year at high school.
2. *While / When* I felt too tired to continue, I stopped studying and went to bed.
3. *During / When* the lunch break, I suddenly remembered that I hadn't called my mum.
4. *During / While* I was waiting to see the doctor, I read a magazine.
5. It started to rain *when / during* I was cycling to school.
6. There were no seats left *when / while* we arrived.

GRAMMAR Pronouns

Pronouns are words that are used to avoid repeating nouns or noun phrases. A pronoun can be the subject of a sentence (*I, she, it*, etc), the object of a sentence (*her, it, us, them* etc), or show possession (*mine, hers* etc.). When we want to avoid repeating a noun, but want to add an adjective or other word, we use *one / ones*.
This bag was a bit small but I didn't have a bigger one.

We often use *they / them* to refer to people or organisations which normally do a particular action.
They arrested a pop star. (they = the police)

A Work in pairs. Look at the underlined pronouns in Kaori's email and say what you think they refer to.

B Now r the account of a climbing trip below. Replace the underlined nouns with pronouns.

My friend Ana had persuaded me to climb the mountain near the town, but as we walked towards the mountain, I wondered if I could really climb ¹the mountain. I'm very unfit and this was the first time I'd done something like this.

We started climbing, and ²climbing was really hard work. I was really sweating and finding it hard, but Ana kept encouraging me.

At midday, we stopped to have lunch. But when I opened my pack, I discovered that I'd left ³my lunch at home. Ana had plenty of sandwiches and ⁴Ana was happy to share ⁵her sandwiches! I had some sweets, so I shared ⁶the sweets with ⁷Ana!

After lunch, we continued to walk up and we reached the top! I couldn't believe it – I'd done it! ⁸The top is really high, and from there we could see all the way to the sea! ⁹Seeing all the way to the sea was beautiful. There were some other people there and we asked ¹⁰the people to take a picture of ¹¹Ana and me.

We couldn't stay long, because we still had to walk all the way back, but somehow I didn't mind.

VOCABULARY Adverbs of attitude

To show our feelings or opinions about something, we can use a range of adverbs, for example: *unfortunately* or *luckily*.

He took me to a very special fish restaurant, but, *unfortunately*, when we got there, it was very crowded.
I complained and, *luckily*, they changed it really quickly.

A Choose the best adverb.
1 None of the students could answer the last question in the test. It was *obviously / luckily* too difficult.
2 I was going to go skiing, but *unfortunately / amazingly*, I broke my leg in a car accident the day before I was due to leave.
3 I was late for school, but, *luckily / obviously*, the teacher was late too!
4 I usually get really nervous before an exam, but *amazingly / unfortunately*, this time, I was very calm.
5 *Sadly / Stupidly*, Mike and Cristina have decided to get divorced. It's a shame.
6 *Stupidly / Fortunately*, I left the keys in the car, and someone stole it!

B Look back at the account of the climb in *Grammar*, exercise B, and add at least three adverbs to show how the writer feels.

C Compare your text with a partner. Did you use the same adverbs in the same places?

PRACTICE

A You are going to write an email to a friend to tell them about one of the following:
• a particularly good or bad experience at a restaurant
• a particularly good or bad experience on a day out
• something you achieved

Choose the experience you want to write about and think about the things that happened.

B Work in pairs. Tell your partner about what happened to you. Ask each other questions to make sure you both understand the events properly.

C Write an email of about 150 words. Use as much language from these pages as possible.

WRITING

You are going to read two postcards from a couple – Sara and Bruce – on their honeymoon.

A Check the meaning of any words in the box you don't know. What type of holiday do you think all the words refer to?

movies	captain	sights	ship	tour	parties	galleries	ruins	port	seasick

B Work in pairs. Do you think this is a good kind of holiday for a honeymoon? Why? / Why not?

C Read the postcards and answer the questions.
1 How do Sara and Bruce feel about their holiday?
2 What do they have the same opinion about?

Hi Mum,
Well, here we are on our cruise. We get to a new port every two days and go on guided tours and see the sights - cathedrals, ancient ruins, galleries, museums. It's a very full schedule!

Life on the ship is great - discos, parties, dinner with the captain (the food's great), even movies and concerts!

Weather's great, although the evenings are quite cool. Wish you were here.

Looking forward to telling you all about everything. (Have about 300 photos to show you!).

Lots of love,
Sara xxx

Charlotte Jenkins,
The Manor House,
Briardene,
Oxfordshire,
England OX6 4PC

Hi Mike,
Greetings from paradise! Writing this from a ship somewhere near Italy, although it might be Greece – everywhere looks the same to me! Ruins, cathedrals, and crowded art galleries and museums – non-stop sightseeing tours! Despite trying hard to enjoy myself, I can't say I'm having a good time. What's more, although it's our honeymoon, we're never alone – there's always a crowd of 'friends' with us. The best thing is the food – amazing! Unfortunately, I sometimes get seasick, despite the good weather!

Can't wait to get back! Hope you're well.

All the best,
Bruce

Mike Thomspon,
9 Shearer Way,
Toonton,
County Durham,
England

SPEAKING

Work in pairs. Discuss these questions.
- What kind of holiday do you think Bruce prefers?
- Does everyone in your family like doing the same things on holiday? What happens when you go on holiday together?
- Is it good that couples have different tastes and interests?
- Do you know any couples who are quite different to each other? In what ways?

VOCABULARY

Postcard expressions

> We use special expressions in postcards. There's often no subject for the verb – or no verb at all. For example:
>
> *Greetings from paradise.*
> *Weather's great.*
> *Writing this from a ship somewhere near Italy.*

A Put the words in order to make expressions.
1 here were you wish
2 all you're hope well
3 to wait you tell can't about it
4 are here we in Panama
5 forward soon looking to you seeing
6 from greetings Greece
7 in this writing café a
8 in a having London time great here

KEY WORDS FOR WRITING
although and *despite*

> ***Although*** and ***despite*** both introduce contrasts – often something that makes the main statement surprising or unlikely. Notice the different grammar after each word.
> ....
> *Although* <u>it's</u> our honeymoon, we're never alone.
> Weather's great, *although* <u>the evenings</u> are quite cool.
> *Despite* <u>trying hard</u> to enjoy myself, I can't say I'm having a good time.
> I sometimes get seasick, *despite* <u>the good weather</u>!

A Complete the sentences with *although* or *despite*.
1 .... the horrible weather, we had a great trip.
2 The beaches are fantastic, ... you have to watch out for sharks.
3 I enjoyed the cruise, ... I got seasick.
4 .... getting very sunburnt, I enjoyed the holiday.

B Rewrite these sentences, using the word in bold.
1 We had a great time, although it rained a lot.
    We had a great time, ... **rain**
2 Despite the crowds, we enjoyed the concert.
    ...., we enjoyed the concert. **crowded**
3 Despite being really tired, we stayed up studying all night.
    We stayed up .... **were**
4 Although it was really sunny, it was still quite cold.
    It was quite cold, ... **being**
5 Although I had a headache, I still went skiing.
    I went skiing, ... **having**

C Complete each sentence in three different ways. Then compare your ideas in groups and decide who has the funniest / saddest sentence.
- The holiday was great, although ... .
- We managed to catch our flight, despite ... .

PRACTICE

A You are going to write a postcard to a friend or relative. Before you write, think about these questions:
- Where are you on holiday?
- What type of holiday is it?
- What things have you done?
- What are you doing at the moment?
- Are you enjoying yourself?

B Write your postcard. Write 100–120 words. Use as much language from these pages as you can.

SPEAKING

A Work in groups. Discuss these questions.
- Have you ever bought anything that didn't work?
- What did you do? Did you return it to the shop where you bought it?
- If yes, what was the result?
- If you have a problem with something you've bought, do you usually go back to the shop, or do you email or phone?

VOCABULARY Problems

A The sentences below all come from different emails written to complain about MP4 players. Translate the words in **bold**.

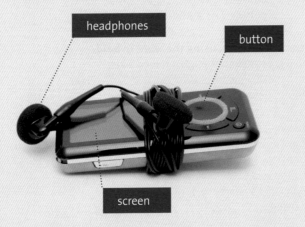

headphones

button

screen

1 The screen is **cracked** and you can't see the menu or video clearly.
2 The **delivery service** was very slow. It took a long time to arrive.
3 The box that it was in was **damaged**.
4 The main button does not work **properly**. It **gets stuck** and you cannot access the main menu.
5 I paid for it four weeks ago, but I still have not **received** it.
6 There is something wrong with the **battery**. The player stops working an hour after you **recharge** it.
7 The headphones are **faulty**, so the sound is quite bad.

B Work in pairs. Discuss if each problem is *very serious*, *quite serious* or *not very serious*. Give reasons.

WRITING

You are going to read a letter of complaint.

A Read the letter and list the problems the writer has had.

B Tarlon   4th August
45 Doone Street
Adderbury
OX17 3AZ

The Manager
Electronics Biz
Shop 16, The Marketplace
Banbury
OX15 1LN

Dear Sir,

Further to my email of 26th July, I am writing to enquire where my replacement MP4 player is, and make a formal complaint about the quality of service your company provides.

I requested a replacement for a faulty MP4 player that I returned to your shop on 19th June, but it never arrived. After many phone calls to your call centre, I sent an email last week, describing the problems I was having. In the reply I received, I was told that a replacement had been sent. However, I still have not received it. I am not at all satisfied with the quality of the after-sales service you provide.

If I do not receive the MP4 player by next Monday, I shall take my complaint to Consumer Affairs.

Yours faithfully,

Brad Tarlon

Brad Tarlon

B Match 1–8 to their meanings a–g.

1 further to
2 enquire
3 request
4 a replacement
5 faulty
6 after-sales service
7 Consumer Affairs

a a new one for something broken, lost or finished
b government office that protects customers.
c as a follow-up to
d help that a company provides to people who have bought products
e ask for
f ask
g not working properly

C Complete each gap with one word from exercise B.

1 .... to my telephone call of 10th May, I am writing to complain about your .... service.
2 The laptop is ...., and I would like a ....
3 I am writing to .... about your delivery service.
4 I would like to .... a refund.
5 I have contacted .... Affairs to complain about your service.

D Discuss the questions in groups.

• Do these adjectives describe Mr Tarlon? Why?

| reasonable | impatient | stupid |

• Do you have an office like Consumer Affairs in your country? How does it work? Is it effective?

"If she doesn't get well do I get a refund?"

KEY WORDS FOR WRITING *but* and *however*

But and *however* both connect two opposing ideas, or introduce surprising information.

But connects two clauses in one sentence and starts the second clause.
I was promised a replacement for a faulty MP3 player that I returned on *19*th June, *but* it never arrived.

However connects two sentences and usually comes at the beginning or in the middle of the second sentence.
...you told me the replacement had been sent. *However*, I still have not received it.

A Use *but* or *however* to complete the sentences.

1 The camera was damaged when I bought it, ... the company won't give me a new one.
2 I have asked for my money back. ...., the company say that I caused the damage to the camera.
3 I have tried to speak to your sales manager three times. The line, ..., is always busy.
4 The shop says I dropped the box, ... I didn't.

B Complete 1–4 with your own ideas. Compare what you write with a partner.

1 I called your company to complain, but
....

2 I bought the book online three weeks ago, but
....

3 I received the camera yesterday, as requested. However,
....

4 You stated the total cost would be $15. However,
....

PRACTICE

A Work in pairs. Think of a situation that requires you to write to complain about something. This could be about something you bought or something you are trying to organise.

Talk about:
• the situation and why you are writing.
• the problem and what has caused it.
• what action you want from the person / company.
• what action you will take next if you don't receive a satisfactory response.

B Write your email / letter. Write 100–150 words. Use as much language from these pages as you can.

08 WRITING INVITATIONS

SPEAKING

A Make a list of events, receptions or parties in the last year that:
- you have been invited to.
- you have invited other people to.

B Compare your lists. Explain:
- what the events were.
- who held the event and why.
- why you were invited or who you invited.
- if the events were successful or not.

WRITING Invitations

A Read the two emails and decide if you would accept the invitation or not. Then explain your decisions to a partner.

B One email is more formal and the other is more informal. Decide if the following indicate formality or informality:
1 contractions (*I'm, he's* etc.)
2 longer, more complex sentences
3 dashes (-) and exclamation marks (!)
4 direct questions
5 more passives

C Work in groups. Discuss these questions.
- How do you show different levels of formality in your language?
- Do you think it's OK:
  - to ask guests to bring food to a party?
  - to ask people to give to charity instead of a present?

To	Salma.Abad@ozmail.com
From	Carlos66@ozmail.com
Subject	Housewarming!

Hi Salma!

How're you? It's so long since we last talked! What's new with you? I've just moved into a new flat in Bondi. It's great to live near the beach.

I'm having a housewarming party next Saturday. I hope you can come. Bring your brother if you like – he's really funny! Unless it rains, we'll have a barbecue in the garden! I'm going to make some salads, and there'll be drinks, but I'm asking people to bring something to cook on the barbecue, if that's OK.

Send me an email and let me know if you can come. It'd be great to see you.

Love,

Carlos

To	Marketing@BLTLtd.com
From	BMarchant@ BLTLtd.com
Subject	Reception for Simone Lacroix

Dear Colleagues,

You are invited to a reception to mark the retirement of our business manager, Simone Lacroix. The reception will take place in the main boardroom on the first floor at 4 o'clock on Friday afternoon. Drinks and snacks will be served.

Simone has been with us for the last fifteen years and has helped us through some difficult times. I am sure you would like to join us in giving her a proper good-bye as she returns to her native France.

If you are able to attend, I would be grateful if you would respond to this email so that we can confirm numbers.

Simone has asked if people could make a donation to the charity *Southern Cat Rescue* rather than give her a leaving present. If you wish to donate, please contact Ken in Sales.

Yours,

Ben Marchant
Communications Director

VOCABULARY
Formal and informal language

> Some vocabulary such as *attend* or *Yours* (to end an email) sound very formal. A less formal way to say these things is *come* and *All the best*.

A **Mark the following F (formal) or LF (less formal).**
1 if you are able to
2 Dear Mr Chopin
3 Hiya
4 if you can
5 if you like
6 Dear Pete
7 Love
8 Give me a call
9 Respond by email
10 We look forward to seeing you
11 Cheers
12 If you wish
13 Kind regards
14 We're having some friends round
15 Yours sincerely
16 It'd be great to see you
17 Let us know
18 Please contact us on 020-034–501
19 We are delighted to announce
20 I would be most grateful if …

B **Compare your ideas with a partner. Which expressions can start an invitation – and which might come at the end?**

KEYWORDS FOR WRITING
If, when and *unless*

> *If, when* and *unless* + present can express future time.
>
> *If* shows something will possibly or probably happen. *When* shows we expect something to happen
> *Unless* = if … not
>
> Bring your brother *if* you like.
> Give me a call *when* you have time.
> *Unless* it rains, we'll have a barbecue in the garden!

A **Match the sentence beginnings 1–6 with the endings a–f.**
1 If the train is late,
2 Unless there's a problem,
3 Give me a call
4 You can bring the kids
5 John says he'll come to the party,
6 I'll give you a call

a unless he has to work.
b when you've got a minute.
c when I know which hotel I'll be in.
d we'll give you a call.
e you don't need to reply to this invitation.
f if you think they would enjoy it.

B **Complete the sentences with *if, when* or *unless***
1 Give me a call .... you arrive and I'll open the gate for you.
2 .... you require picking up from the station, please send us details of your train and arrival time.
3 You may bring a guest .... you wish.
4 I am afraid I will be unable to attend, ... I can change the date of my flight.
5 We're going to have a party .... we finish our exams.
6 We'll go swimming in the river in afternoon, ... it's too cold.

PRACTICE

In pairs, you are going to write two email invitations to a reception or party. The first is an informal, personal invitation to something you are organising. The second is a formal one in a school, company or similar situation

A **Work with your partner. For each invitation, think of:**
- the reason for the reception / party.
- where it will be and when.
- if guests should bring anything.
- anything else special about it.

B **Student A:** write the informal invitation.
Student B: write the formal invitation.

C **Check each other's invitations. Discuss anything you think should be written differently in each invitation.**

01 FAMILY AND FRIENDS

QUESTION FORMATION

Tense	Auxiliary	Subject	Verb
Present simple	Do	you	like it here?
	Does	she	work?
	Do	they	live near here?
	Do	you	both work here?
Past simple	Did	you	call Mike?
		Paula	speak to you?
		they	get home OK?
Present continuous	Are	you	coming with us?
	Is	he	driving here?
	Are	they	staying?
Present perfect	Have	you	had lunch?
	Has	she	decided yet?
	Have	they	met her before?
Modal verbs	Can	I	help you?
	Could	you	pass the salt?
	Would	they	move, please?

With the verb *be*, we add adjectives, adverbs, nouns.

	be	Subject	Adj, adv or noun
Present	Are	you	ready?
	Is	it	easy to do?
	Is	she	your teacher?
	Are	they	here now?
Past	Were	you	late?
	Was	it	busy in town?
	Were	there	many people?

Question words
With question words, the same patterns as above follow.
How *did you get* here?
Who *did she go* with?
Where *are they staying*?
How long *have you been* here?

How and *what*
How + adjective or adverb
How old is he?
How far is it from here?
What + noun
What kind of films do you like?
What time did you get home?

Prepositions and questions
Prepositions usually go at the end of the question.
Who did you stay *with*?   Not   ~~With who ...?~~
What are you listening *to*?   ~~To what ...?~~
What are you worried *about*?   ~~About what ...?~~
Where's she *from* originally?   ~~From where...?~~

Exercise 1
Rewrite the sentences using the words in brackets.
Present simple
1 A: ....? (where / she / work)
   B: In a café in the centre of town.
2 A: ....? (you / like / football)
   B: Yeah. I'm a Leeds fan. Who do you support?
Past simple
3 A: Sorry, ...? (what / you / say)
   B: I said 'Do you want a cup of coffee?'
4 A: ....? (he / have a nice time)
   B: Yes, he really enjoyed it.
Present continuous
5 A: ....? (what / he / studying)
   B: Civil Engineering.
6 A: ....? (you / looking for something)
   B: Yeah, I can't find my book. Did I leave it here?
Present perfect
7 A: ....? (you / been to the States).
   B: Yeah, once. I went to New York a few years ago.
8 A: ....? (how long / they / been married)
   B: 20 or 21 years.

Exercise 2
Complete the questions with *how* or *what* + a word in the box.

far	film	kinds	long
many	old	questions	way

1 A: .... is your gran?
   B: 83.
2 A: .... of things do you do at the weekend?
   B: I always play tennis on Saturdays. Apart from that, I go to the cinema, watch TV ... nothing much.
3 A: .... did you see in the end?
   B: *Forever*. It's a romance. My wife wanted to see it.
4 A: .... have you lived here?
   B: About six months.
5 A: .... did they ask in the exam?
   B: How old are you?; Where do you live?; things like that.
6 A: .... is the best .... to get there?
   B: It's a bit difficult to explain. I'll draw you a map.
7 A: .... do you have to travel to get to work?
   B: It's 50 minutes by train and then a ten-minute walk.
8 A: .... students are there in your class?
   B: There are 12 of us, I think.

Exercise 3
Put the words in brackets in the correct place.
1 what are you talking? (about)
2 you seen that new Kate Winslet film? (have)
3 where you get your book? (did)
4 who did you go? (with)
5 what are you listening on your iPod? (to)

THE PRESENT SIMPLE

Use the present simple to talk about facts, habits and regular activities.

Remember that the verb *be* is irregular. The verb *be* is followed by adjectives or nouns.

I'm a student.   *It's* really cold in here.
Are you OK?   *We're* flatmates.
She isn't here today.   *They're not* Japanese!

With other verbs (apart from *can* and *have*), add *–s* when talking about *he / she / it* and make questions and negatives using *do / does*.

I see my grandparents once or twice a month.
You don't sound French.
How often *does she come* here?
We're twins, but *we don't look* very similar.
They both *wear* glasses.
Do your parents like your new boyfriend?

We often use adverbials of frequency with the present simple to explain how often we do things. Many adverbs go between the subject and the main verb.
We always meet in the same place.
I usually order the same meal.
We often go shopping together.
He's so lazy! *He never does* any exercise!

When we use the adverbs above with *be*, they appear after the verb!
It's always quite cold here in the winter.
I'm never home before seven in the evening.

Look at this way of using adverbs in negative sentences:
I don't like this kind of music *very much*.
We don't see each other *very often*.

The adverbials below usually go at the end of a sentence.
I email her *every day*.
I go swimming *twice a week*.
I visit my mum *two or three times a month*.
He goes abroad on business *once or twice a year*.

Exercise 1
Find six mistakes and correct them.
1 Does your sister married?
2 Does your brother have any kids?
3 He doesn't work any more. He's retired.
4 Why you still live at home?
5 My brother and I go always to watch the football on Saturday.
6 My sister's quite shy. She don't have many friends.
7 Do you get on OK with your uncle?
8 My brother work for my father's company.
9 I eat fast food once twice a week.
10 He's never late. He always arrives early.

SIMILARITIES AND CONTRASTS

To show two people have positive things in common use *both*. Use *neither* when they have negatives in common.
Both (of) my parents are quite religious.
I don't see them often because *they're both* working.
We eat out a lot because *neither of us* like cooking.

Don't use *both* or *neither* before a negative:
~~Both my kids can't swim~~. = Neither of my kids can swim.
~~Neither of us don't like it~~. = Neither of us like it.

We often use *either* after a negative to show there are two.
I don't get on very well with either of my neighbours.

To talk about more than two, use *all* for positive things in common and *none of* or *no-one* for negatives.
We're also all very messy in our family.
None of us are good at cleaning or putting things away.
No-one in my family likes sport.

Don't use *all* or *none* with a negative verb or other negative word:
~~All of us don't smoke~~. = None of us smoke.
~~He never met none of them~~. = He never met any of them.

We often use *any* after a negative.
He had five exams and *he didn't pass any* of them.

We show a contrast by using *whereas* or *but* and it's often followed by an auxiliary – *be / do / have*, etc.
My dad's quite religious, *whereas* my mum *isn't*.
Neither of my parents speaks English, *but* I *do*.

Exercise 1
Complete the sentences with one word.
1 I've got two brothers and a sister and we're .... doctors.
2 I see my two grans a lot because they .... live nearby.
3 My girlfriend and I often play tennis together. .... of us are very good, but we enjoy it anyway.
4 Although they're twins, they're .... quite different.
5 People in the south are generally quite wealthy, ... the north is quite poor.
6 We saw several flats, but we didn't like .... of them.
7 I didn't know .... of my grandparents. They .... died before I was born.
8 There are a couple of bars in our road but I never go to .... of them.

02 SHOPS

THE PAST SIMPLE

To make verbs in the past simple, we usually add –ed. When verbs end in –e, we just add –d. Note the spelling with some verbs.

They wanted to get there early.
Sorry. *I used* all the paper.
I tried to tell him. (-ied often added to verbs ending in -y)
It stopped raining briefly. (double consonant when a verb ends in a vowel + consonant)

Use *did / didn't* + verb to form questions and negatives.
Did you get anything nice?
Sorry. *I didn't hear* what you said.

Avoid repeating the past tense by using only *did* or *didn't*.
A: Did you speak to him about changing class?
B: Yes, *I did* and he said it was fine.
They thought the film was really good, but *I didn't*.

Use the past simple to talk about completed events in the past. Time expressions are often used with the past simple.
I went there *last week*.
Did you go out yesterday?
I was there *five minutes ago*, but *I didn't see him*.

Use the past simple to talk about past states or habits.
We went to France *every year* for our summer holidays.
He lived in Indonesia *when he was younger*.

Exercise 1

Correct the mistake in each sentence.
1   I go there yesterday.
2   Sorry. What do you say? Can you repeat it?
3   I wanted to buy a coat, but I didn't saw anything nice.
4   I love your earrings. Where you did get them?
5   They living in France when they were kids.
6   I have to admit, I cryed at the end of the film.
7   She told me not to say anything, so I didn't.
8   He complained and I do too, but it didn't make any difference.
9   I breaked a glass and cut my finger.
10 It started to rain five minutes after we leaved the house.
11 Why wasn't you in class yesterday?
12 Where did you went last night?

COMPARATIVES

Adverbs and adjectives

Add *–er* to words of one syllable.
Two-syllable words ending in *–y* change to *–ier*.
Use *more* with two- or three-syllable words.
Some two-syllable words can take either *–er* or *more*.
It's a bit *quieter / more quiet* now.

We often use *more* with pairs of adjectives linked with *and*.
I'd like to be *more fit and healthy*.

To compare things in the same sentence, use *than*.
Costsave *is much cheaper than* the other supermarkets.

To say there's a big difference, use *much* or *a lot*.
To say there's a small difference, use *a bit*.
It's *a lot more expensive* here than in Brazil.
I'm *a bit taller* than my brother – maybe 2 centimetres.

Negative comparisons

Make negative comparisons using *less* or *not as*.
Don't use *less* with adjectives of one syllable.
I never go to Booths. I shop at Costsave. It's *less / not as expensive*. Of course, the quality is *less good / isn't as good* there.

To compare two things in the same sentence, use *less ... than* and *not as ... as*.
I *don't* usually finish *as late as* this. I normally finish at six.
Their selection of clothes is *less varied than* at Harrods.

Exercise 1

Complete 1–7 using the words in brackets to make a comparative.
1   Shall we take the underground? It'll be .... (quick)
2   No, let's take the bus. It's a bit .... – especially on a nice day like today. (pleasant)
3   I'll call you later when I'm .... (busy)
4   A: What time shall we leave? Eight? Eight thirty?
    B: I think you'd be .... to leave a bit .... The traffic is .... before seven thirty. (wise, early, heavy)
5   I speak English and French. I guess my English is .... My French isn't bad – just .... my English. (fluent, good)
6   My dad's .... my mum when it comes to bedtimes, so he'll let me stay up .... (strict / late)
7   I wouldn't say I'm .... my brother – he's very bright. I'm just a bit .... and study .... (intelligent, determined, hard)

PASSIVES

Form
The passive is formed with *be* + a past participle.
We also sometimes use *get* instead of *be*.

The past simple passive
My bag *was stolen* when I went shopping.
The goods *got damaged* in the post.
Was anyone *injured* in the crash?
They didn't come because they *weren't invited*.

The present simple passive
Most of their clothes *are made* in India.
I*'m* often *confused* with my sister. We look very similar.

Other tenses
Passives are used in most tenses.
I*'ve been asked* to help organise. (the present perfect)
The washing machine *will be delivered* on Friday. (*will*)
Selling pirate DVDs *should be stopped*. (*should*)

You will look at these tenses more in later units.

Adverbs
Adverbs usually go between *be* and the past participle.
This dish *is usually served* with rice.
I *wasn't badly hurt* when I fell – just a few small cuts.

Use
We usually use the passive:
1 when we don't know who or what did / does the action we want to talk about
2 when it's simply not important who did / does the action.

We sometimes include the doer of the action in passive sentences with *by* after the verb.
Her wedding dress *was designed by* John Paul Gaultier.
We*'re encouraged by* our teacher to read in English.

We sometimes avoid passive sentences by using *they* – especially for organisations / government.
They've introduced a new law against chewing gum.
(= *A new law has been introduced* ...)

The verbs below don't take an object in the active and can't be used in the passive. Verbs like these are often marked with an [I] in dictionaries, meaning 'intransitive'.

appear	behave	come	disappear
exist	go	happen	last
progress	rise	seem	sleep

It *is happened* happens to me all the time.
His English *has been progressed* a lot.

Exercise 1
Write the past participles of the verbs below.

blow	...	hit	...	sell	...
break	...	keep	...	show	...
bring	...	leave	...	steal	...
build	...	lend	...	take	...
buy	...	pay	...	teach	...
catch	...	put	...	throw	...
find	...	run	...	wake	...
gave	...	see	...	write	...

Exercise 2
Rewrite each sentences using a passive. The first one is done for you.
1 They told me I couldn't take my bag into the shop.
 I was told I couldn't take my bag into the shop.
2 They caught him stealing some perfume.
3 They send me junk emails all the time.
4 They knocked down the building over two years ago.
5 They usually make it with lamb, but you can use beef.
6 They broke into my house last night.
7 They introduced a new tax on luxury goods last year.
8 They've built a huge shopping centre nearby.

Exercise 3
Complete 1–5 by adding one verb in the active form and one in the passive.
1 **teach**
 a My mum .... me to always say 'Please'.
 b I .... to always say 'Please'.
2 **leave**
 a My granddad .... me his car when he died.
 b Apparently, she .... a fortune when her dad died.
3 **show**
 a We .... round this morning, so we won't get lost.
 b We'll be fine. Tom .... us how everything works.
4 **wake up**
 a I .... at three by some noise outside.
 b I've been in a rush all morning because I .... late.
5 **give**
 a My gran .... me some socks for my birthday.
 b It .... to me as a leaving present.

Exercise 4
Find the four mistakes and correct them.
1 The Internet didn't exist when I was at university.
2 How was the accident happened?
3 A dog was suddenly appeared in front of me.
4 Fortunately, none of us badly was hurt.
5 Prices in the shops have risen a lot recently.
6 Those batteries weren't lasted very long.

03 EAT

THE PRESENT PERFECT SIMPLE

The present perfect simple is formed using *have / has* + the past participle. It shows something happened before now at an unspecified time in the past.
I think I've *seen The Fantastic Four* ten times now.
She's *travelled* a lot. She's *been* to most countries in Europe.

Negatives are formed with *not* or *never*.
I *haven't ever read* anything by José Saramango.
He's *never been* abroad.

Questions are formed like this:
Has she arrived yet?
What countries *have you been* to?

Passives in the present perfect are formed with *have / has been*.
The restaurant *has been closed down* because it has rats!

Use *have / haven't*, etc. to avoid repeating the whole verb.
I haven't been to that restaurant, but Javi *has* (been there).
A: Have you talked to Karen recently?
B: *I haven't* (talked to her). *Have you* (talked to her)?

Use

The present perfect is often used to begin a conversation about an experience. We often use *ever* in questions to ask about a life experience. We use *never* to mean 'not in my life'. We use the present perfect to talk about the number of times before the present.
A: *Have you ever tried* horse meat?
B: *No, never* (= I've never tried it). I don't like the idea of it.

A: *Have you visited* Belgium before?
B: *Yes, I've been* here several times, actually.

Present perfect actions often have a present result.
I *haven't eaten* anything all day, so I'm really hungry.
He's *gone* to the shops. (= He's not here now.)

Use *yet* to ask about events you're expecting to happen. and *not yet* to show you still plan / expect to do it.
A: *Have you spoken* to Jens *yet*?
B: *Not yet*, but I'm going to see him later.

Use the present perfect simple with some verbs to talk about duration of events that are still not finished now.
A: How long *have you lived* here?
B: Not long. We moved here in February.

Don't use the present perfect with time phrases that show something happened at a specific time. Use the past simple.
~~Have you gone out~~ *Did you go out* last night?
~~We've had~~ *We had* dinner there the other day.
~~I've spoken~~ *I spoke* to him two minutes ago.
~~We have never eaten out~~ *We never ate out* when I was a kid.

Exercise 1

A Make present perfect questions from the notes.
1 you / be / here before?
2 you / ever / eat / snake?
3 you / try / that new restaurant round the corner?
4 Dave / speak / to you about tonight yet?
5 you two / be introduced?
6 how long / she / live / there?

B Match the answers to the questions.
a Yeah, I had it once when I was in Hong Kong.
b Yeah, we've met before actually.
c Yeah, I came on holiday here a few years ago.
d No, but I've had my phone switched off.
e About six years now.
f No, but I'd like to go there. It looks nice.

Exercise 2

Choose the correct tense.
1 A: Shall we go to that Thai place on Grove Lane?
  B: *I've never been / I didn't go* there. What's it like?
2 A: *Have you gone out / Did you go out* yesterday?
  B: No, I just stayed in.
3 A: *Have you had / Did you have* anything to eat?
  B: Yes thanks. *I've made / I made* myself a sandwich before I left home.
4 A: I went to Italy last summer.
  B: Really? What part *have you been / did you go* to?
  A: Umbria.
  B: Oh yeah, lovely. *We've been / We went* to Italy quite a few times now. It's a fantastic country – great food.
  A: Yes, *we've had / we had* a great time.

Exercise 3

Complete each pair of sentences with the verbs in **bold**. Use the present perfect in one sentence and the past simple in the other.
1 **lose**
  a I .... my mobile two weeks ago, so I'm in a mess! It had all my contacts on it.
  b My brother .... his mobile about 15 times.
2 **visit**
  a .... you .... the Taj Mahal when you were in India?
  b .... you .... the Taj Mahal yet?
3 **try**
  a I .... never .... coffee. I don't like the smell.
  b I got these jeans on holiday, but I .... not .... them on before I bought them.
4 **see**
  a .... you ever .... that film *Babette's Feast*? It's on tonight.
  b .... you .... the news last night? I was on it!

TOO / NOT ... ENOUGH

too

Use *too* + adjective / adverb to explain why we don't like something or to talk about problems.
I need to lose weight. *I'm getting too big for my jeans.*
The service wasn't very good. *We had to wait too long.*

Don't use *too* for positive feelings. Use *really / a lot.*
I loved the curry. *It was ~~too~~ really spicy!*
I like it ~~too much~~ a lot. It's my favourite restaurant.

Don't use *too* + noun. Use *too many* + countable noun (people, cars, etc.); *too much* + uncountable noun (sugar, traffic, etc.).
There are *too many bars and cafés* round there.
I don't like the food they serve. They use *too much salt.*

not ... enough

Use *not* + adjective / adverb + *enough* when you need more.
It's not hot enough to have an ice-cream!
We had to wait because *we didn't get there early enough.*

Use *not enough* + noun. Note: *enough* goes after an adverb, but before an adjective.
They said *I didn't have enough experience* to get the job.

to + verb

to + verb after *too / not enough* shows what you can't / don't do – i.e. the negative result.
It's too hot to drink. (Don't drink it.)
They didn't have enough people to serve everyone.

Exercise 1

Complete the sentences with ONE word in each space.

1 I didn't speak to him. We were sitting .... far apart.
2 I love that cheese. It's .... strong.
3 I know you said it wasn't spicy, but it actually wasn't mild .... for my taste.
4 There really were too .... people there, and it just got so noisy I had a headache by the end of the evening.
5 I didn't feel .... good after dinner. I ate too ....
6 He has an unhealthy diet. He eats too .... fast food.
7 I didn't understand her. She was talking .... fast.
8 It would be nice to be able to eat in the kitchen but there's not enough room .... put a table and chairs.

OFFERS, REQUESTS, PERMISSION, SUGGESTIONS

would, could, shall

Use *would*, *could* and *shall* to add meaning to other verbs. They are often used when you want to offer, request, ask for permission, suggest or show politeness. *Would*, *could* and *shall* are modal verbs and form questions in the same way as each other.

modal	pronoun	verb phrase
Would	you	like me to order?
Could	I	have another knife?
Shall	we	go?

Replies to these questions don't usually use the modal verb.

Would

We use *would you like* instead of *do you want* – and *would you mind* instead of *do you mind* – to sound more polite. Note some typical replies.
Would you like me to sit there? (Do you want me to ...?)
    Yeah, thanks / If you don't mind / No, it's OK / I'm fine.
Would you mind closing the window? (Do you mind ...?)
    Of course not / I'll do it now / Actually, I'd rather ...

Could

Use *could* to make polite requests (and avoid imperatives). *Could I / we* is also used to ask for permission. Note the typical replies.
Could you bring me another glass? (Bring me ...)
    Of course / Sure / I'll do it now / I'm afraid I can't.
Could I / we change tables? (Is it OK if I ...?)
    Of course / Sure / Go ahead / Actually, I'd rather ...

Shall

We use *shall I / we* to make a suggestion or to start a discussion about what to do. Note some typical replies.
Shall we get a set menu?
    Fine / Why not? / I'd prefer to ... / How about...instead?
Shall we stay here or do you want to go somewhere else?
    Let's (stay here) / I don't mind / I'd rather (go) ...

Exercise 1

Use *would*, *could* or *shall* and the words in brackets to rewrite 1–8 as questions with the same meaning.

1 Do you want more of anything? (like)
2 Is it OK if I close the window? (I)
3 How about going for a Thai meal? (we)
4 Pour me some water. (you)
5 Is it OK if we wait till our friend arrives? (we)
6 Do you want me to hang your coat up? (me)
7 Do you want me to pay with my card? (I)
8 Turn down the air conditioning. (mind)

04 JOBS

PRESENT CONTINUOUS AND PRESENT SIMPLE

Form the present continuous with *be + –ing*.

Can't you see *I'm working*?

He's chatting online. (double letters with short verbs)

They're using my car while I'm away. (remove final *–e*)

Negatives

I'm not working at the moment.

He's unemployed, but *he isn't / he's not looking* for a job.

Questions

Where *are you going*?

What's *the government doing* to sort out the problem?

Passive

My car's being repaired at the moment.

Use the present continuous when you see an action as temporary and / or unfinished. It is often used with *at the moment*.

Listen, I can't speak now. *I'm driving*. I'll ring you back.

Unemployment is going up at the moment.

Use the present simple when the verb describes something generally true, a habit or a permanent state. It is often used with adverbs such as *usually, generally, normally, often, sometimes, never*, etc.

Where *do you work*, then? (= always)

I usually visit Paris once or twice a month. (= habit)

These verbs are generally used in the present simple – even to describe unfinished or temporary states.

agree	believe	belong	depend	hate
know	like	need	owe	own
seem	sound	suppose	taste	want

Exercise 1

Complete the pairs of sentences with the verbs in **bold** – one in the present simple and one in the present continuous.

1 **do**

   a I'm very busy because we .... the end-of-year accounts.

   b We .... most of our business in the States, so a strong euro is bad for us.

2 **run**

   a They .... a hotel. They've had it for 30 years.

   b I .... the shop while my boss is away.

3 **try**

   a As a good businessman, I always .... to meet my customers' demands.

   b He .... to get a job in TV, but it's hard!

4 **wait**

   a I've had the interview. I .... to hear if I got it.

   b All good things come to those that ....

PLANS AND WISHES FOR THE FUTURE

Use *be going to* + verb to talk about personal plans / intentions for the future – things that are already decided.

I'm just going to apply for lots of jobs and see what happens.

Are you going to book a table for tonight?

Use *would like to* + verb or *be hoping to* + verb to talk about things that you want to do – or want to happen – in the future. *Be hoping to* suggests there is already a reason for your hope.

I'd like to work in the media – maybe as a journalist.

She's hoping to save enough money to buy a new car.

Use *be planning to* + verb when you have already thought carefully about something in the future – and have a plan.

My brother is planning to get married next year.

We're not planning to open any more shops this year.

Use *be thinking of* + *–ing* to talk about possible future plans that are not yet certain or fully decided. It is often used with *maybe*.

I'm thinking of maybe doing a French course next year.

Where *are you thinking of applying*?

Exercise 1

Write full sentences using the ideas below.

1 What / you hoping / learn on this course?

2 Next year, we / planning / open a factory in China.

3 I really / not like / work night shifts!

4 Where / you thinking / moving to?

5 Who / going / organise the launch party?

6 We / hoping / develop a new anti-cancer drug.

7 What kind of work / you / like to do / the future?

8 He / thinking / applying to do some voluntary work.

9 I / not planning / start work immediately. I / hoping / go travelling for a while first.

10 When / you / going / realise that your boss / never / going / change?

Exercise 2

Match the sentences 1–5 with the follow-up comments a–e.

1 I'm really interested in languages.

2 We're planning to start a family next year.

3 I'm doing my Master's at the moment.

4 I'd like to run my own business.

5 I'm planning to work part-time while I study.

a I'm hoping to do a PhD next.

b I'm thinking of going part-time after the baby is born.

c My parents aren't going to pay for me to study any more!

d I'd like to do Russian and Arabic at university.

e I'm planning to open a restaurant.

THE PAST CONTINUOUS AND PAST SIMPLE

Form the past continuous with *was / were + –ing*. If the verb ends with a consonant + *–e*, remove the *–e* before adding *-ing*.
We were both *working* for BMI when we met.

Negatives

I wasn't feeling very well, so I went home.
He wasn't doing well at work, so they fired him.

Questions

Where *were you living* at that time?
Were you dating Diane then or did that start later?

We use the past continuous to show an action or event was unfinished – and continuing – when another action happened. Verbs in the past continuous and simple are often linked together using *and*, *when* or *while*. The past continuous is also often used to give the background situation to a story.
It was late and *I was driving* back home from the office. *It was raining* and *I wasn't feeling* very well. Suddenly, *a dog ran* in front of my car. *I tried* to stop, but I couldn't.

We can also use the past continuous on its own to emphasise that an action continued for some time.
I was studying until two in the morning last night.
You were making a lot of noise! What *were you doing*?
Sorry. What was that? *I wasn't listening.*

The following verbs are not generally used in the past continuous.

agree	believe	belong	depend	hate
know	like	need	owe	own
seem	sound	suppose	taste	want

When one action happens after another, use the past simple. Also use the past simple to talk about completed events in the past. We often use a time expression with the past simple.
I tried to make a good impression at the interview, but *failed*!
They arrested him *last week*, but *his lawyer negotiated* his release.
He worked in Japan *for ten years* and then *he moved* to Korea.

Exercise 1

Complete the sentences with the past continuous form of the verbs in brackets.

1 Yrais went home early because she .... very well. (not / feel)
2 I can't believe they did that! What .... they .... ? (think)
3 Where .... you .... when this photo was taken? (live)
4 I left my old job because I just .... it any more. (not / enjoy)
5 We .... (have) a meeting at work yesterday when the fire alarm suddenly started ringing.
6 I wasn't very impressed with their sales presentation. They .... anything new or different. (not / offer)
7 It .... for hours yesterday. It was great! (snow)
8 I was in Portugal last week. I .... a paper at a conference there. (present)

Exercise 2

Complete the stories by putting the verbs in brackets into the past continuous or past simple.

1 A few years ago, I [1] .... (go) to Singapore to visit some friends. They [2] .... (offer) to let me stay in their flat, but I [3] .... (decide) to stay in a hotel instead. One day, I [4] .... (have) breakfast in the hotel restaurant when suddenly Jackie Chan [5] .... (walk) in and [6] .... (sit) down next to me. I couldn't believe it!

2 I [1] .... (do) something really stupid last month. I [2] .... (write) an essay for college and I [3] .... (start) to feel tired, so I [4] .... (go) to the kitchen and [5] .... (make) a cup of coffee. I [6] .... (put) the coffee next to my computer and [7] .... (start) working again. Then the phone [8] .... (ring) and I [9] .... (jump) up to answer it – and [10] .... (spill) coffee all over my computer! It's going to cost a fortune to repair it.

3 I first [1] .... (meet) my girlfriend three years ago. We [2] .... both .... (work) part-time in a big department store in Brno. None of us who worked there [3] .... (like) our boss and a group of us often [4] .... (go) out after work for a drink and chat – and to complain about work! One day, we [5] .... (sit) and talking and our eyes [6] .... (meet) – and I just [7] .... (know) that she was the one for me! It [8] .... (take) a while before we starting going out together, though, but we've been together for two and a half years now and it's still going well.

05 RELAX

MIGHT, THE PRESENT CONTINUOUS, *BE GOING TO* + VERB

Use *might* to talk about possible plans in the future that are not yet definite – things that maybe will happen. *Might* is not usually used in questions. Instead, we often use *be thinking of*.

I might come out with you tonight. *I might not*. I'm not sure.

Where *might you go*?

Where *are you thinking of going*?

Use the present continuous to talk about future arrangements with other people – usually in the near future.

A: What*'re you doing* tonight?

B: *I'm meeting* a friend at six for a drink. What about you?

A: *I'm having dinner* with my boyfriend's parents!

Use *be going to* + verb to talk about personal plans / intentions for the future – things that you have already decided to do.

I'm not going to do anything tonight. *I'm just going to stay* at home and sleep instead!

Exercise 1

Complete the sentences with the correct form of the verbs in the box.

do	get	have (x2)	hire
meet	see	play (x2)	watch

1 A: What .... you .... later?
   B: We .... Gary and Sam at the cinema, if you'd like to come.
   A: Yeah, that sounds good. What are you going ....?
   B: *Juniper Love* – the one that won the Oscar.
2 A: We're thinking of .... a party to celebrate finishing school.
   B: That's a good idea. Are you thinking of .... it at your house?
   A: I don't know. We might .... a room somewhere. It depends how expensive it is.
3 A: Simon and Matt told me to tell you they .... tennis tomorrow, if you're interested.
   B: What time are they going ....?
4 A: We're going .... the Madrid–Malaga match in a bar in town.
   B: OK. What time are you going .... there?
   A: Quite early, so we can get a seat. Seven?

SUPERLATIVES

To make superlatives, add *–est* to adjectives or adverbs of one syllable. Two-syllable words ending in *–y* change to *–iest*. Use *most* with most other two- or three-syllable words.

I'm *the youngest* of four brothers.

The easiest way to get there is actually by bus.

Moscow is one of *the most expensive* cities in the world.

For some short adjectives – *big*, *fit*, *sad*, etc. – double the final consonant when you add *–est*. Some two-syllable words can take either *–est* or *most*.

Wimbledon is probably *the biggest* competition in tennis.

Two o'clock is our *quietest / most quiet* time of the day.

Superlatives usually start with *the*, but sometimes we use *my*, *his*, etc. With general statements, you don't need *the*, *my*, *his*, etc.

My best time for running a kilometre is four minutes 20.

I usually work (*the*) *best* in the mornings.

Superlatives + the present perfect

Superlatives often go with the present perfect.

It's *the best* book I've (*ever*) *read* in my life.

I think this is *the fittest I've ever been*.

He's *the most successful* striker who's ever *played* for us.

That's *the most exciting* match I've *seen* in a long time.

The least

You can use *the* (or sometimes *my*, *his*, etc.) *least* before an adjective to show that they are bottom of the group of things being compared.

I'm *the least competitive* person I know!

It's not a cheap hotel, but it's *the least expensive* in the area.

Exercise 1

Correct the mistake in each sentence.

1 I think it's the most bad film I've ever seen.
2 It's freezing outside so wear your most thick coat.
3 My mum's probably most generous person I know.
4 We're busyest in the afternoons, so ring in the morning.
5 Ironing is my worst favourite job.
6 That must be the sadest thing I've ever heard!
7 Honestly, it's the disgustingest thing you'll ever see.
8 Deano's has the widdest selection of clothes in town.

Exercise 2

Write sentences with a superlative + the present perfect.

   it / long time / he / be / away from home.
   It's the longest time he's been away from home.
1 he / nice person / I / ever meet.
2 it / exciting race / I / take part in.
3 that computer / reliable / we / ever have.
4 this / complicated game / I / ever play.
5 it / funny book / I / read / in a long time.
6 that / smart / I / ever see you look.

06 HOME

HAVE TO, DON'T HAVE TO, CAN

Use *have to* + verb to talk about things you feel are essential or necessary to do.

I have to walk about ten minutes to get to the train station.

Do *you have to do* much housework?

My brother has to help my dad run the family business.

Have to is also used to talk about rules.

We have to pay a month's deposit before we can move in.

If you *don't have to* do something, it means it is not essential or necessary, but you can do it if you really want to.

I don't have to do any housework, but I like to do the cooking.

It's Sunday tomorrow, so *I don't have to get up* early!

It's OK for her! *She doesn't have to work* evenings!

Use *can* when it is possible to do something. The negative form is *can't*.

I live near the river. *You can walk* along there. It's nice.

Can we stay with you when we come to Berlin?

I can't help you, I'm afraid.

Exercise 1

Correct the mistake in each sentence.

1 We have to telling our landlord three months in advance if we want to move out.
2 My sister cans stay with my uncle whenever she visits the capital.
3 My friend Juan have to find a new place to live.
4 You doesn't have to do it if you don't want to.
5 If you want, I can to drive you home.
6 I'd love to get my own place, but I don't can afford it.

Exercise 2

Match the sentences 1–6 with the best follow-up comments a–f.

1 You don't have to come to the party if you don't want to.
2 We have to study English for five years at school.
3 We can do Mandarin, Arabic or Spanish too if we want.
4 I have to work six days a week.
5 I can work from home two days a week if I want to.
6 All the bills are included in the rent.

a I'm not happy about it, but what can I do!
b It's one of the big advantages of my job.
c It's your choice.
d It's one of the compulsory subjects.
e They're all optional.
f We don't have to worry about how much gas we use.

WILL / WON'T

Will / won't + verb is mainly used to make immediate responses to situations or to things people say. For example:

To say decisions made at the moment of speaking

I'll have the roast chicken, please.

I won't eat now. *I'll wait* till later.

To offer to do something

I'll open the door for you.

To promise to do something

Thanks for that. *I'll pay you back* next week.

Thanks for your help. *I won't forget* it.

We also use *will* to talk about things we see as facts in the future, things we feel sure will happen.

The sofa will be delivered next Monday.

It's a nice coat. *It'll keep* you warm in the winter.

Remember that when we talk about definite personal plans for the future – decisions about the future we have already made – we use *going to* + verb. When we talk about future arrangements with other people, we use the present continuous.

Exercise 1

Complete the sentences by adding *'ll* or *won't*.

1 I have to go to the doctor's tomorrow, so I .... be at the meeting in the morning.
2 It's my turn to pay. I .... get this.
3 You .... believe who I saw today!
4 Shall we take the bus into town? It .... be cheaper – and it .... take as long as driving.
5 I don't think it .... be very expensive. It certainly .... cost more than 100 euros.
6 I need to get good results in my exams. Otherwise, I .... get into the university I want to go to.
7 Ask Kenny to lend you some money. I'm sure he .... mind.
8 We .... eat at about nine, if that's OK with you.

Exercise 2

Choose the correct form.

1 I can't meet you tonight. A friend of mine *will come / is coming* to my house for dinner.
2 Don't worry. The dog *won't bite / isn't biting*.
3 A: *What're you doing / What will you do* tonight?
   B: Nothing. *I'm just going to / I'll just* go home and have an early night.
4 Our oldest son *is getting / will get* married next month.
5 That looks hard. *I'll help / I'm helping* you, if you want.
6 A: I need to send some letters sometime today.
   B: *I'll go / I'm going* into town later, so *I'll post / I'm going to post* them for you, if you want.

07 MIND AND BODY

GIVING ADVICE

should, ought to, why don't you

The most common way of giving advice – to say what you think is the best thing to do – is *should* + verb. We often soften advice by adding *Maybe* at the beginning of sentences. It's also common to say *I think you should*.

Should is a modal verb. The forms of modal verbs are the same for all persons. There is no third person –s; there is no *do / does* in questions; and no *don't / doesn't* in negatives. The negative form is *shouldn't*.
Maybe we should phone the restaurant and book a table.
This place is great. *We should come* here again.
You shouldn't worry about it. It'll all be fine.
What do you think *I should do*?

Two other common ways of giving advice are *ought to* + verb and *why don't you* + verb. They basically mean the same as *should*.
(Maybe) you ought to stop drinking so much coffee.
Why don't you take a few days off work?

Exercise 1
Complete the sentences with *should / shouldn't* and the verbs in the box.

do eat go ignore miss take watch

1 You .... so much! You'll get fat if you're not careful!
2 I'm not surprised your eyes are sore. You .... less TV!
3 If it hurts, you really .... and see a doctor about it. You .... just .... it. It might get worse.
4 This phone doesn't really work properly! I guess I .... it back to the shop and complain.
5 The government .... more to sort the problem out.
6 If you go to Seville, you really .... the cathedral there.

Exercise 2
Use the words in brackets to rewrite the sentences so they have a similar meaning.
1 You should go on a diet. (why)
2 You ought to put some cream on that rash. (should)
3 What do you think we should do? (ought)
4 You should phone and make an apointment. (don't)
5 Selling pirate DVDs should be stopped. (to)
6 Why don't you drink less coffee? (maybe)

IMPERATIVES

Use
Imperatives are used to do lots of different things.
Be quiet. (order)
Take twice daily with food. (instructions)
Go and see your doctor if you're worried. (advice)
Don't buy that one. It's bad quality. (warning)
Come on! You can do it! (encouragement)
Have a seat. (offer)
Don't worry. It'll be fine. (reassurance)

With friends, we sometimes use imperatives as requests, but it's better to use *Could you / Can you* because imperatives can sometimes sound rude and too direct.
Pass me the salt, please?(= with close friends)
Could you pass me the salt, please? (= more polite, less direct)

Structures with imperatives
We often use a conditional *if*-clause with an imperative, especially when giving advice
Don't worry if you find it difficult. (= you shouldn't worry)
If you need anything, just *email* me.
If you can't sleep, *try* counting backwards from 100.

We often use *will* after imperatives.
Hurry up or *we'll miss* the train.
Have a seat. *I'll stand*.
Don't worry about cleaning up. *I'll do* it.
Don't make so much noise. *You'll wake* the baby!

We often use *so* + adjective after negative imperatives.
Don't be so lazy!
Don't be so rude!

Exercise 1
Make one of the imperatives in each of 1–8 negative.
1 Panic. Stay calm.
2 Whisper. Speak up. We can't hear you.
3 Be careful. Slip.
4 Just sit there. Do something.
5 Take your time. Rush.
6 Be quiet. Make so much noise.
7 Get up. Be so lazy.
8 Wait for me. Go ahead. I'll catch you up.

Exercise 2
Rewrite the imperatives below with *could* for requests and *should* for advice or instructions.
1 Pour me some water, please.
2 Try talking to someone about it.
3 Bring me the bill.
4 Help me carry these bags to the car.
5 Don't drive if you're taking that medication.
6 Don't call him now. It's too late.

08 GETTING THERE

ARTICLES

a, an and *the*

We use *a* (or *an* if the following word starts with a vowel) the first time we talk about something.
We stayed in *an old hotel* in *a small town* near Naples.

Use *the* when you think the listener knows the specific thing because:
it's already been mentioned
The town was nice, but I didn't like *the hotel*.

you share knowledge with them
I'm just going to *the shops*.

there is only one of the thing present
Can you turn *the light* on?

a clause or prepositional phrase makes it clear
The dance music that they played at the party was terrible.

only one exists (names of seas, rivers, theatres etc.)

the Atlantic Ocean	*the Red Sea*	*the Seine*
the Hilton	*the Globe*	*the Pyrenees*

We do NOT use *the* or *a* to talk about things:
in general or the whole of a type / group
~~The~~ *life* can be strange sometimes.
I listen to ~~the~~ *dance music* a lot.

in certain prepositional phrases
I'm going *to work*.   He's *at university*.

with continents, countries, cities, and some other place names

Asia	*Tanzania*	*Cuba*
Oxford Street	*Mount Fuji*	*Lake Como*

Exercise 1
Correct the mistakes in the sentences below.
1 We hired a boat and sailed down River Nile.
2 I usually come to school by the train.
3 Our friends have the lovely cottage in the Black Forest.
4 I'm meeting one friend of mine later.
5 One day I'd love to try and climb the Mount Everest.
6 My father is pilot, so he's away from home a lot.
7 The happiness is more important than money.
8 I don't like the eggs. I don't know why. I just don't.

Exercise 2
Put *a, an, the* or nothing in each gap.
1 ... food in Laos was quite strange. Most days, we had ... spicy noodles for ... breakfast – sometimes with ... egg on top.
2 I'm from ... Quito – ... capital of ... Ecuador.
3 ... life always seems better when ... sun is out!
4 ... hotel we were in had ... great view of ... sea.
5 Did ... police find ... guy who stole your luggage?

QUANTIFIERS AND UNCOUNTABLE NOUNS

We use *many, much, a lot of, (a) few, (a) little, some, hardly any, no, any*, etc. before a noun to show quantity.

Many and *(a) few* are only used with plural countable nouns.

children	feet	fish	people	sheep

Much and *(a) little* are only used with uncountable nouns.

water	liquid	bread	cheese
work	traffic	chaos	anger
news	information	advice	help
progress	accommodation	luggage	traffic

A lot of, some, hardly any and *no* can be used with both countable and uncountable nouns.

Don't use *no* or *some, (a) few, hardly any* or *(a) little* after a negative. Instead, use *any, much* or *many*.
I *don't have* ~~some~~ *any* brothers and sisters.
We *didn't take* ~~hardly any~~ *much* luggage with us.

We often use *much, many, (a) few* and *(a) little* with *so* and *too*.
We bought *so many things* we couldn't carry them all.
There are *too few trains* running.

A lot of / Lots of is more commonly used with positive sentences in spoken English. *Many* and *much* are more common in formal written English.
There were *a lot of / lots of* people at the party.
Many people believe that car use should be limited.

Use *any* in positive sentences to mean 'it's not important which one or how little'.
I'd be grateful for *any* help.

We generally use *any* in questions, but *some* is often used as well – especially when offering people things.
Would you like *any / some* coffee?

Exercise 1
Complete the sentences with ONE word in each gap.
1 It doesn't cost .... money to take a taxi here.
2 I fainted because I'd eaten so .... food.
3 There aren't .... things to do there.
4 There was so .... noise in the room that I couldn't hear what anyone was saying.
5 He can't give .... information yet – only the date of the course. He needs to speak to a .... people first.
6 There's a .... of anger about the train strike.
7 .... anyone cycles here. It's too dangerous.

09 SCIENCE AND NATURE

THE PAST PERFECT SIMPLE

Form

The past perfect simple is *had* + the past participle.

I didn't recognise her at first because she*'d cut* her hair.

The past perfect passive is *had been* + the past participle.

I was upset I lost my watch. It*'d been made* by my dad.

To make a negative, use *hadn't* or *had never*.

I was nervous because I*'d never met* her parents before.

Use

Use the past perfect simple to show that something happened before another past action. The past perfect is common after *realise, find out, discover* and *remember*.

I suddenly *remembered* I *hadn't packed* my passport.
I *realised* I*'d made* a mistake and changed the answer.

If we write the sentences in the order in which they really happened, we usually use the past simple.
I *made* a mistake but I *realised* later and *changed* it.

However, in past sentences with *after, as soon as, until* and *before*, we can use past simple or past perfect for the action that happened first. It doesn't matter which order the actions are written in.
He changed his mind *after he'd spoken / he spoke* to me.
I*'d heard / I heard* a lot about him *before* we met.

Exercise 1

Complete the sentences using the past perfect form of the verbs in brackets.

1 That's it! We met at Mina's party! I knew I .... you somewhere before. (see)
2 I suddenly remembered I .... to bring my homework. (forget)
3 When I got home, I realised I .... my keys in the office. (leave)
4 We found out we .... at university at the same time, but we .... (be / never meet)
5 I was surprised because there was no-one there and I .... the class .... (not be told / be cancelled)
6 They were surprised he .... so well in his exams, but then they discovered he .... (do / cheat)

Exercise 2

Put the actions that happened first into the past perfect.

1 After they had one date, he asked her to marry him.
2 I rang you as soon as I heard the news.
3 I never went on a plane until I went to Japan.
4 They had an argument before I arrived, so there was a bad atmosphere. It was quite uncomfortable.
5 I was fed up after I found out I didn't get the job.

REPORTING SPEECH 1

We use lots of different verbs to report speech. The most common are *say, tell* and *ask*. You always *tell someone something*, but you *say something*. Look at these mistakes:.
He said ~~me~~ he was a biologist.
~~He told he~~ *He told me he was* a biologist.

We can ask *someone* or *something*.
I *asked him if he likes fish* and he said no.
I *asked where the shop was*, but no-one knew.
I *asked to change classes*.

Report requests or orders from other people using the following pattern:
Your teacher asked me to discuss your marks with you.
The doctor told me not to eat for 24 hours.
NOT
~~Your teacher asked that I discuss it with you.~~
~~The doctor told me that I don't eat for 24 hours.~~

Tell and *ask* are often used in the passive as well as in the active.
They were *told* to carry on with the experiment.
Students were asked what they thought about the results.

Exercise 1

Choose the correct words.

1 The doctor *said / told* I need to lose weight.
2 I *asked / told* him he wasn't allowed to come in, but he *told / said* he had permission to enter.
3 I enjoyed the talk, but I was surprised he didn't *tell / say* anything about experiments on animals.
4 Researchers *were asked / were said* to find out how the disease was spreading.
5 Participants *were told / were asked* that they were part of a study of eating habits.
6 I *told / asked* to leave the room, but I *was told / was said* to stay and finish the experiment.
7 I *was told / was asked* if I wanted to take part in an experiment, but I *told / said* them I wasn't interested.
8 My teacher *said / told* that I should think about studying Physics at university.
9 The research looked at attitudes towards the health service. 100 people *were told / were asked* about their experiences of hospitals.

Exercise 2

Find the five mistakes and correct them.

1 I said him to stop, but he ignored me.
2 When you see him, say hello from me.
3 My science teacher told we only use 10% of our brains!
4 I've been asked to say a few words about our project.
5 My teacher told me to don't to text in class.
6 I asked my dad I could go to the party, but he said no.
7 I asked them what the experiment was for.
8 He asked that I help him with his Chemistry homework.

10 SCHOOL AND UNIVERSITY

FIRST CONDITIONALS

We use first conditionals to talk about things we think are likely to happen in the future. The *if*-clause describes a probable – but not definite – future situation. We use present tenses in this clause. The other clause(s) describe(s) the future result. We usually use *will / won't* + verb in this clause.

If it's still cold later, *I'll* probably just *stay* at home.
If you don't apply soon, all the places *will go*.
If you try your best, *you won't feel* bad about it later.
If I'm working on Saturday, *I won't be able to meet* you.
You won't pass if you don't work harder!
Where *will she live if she gets into* university in England?

It is also possible to use *might* + verb and *going to* + verb.
I might call you later *if I have* time. (= maybe I will)
If it happens again, *I'm going to complain*. (= I've already decided to do this)

The *if*-clause can come first or second in a sentence. If we start with the *if*-clause, we use a comma after it. If we start with the result clause, we don't use commas.
If I save enough money, *I'll take* a few months off.
I'll take a few months off *if I save* enough money.

Exercise 1
Match 1–8 with a–h to make complete sentences.
1 If you copy anything directly from the Internet,
2 If I do well in the entrance exam,
3 I'll give you hand with that
4 If the bank won't lend me money,
5 I'm not going to support you
6 We'll be late for the lecture
7 If you go to room 605,
8 I might do some research for my project today

a you'll find the finance department. Ask there.
b they'll then ask me to go for an interview.
c if you decide to leave university early.
d you'll automatically fail.
e if you want.
f I might need to borrow some from you.
g if I'm not too busy with everything else!
h if we don't hurry up!

Exercise 2
Find the four mistakes and correct them.
1 If I'll go to England, my English will get better.
2 You don't do well at the interview tomorrow if you don't dress well for it.
3 I'm sure your tutor will help if you ask her to.
4 If I find the website address, I send it you later.
5 If I'm still feeling bad, I won't come to class.
6 If I won't go to university, my parents will be really upset.

HAD TO / DIDN'T HAVE TO

Use *had to* + verb to talk about things that were necessary.
Sorry I'm late. *I had to go* to the dentist.

Use *Did ... have to* + verb in questions.
Did you have to wear a uniform at school?

Note: *must* has no past form – we use *had to*.
She ~~must~~ *had to go* and speak to someone.

Use *didn't have to* + verb for things that were not necessary.
She *didn't have to do* much homework in England.

Note: *needed / didn't need to* has the same meaning as *had to / didn't have to*.
I didn't need to go to the meeting in the end.

COULD / COULDN'T

Can is not used in the past. Use *could* or *was able to*.
Sorry I ~~can't~~ *couldn't / wasn't able to* come yesterday.

Use *could* + verb for things in the past that were possible – that you had a choice about.
When I was at school, *we could go* home for lunch.

Use *couldn't* for things that were impossible
- **because of a rule / law**
  We couldn't take mobile phones with us to my school.
- **because of a problem**
  I couldn't see, because there were people in front of me.
- **because you didn't have the ability**
  I couldn't swim until I was 20.

Exercise 1
Choose the correct form.
1 *I could / couldn't* go home for lunch when I was at school, but now I'm working, I don't have time.
2 *I had to / I didn't have to* get up early when I was at school, but at university the classes start later.
3 When I was living at home, *I had to / didn't have to* cook, but now I'm on my own, *I had to / have to*.
4 When I was at school, you *couldn't / could* call a teacher by their first name. You *had to / have to* call them 'Sir' or 'Miss'. Now, at university, we *can / could*.

Exercise 2
Which five sentences are incorrect? Correct them.
1 We can't come yesterday, because of the train strike.
2 I must go to the bank. I have to get some money.
3 We don't have to do exercise 4 – we only needed to do exercise 3.
4 The question was so difficult, I couldn't to answer it.
5 When I was at school, we must always stand up when the teacher came into the classroom.
6 Could you move, please? I can't see the board.
7 He has to re-take the test twice before he passed.

11 PLACES TO STAY

SECOND CONDITIONALS

We use second conditionals to talk about imaginary situations – or situations that are impossible to change – now or in the future. The *if*-clause describes an imaginary situation. We use past tenses in this clause. The other clause describes the imaginary result. We usually use *would / wouldn't* + verb in this clause.
I'd help you *if I had* time, but I'm too busy, I'm afraid.
I'd respect her more *if she wasn't* so demanding.
I wouldn't be so annoyed about it *if they were* more polite!
What *would you do if something like that happened* to you?

It is also possible to use *might* + verb to talk about uncertain or possible imaginary results.
They might attract more people *if they weren't* so expensive! (= maybe they would attract)

The *if*-clause can come first or second in a sentence. If we start with the *if*-clause, we use a comma after it. If we start with the result clause, we don't use commas.
I'd love to travel more *if I had* the time and money.
If I had the time and money, *I'd love to travel* more.

We use the expression *If I were you, I'd ...* to give advice.
If I were you, I'd book online. It'd be cheaper.

Exercise 1
Match 1–6 with a–f to make complete sentences.
1 They wouldn't have these problems
2 I'd be more willing to try camping
3 It's a nice hotel, but it'd be better
4 I think that, if they opened a branch in Brighton,
5 If we booked an earlier flight,
6 If something like that happened to me,

a if the rooms were a bit more child-friendly.
b I'd complain. I'd be really angry about it!
c if they employed staff who spoke better English!
d we could just get a bus to the hotel.
e if the weather here was a bit better.
f it'd be a big success.

Exercise 2
Choose the correct form.
1 I might think about staying there if it *was / would be* nearer the beach.
2 *I'd / I'll* pick you up from your hotel if it *was / wasn't* so far from the centre of town!
3 If I *am / were* you, I *wouldn't / don't* have the hotel breakfast. *I'll / I'd* eat somewhere else instead.
4 *It'd / It's* be better if the website *was / will* be more user-friendly.
5 I'm having a good time here, but it *will / would* be even better if it *didn't / wasn't* raining all the time!
6 If we *was / were* earning more money, we *can / could* stay in nicer places.

USED TO

Used to + verb often replaces the past simple when we describe past habits or states – especially to talk about changes.

Note that we often don't say a time phrase with *used to*.
My parents *lived* in Holland *in the 80's*.
My parents *used to live* in Holland.

I *did* acting *when I was at school*.
I don't mind speaking in public. I *used to do* acting at school.

I *didn't like* vegetables *when I was younger*.
I *never used to like* vegetables but I love them now.

Passives use *used to be* + past participle.
Lots of things that *used to be made* here are now made abroad.

The most common way to form the negative is with *never*.
I *never used to worry* about anything, but as you get older...
My parents were quite strict, but *they never used to hit* us.

You can also form negatives of *used to* in the following ways:
My dad *didn't use to do* any housework when I was a kid.
A: There are lots of shops round here.
B: Yes, it's better than it was. *There didn't used to be* any!
Some say *didn't used to* is incorrect, but it is very common.

There is no present form of *used to*. It is only used to talk about the past. For habits in the present, use present simple + *usually* (see page 137).
I ~~use to~~ *usually go* back to my hometown during the holidays.
I don't ~~use to~~ *usually watch* TV much during the week.

Exercise 1
Find the five mistakes and correct them.
1 When I was a kid, we usually go to the mountains during the summer.
2 I used work as a researcher for a drug company.
3 He's lost a lot of weight. He used to weigh 100 kilos.
4 I didn't never used to have lunch at school. I always had lunch at home.
5 I didn't use to like swimming, but I go quite a lot now.
6 On Fridays, we use to watch a DVD at home together.
7 Last week, I used to have to study for my exams.
8 My grandparents usually come to stay with us at Christmas.

12 PHONE

JUST, ALREADY, YET AND STILL

Just

Just + the perfect perfect simple shows an action happened very recently. It often goes with *only*.
He's definitely here. *I've just seen* him. Maybe he's in the loo.
A: Would you like a cup of coffee?
B: No thanks. *I've only just had* one.

With other tenses, *just* means '*only*' – or shows that something is not important or difficult.
I just have three euros.
I didn't do much. *I just relaxed* at home.

Already

Already + the present perfect shows something happened before, often sooner than expected. It's usually used in positive sentences.
I've already seen that film. Let's see something else.
I can't believe *you've already finished* those biscuits.

We can use it with other tenses too.
Come on! *We're already late*!

Yet

Yet + the present perfect shows we expected – or expect – something to happen. It's used in questions and negatives.
Have you seen the latest Almodovar film *yet*? You'll love it.
I haven't done my homework *yet*, but I'll do it later.

You can use *yet* with the verb *be* as well.
He's not here yet.

Still

Still shows that an action continues unchanged. It's used more with the present simple / continuous than the present perfect.
Are you still working in McDonald's?
She's 45, but *she still lives* with her parents.

We use *still* + *not* + the present perfect when we wanted something to happen, but it didn't and probably won't.
He still hasn't cleaned his room. I've asked him six times!

Exercise 1

Write sentences with *just, already, yet* and *still* using the notes below.
1 you / speak / the bank yet?
2 I / have / time yet. I'll do it tomorrow.
3 she / only just / graduate.
4 she / still / try / to decide / what to do with her life.
5 I'm afraid he / be / back yet.
6 don't worry! I / already / sort out / everything.
7 she / just / hand / the work to me this second. I'll put it in the post now.
8 he / already / make $1 million / and he's only 26!

REPORTING SPEECH 2

To report things people said, we often move 'one tense back'.
Present simple / continuous → Past simple / continuous
Present perfect → Past perfect
Past simple → Past perfect
Will → *Would*
Can → *Could*

Time expressions often change as well. For example:
This week → *Last week* / *That week*
Today → *Yesterday* / *That day*

However, when we report something that is still true now – or that will happen in the future – we don't have to move 'one tense back'. For example:
'I'm from Greece.
He told me he was from Greece.
OR
He told me he is from Greece.

When we report questions that start with a question word, we don't use *do / does / did*. The word order becomes subject + verb.
'Where do you live?' → She asked me where I lived / live.
'How old are you?' → He asked me how old I was / am.

For yes / no questions that start with *do, can, would*, etc. add *if*.
'Can you help me?''→ He asked *if I could* help him.
'Have you been there?' → He asked me *if I'd been* there.

Exercise 1

Complete each of the sentences that report direct speech.
1 'My dad is in hospital.'
   > I saw Dan last week and he said his dad
   ....
2 'Phil is working in an ice-cream factory.'
   > The last time I heard, Phil ....
3 'Guess what? Ivy's had a baby.'
   > I saw Lee the other day and he told me that Ivy
   ....
4 'I'll tell Mr Jackson you called.'
   > I spoke to his secretary. She said she .... Mr Jackson I'd called.
5 'Why do you want to work for us?'
   > They asked me why ....
6 'What are your career goals?'
   > They asked me what ....
7 'Have you had many other interviews?'
   > They asked me ....
8 'Is there anything you'd like to ask us?'
   > They asked me ....

13 CULTURE

–ED / –ING ADJECTIVES

A small group of adjectives can end in either –ed or –ing. When they end in –ed, they describe people's feelings. When they end in –ing, they describe the situation, thing or person that causes the feeling. These words come from verbs.

I was *annoyed* when it happened!
I just find him really *annoying*!
You're starting *to annoy* me now.

Here are some common adjectives with two forms.
I'm *bored*! / My job is really *boring*.
I'm not *interested* in history. / She's really *interesting*.
I'm *surprised* I passed the exam. / It's a *surprising* decision.
I'm *disappointed* I failed the exam. / A *disappointing* game.
I'm too *tired* to cook tonight. / I've had a really *tiring* day.
I'm really *excited* about it. / It's very *exciting* news.
I was *amazed* when she told me. / The food is *amazing*!
I was really *shocked*. / The ending was really *shocking*!
I'm *disgusted* by your behaviour. / The food was *disgusting*!
I'm really *confused*. / This grammar is so *confusing*!
I feel *depressed* all the time. / It's very *depressing* news.
I was so *worried* about you. / It's quite a *worrying* situation.

Exercise 1
Choose the correct form of each adjective.
1   I didn't understand the film. The plot was really *confused / confusing*.
2   I can't wait to see the Brad Schmidt film! I'm really *excited / exciting* about it!
3   I don't like his films. I find them quite *bored / boring*.
4   We couldn't get tickets because they were sold out. I was so *annoyed / annoying* about it.
5   I thought the film was *disappointed / disappointing*.
6   I was *amazed / amazing* when I heard who the new James Bond is!
7   The costumes in the film were *amazed / amazing*.
8   I'm *bored / boring* with this. Can we just turn it off?
9   It's violent. The murder is really *shocked / shocking*.
10 I'm really *worried / worrying* about my son. He watches too many violent war movies!

Exercise 2
Rewrite the sentences using the verb form of the adjectives.
1   Can you stop doing that? It's really annoying!
    Can you stop doing that? It's ....
2   I'm not interested in that job.
    That job ....
3   I found the ending really shocking!
    The ending ....
4   His behaviour is really worrying.
    His behaviour really ....
5   I was surprised how good Bill Fox was in that film.
    Bill Fox's performance in that film ....

THE PRESENT PERFECT CONTINUOUS

The present perfect continuous is *have / has + been + –ing*.

Use it with *for* and *since* to talk about an activity that started in the past and is unfinished. Don't use the present continuous.
~~I'm living~~ *I've been living here for three years*.
How long ~~are you working~~ *have you been working* here?

For is used to say the amount or period of time:
for five years, for a few days, for an hour, for a while, etc.

We don't use *for* with phrases that use *all*, such as *all day, all night, all week, all year, all my life*, etc. *Since* shows when something started:
since the year 2000, *since I was* 15, *since yesterday*, etc.

We use these phrases as well: *since then, ever since*.
I started judo when I was six. *I've been doing it ever since*.
We met at school and *we've been good friends since then*.

We often use the present perfect continuous to refer to recent activities – and with *recently*.
A: What *have you been doing recently*?
B: *I've been studying* for my exams.

THE PRESENT PERFECT CONTINUOUS AND PRESENT PERFECT SIMPLE

Use the present perfect simple with *be, believe, belong, hate, have (= possess), know, like, love*.
I've had this car for 15 *years and it still runs perfectly*.
I've belonged to the club since last year.

Use the present perfect simple with passive verbs.
The company's been run by my sister *for the last ten years*.

Use the present perfect continuous to focus on the activity – and to talk about how long. Use the present perfect simple to focus on finished achievements in the time up till now – and to talk about how many.
Compare:
I've been phoning him all morning, but he's not answering.
I've phoned ten shops, but none of them had the book!
They've been meeting since April to discuss the project.
We've met several times before.

Exercise 1
Write sentences in the present perfect continuous or simple with *for* or *since*, using the notes below.
1   I / learn Chinese / I was eight.
2   I / go to the gym every day / the last two months.
3   They / be together / quite a long time.
4   The Conservatives / be in power / the last election.
5   He / live there / last year.
6   I / try to find / a job / months.

14 THINGS

RELATIVE CLAUSES

We use relative clauses to add information after nouns. The relative clause usually comes immediately after the thing / person / place it describes. Relative clauses usually begin with a relative pronoun. We use *that / which* for things, *that / who* for people and *where* for places.

When the relative pronoun is the subject of the verb in the relative clause, you don't need to add *he, she, it,* etc.
A science-fiction film is *a film which / that it is set* in space and *which / that it is usually set* in the future too.
The Boredoms are a group from Japan *who / that they have released* about ten albums.

When the relative pronoun is the object of the verb in relative clauses, you don't need to add *him, it, there,* etc.
The woman *who I spoke to her was* the manager.
That's the place where I used to work there.

Note that in these relative clauses we don't always use a relative pronoun at all.
The woman I spoke to was the manager.

Exercise 1
Complete the sentences with *who, which* or *where.*
1   That's the woman .... lives upstairs from me.
2   It's one thing .... just really annoys me.
3   That's the shop .... I bought my shoes.
4   He's the guy .... owns the whole factory.
5   English is the subject .... I enjoy most.
6   That's the room .... you get your lunch.

Exercise 2
Join the pairs of sentences using a relative clause.
1   Sertab Erener is a Turkish singer. She won the Eurovision Song Contest in 2003.
    ....
2   Storaplan is a very trendy area. There are lots of nice shops and restaurants there.
    ....
3   Sue Briggs was an English teacher. She persuaded me to go to university.
    ....
4   A campsite is a place. You stay there when you go camping.
    ....
5   Shostakovich was a Russian composer. He wrote some amazing pieces of music.
    ....
6   Istanbul is a city. Europe and Asia meet there.
    ....
7   What do you call those machines? They do the washing-up for you.
    ....
8   I need to buy one of those things. You wear it round your waist and keep your money in it.
    ....

MUST / MUSTN'T

Must shows something essential because of natural or legal laws, because of an order or because you personally think it's essential. You can also use *have to* in all these cases.
The doctor said *I must lose* some weight.
I must go or I'll miss my train.

Mustn't shows it is essential not to do something.
You mustn't eat in the library at all.

You can't use *don't have to* here. *Don't have to* means that it's not necessary to do something.

We often prefer *can't* or *be not allowed to* for rules.
You can't / You're not allowed to eat in the library.

If you (I, etc.) must shows we understand someone else feels it's essential to do something, but we don't agree.
If you must smoke, go outside.
If they must wait here, tell them to be quiet.

Must for commenting
It's very common to use *must (be)* to comment on things. It means *I think (you are / it is / he is,* etc.).
He must be really happy to have a holiday.
A: I've been travelling all day.
B: *You must be tired.*

Exercise 1
Complete the sentences with *must* or *mustn't.*
1   I .... rush. I'm late for class.
2   I can't talk now. I .... finish this work.
3   You .... worry. Everything will be OK.
4   We .... remember to pay the gas bill.
5   My parents told me I .... be back by ten.
6   The teacher said we .... be late.
7   I can do the shopping, if I really ....
8   A: I've been waiting for over an hour.
    B: You .... be really fed up.

Exercise 2
Use the words in **bold** to rewrite the sentences so they have a similar meaning.
1   People must pay tax for throwing rubbish away. **have**
    People .... for throwing rubbish away.
2   You mustn't leave rubbish bags on the street. **allowed**
    You .... rubbish bags on the street.
3   I must remember to call him. **forget**
    I .... call him.
4   I imagine you're very excited about going away. **must**
    You .... about going away.

15 MONEY

TIME PHRASES AND TENSE

Some time phrases commonly go with particular forms.

At the moment and *currently* commonly go with the present continuous (see page 142). *Currently* is more common in writing than speaking.
The economy *is doing* very well *at the moment*
I am currently working for an import-export company.

Over / in the last ... and *since ...* commonly go with the present perfect.
She's lost a lot of weight *over the last few months.*
I've had six interviews *in the last month.*
The government's done a lot *since it was elected.*
Each sentence above shows a change happened at some time during the period of time up to now.

In, in ... time, next, over the next, tomorrow, etc. go with future forms.
The recession is going to be over *in a year.*
Unemployment will fall over the next few months.
I'm going away *in two weeks' time.*

Used to is commonly found without a time phrase, but it often goes with *in the past* or *when I was ...* .
Flying used to be a lot more expensive *in the past.*
I used to play basketball *when I was at school.*

Last, the other, ago, yesterday, etc. go with past tenses.
I saw him *the other day / week.*
Last year, inflation *went up* 3%.

Exercise 1

Decide which of these time phrases can go with each sentence below.

over the last five years	in three months' time
in two years	the other week
last month	when I was
three months ago	since last year
at the moment	in the last six months

1 Prices have gone up a lot ... .
2 Unemployment is falling ... .
3 They opened a new factory here ... .
4 There's going to be a general election ... .

Exercise 2

Write full sentences using these ideas.
1 The prime minister / lose popularity / in the last year.
2 I / spend a lot more money / in the past.
3 I / get a loan from the bank / the other month.
4 The recession / get worse / at the moment.
5 They / invest more in schools / over the next five years.
6 He / lose his job / three years ago.

PRESENT TENSES IN FUTURE TIME CLAUSES

Use the present simple or continuous to talk about the future in clauses that start with *when, as soon as, before, after* and *until*. *When* shows we are sure something will happen. *As soon as* shows that one thing will happen quickly after another thing. *Until* shows something stops happening at this time.
The future time clause can come first or second in a sentence.

In the main clause of these sentences, we can use *will / won't, can, be going to* or imperatives.
I'll do it now *before I forget.*
We won't see any improvement *until the economy gets* better.
I can help you with your homework *as soon as I finish* this.
When I leave school, *I'm going to study* Law at university.
After you finish that, *make* me a cup of coffee.

Exercise 1

Choose the correct word.
1 I have to finish this work *before / when* I leave the office tonight.
2 I'll email you *when / until* I get home tonight.
3 I'm not going to lend you any more money *until / after* you pay me the ten pounds you still owe me!
4 *After / Until* this course ends, I'm going to visit my cousin in the States.
5 I'm not going to talk to him *until / as soon as* he apologises.
6 We should book a hotel *before / after* we arrive in Paris. It's going to be very late when we get there.
7 She's still in hospital. *As soon as / Until* I hear anything, I'll call you.
8 My neighbours are going to look after our cat *when / after* we're away on holiday.
9 I'll do it *as soon as / before* I have time, OK?

Exercise 2

Find the five mistakes and correct them.
1 We'll obviously discuss the deal with everyone before we'll make a final decision.
2 When you're ready, tell me, OK?
3 We will can have something to eat when we get home.
4 After you'll register, you'll be able to access your account online.
5 I'll be OK for money when this cheque clears.
6 I'll come and visit you as soon as I'm feeling better.
7 Inflation continues to rise until the government does something about it!
8 I will believe in UFOs until I see one with my own eyes!

16 DATES AND HISTORY

PREPOSITIONS AND NOUNS / –*ING* FORMS

Prepositions go before nouns. If we need a verb to follow a preposition, we use an –*ing* form to make the verb into a noun.

After the revolution, the nation suffered many problems.
Before leaving the room, please turn off the light.
I find it difficult to pay all the bills, *despite having* two jobs.

Some verbs / adjectives are often followed by particular prepositions:

listen to	result in	insist on
lead to	invest in	complain about
belong to	be involved in	argue about
be opposed to	depend on	date from
be caused by	apologise for	vote for / against

Some verbs often have two objects:

accuse someone of something
ban someone from a place
remind someone of something

Notice also this pattern:
The problem *was caused by people* not pay*ing* taxes.
I'm opposed to people smok*ing* in public places.

Exercise 1

Rewrite these sentences using an –*ing* form. For example:
After Napoleon became president, he introduced a new legal system.
After becoming president, Napoleon introduced a new legal system.

1 After the Mongols invaded Kazakhstan, many of them settled in the region.
   After ....
2 Before I saw the film, I knew nothing about the history of slavery.
   Before ....
3 The king brought the two sides together for peace talks and as a result, he basically ended the civil war.
   By ....
4 Because unemployment is rising, there's a lot of competition for jobs.
   Because of ....
5 The country has a good education system but health care is poor.
   Despite ....

VERB PATTERNS
(–*ing* and *to*–infinitives)

When some verbs are followed by another verb, the second verb takes either the -*ing* or the *to*-infinitive form. There are no rules for this. You just have to learn which verbs have which patterns.

Verbs which are often followed by the –*ing* form include:

avoid	feel like	love	prefer
can't stand	finish	mind	recommend
consider	hate	miss	spend
enjoy	like	practise	stop

I've always really *enjoyed* cook*ing*.
I really *hate* be*ing* so tall!

Verbs which are often followed by a *to*-infinitive include:

afford	continue	manage	promise
agree	decide	offer	refuse
arrange	fail	persuade	want
ask	hope	plan	would like

I *asked him to stop*, but he *refused to listen*!
I've *arranged to go out* with some friends tonight.

Some verbs can be followed by an -*ing* or a *to*-infinitive without the meaning really changing.
I *love going / to go* for walks in the countryside.
It's *started raining / to rain*.

With a few verbs, there is a change in meaning when the –*ing* form or to–infinitive form is used.
I *must remember to call* her. (= in the future)
I *can't remember meeting* her. (= in the past)
I *tried to stop*, but I couldn't. (= I wasn't able to do it)
I *tried dieting*, but it didn't work. (= it had no effect)
I *stopped to buy* some petrol. (= this is why I stopped)
I *stopped trying* after a while. (= I didn't try any more)

Exercise 1

Find the seven mistakes and correct them.
1 I like watching tennis, but I prefer play it.
2 I've decided not going to university.
3 I thought we agreed not to talk about politics!
4 Would you mind to go to the shop for me?
5 I don't really enjoy to shop for clothes.
6 I spent six months to travel round Africa.
7 A friend of mine recommended coming here.
8 I don't really feel like cooking tonight. Let's eat out.
9 When I can afford to take some time off work, I'd really like to go to Kazakhstan.
10 Sorry I'm late. I stopped having lunch on the way.
11 Can you please stop to make so much noise?
12 I must remember to buy some stamps later today.

FILE 1

Unit 14 p. 99 Conversation practice
Student B

FILE 2

Unit 3 p. 25 Speaking

Student A (waiter / waitress)
Ask student B if he / she has booked. If not, give choices about what to do. Then show student B to their seat. Show The Globe Restaurant menu. Ask if B needs any help – or recommendations. Answer any requests. You don't have to give positive replies but be polite.

Take their order for the starter and main course. Invent a problem with one of the dishes B orders.

Ask if B wants to see the dessert menu.

FILE 3

Unit 8 p. 56 Reading

'Don't worry,' said the farmer. 'In the next town you come to, you'll find more of the same sort of people!'

FILE 4

Unit 8 p. 55 Conversation practice

Student A
You want to go to the following places. Ask for directions and mark the places on your map.
- the big department store
- a bank
- the football ground
- the town hall
- the station

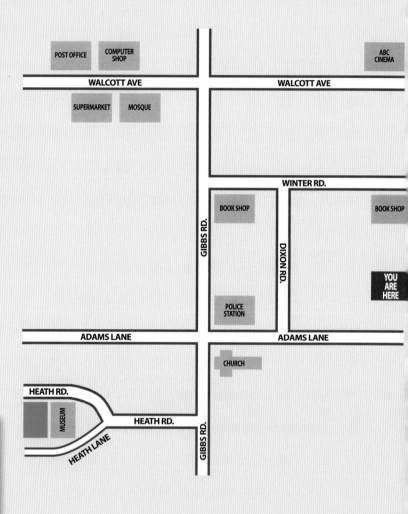

FILE 5

Unit 11 p. 77 Conversation practice

Student B
You have friends who have found a hostel 20km from Edinburgh in Scotland. They want to stay for four days and go to the arts festival in the city. They also want to go on a day trip round the Scottish countryside. They are students and don't want to spend too much money.

Canada
USA
Boston
New York
Venezuela
Brazil
Brasilia
Rio do Janeiro
France
Paris
Lyon
Slovenia
Mali
Africa
St Petersburg
Moscow
Russia
Kazakhstan
China
Beijing
Shanghai
Vietnam
Australia

FILE 6 (ABOVE)

Unit 6 p. 43 Developing conversations

FILE 7

Unit 9 p. 67 Grammar

1 A pigeon was caught and arrested at a jail. The pigeon had carried drugs to prisoners at the jail. Apparently it had flown over 60 kilometres from one prisoner's home town.

2 A woman's pet dog was found on a desert island. The dog disappeared when the woman was travelling on a cruise. The dog had fallen into the sea and swum to the island. Guards who look after the island found the dog several weeks later. It had survived by eating small animals.

3 A couple were saved by their pet rabbit. The couple hadn't turned off a gas ring on their cooker properly and the house was filling with gas. The rabbit detected the smell and ran up the stairs and woke his owners who were sleeping.

FILE 8

Unit 11 p. 77 Conversation practice

Student A
Your parents' friends are going to Canada on holiday. It will be two adults and two children – aged 14 and nine. They have seen an advert for four-bed apartments connected to a hotel. They are interested in going skiing in a place nearby and the adults want to spend some free time on their own. Ring the hotel in Canada and ask for information.

FILE 9

Unit 9 p. 66 Reading
The story about the parrots is not true. However, a Japanese restaurant did train some monkeys to do a similar job!

FILE 10

Unit 15 p. 105, Conversation practice, exercise B

Student A
You are from a country called Remonesia, which is somewhere in South–east Asia.
- Invent exactly where it is.
- Decide what the quality of life is like there and give at least two reasons for this.
- Decide how the economy is doing and give at least two examples.
- Say you are thinking of moving. Explain when / where / why.

FILE 11

Unit 9 p. 65 Conversation practice

Student A
1 They have found a cure for the flu. It's a new drug which deals with 90% of all cases. It could save thousands of lives.
   Ask: Did you hear about the new cure for the flu?
2 There's going to be a storm this weekend. It's going to rain a lot and be very windy.
   Ask: Did you see the weather forecast for the weekend?
3 The right whale is almost extinct. There are only around 500 left in the wild. Scientists don't know if there are enough to survive.
   Ask: Did you see the article about the right whale?

FILE 12

Unit 2 p. 18 Reading

Riot police were called to control a group of a hundred angry tourists in Macau yesterday. The tourists from Beijing were unhappy that tour guides were forcing them to visit shops instead of visiting historic places of interest. Macau was previously occupied by Portugal and there is a famous mixture of Portuguese and Chinese buildings. The tourists wanted to see some of the old temples and churches, but they said the guides were only interested in persuading them to buy things. The protest finally started when the weather became cold and the guides stopped the tourists collecting warm clothes from coaches, which were locked. There was some fighting and the police were called. The tourists finally returned to their hotels after five hours. Four people were arrested.

FILE 13

Unit 9 p. 65 Conversation practice

Student B
1 The police caught some terrorists with nuclear material. The police don't know where it came from. It's not clear what they planned to do with it.
   Ask: Did you see the news about those terrorists with the nuclear material?
2 It's going to snow at the beginning of the weekend and then it's going to be cold and sunny.
   Ask: Did you see the forecast for the weekend?
3 They're going to build a new zoo in a city near you. It's going to cost $3 billion dollars to construct.
   Ask: Did you hear about the zoo that they're going to build in .... (say the place)?

FILE 14

Unit 11 p. 80 Reading
Group B

Sherise Pinto, USA
I went camping for the first time on a field trip to La Laguna in Mexico this year. I'm in the first year of a Biology degree and we went to La Laguna because it has a huge variety of plant and animal life. We walked for miles to get to the campsite and it was just so hot I thought I was going to die, but we eventually got to where we were camping and it was next to a rock pool. We all jumped in to cool down. What a relief!

Sitting outside that night, looking at the stars, I felt great. Unfortunately, though, I couldn't sleep because of the rocks under my tent and I got bitten by mosquitoes or something. After three days without hot water or a proper toilet, I began to miss the comfort of home. La Laguna's fantastic, and waking up to birds singing and amazing views is great, but if I went again, I'd prefer to have more facilities – like a bed!

Marcia Machado, Brazil
I joined the Girl Guides when I was 11 and that's how I started going camping. The first time wasn't very wild – it was in the gardens of a Girl Guide centre, where we had dinner and showers and everything, but staying in a tent at night still seemed like a big challenge. I woke up scared during the night because I thought I heard an animal moving around outside. It took me a while to fall asleep again. It felt like a real achievement when I got up in the morning and we made breakfast outside. I felt like I'd climbed a mountain! The next night, we stayed up late round a fire, telling jokes and singing. Camping gives you that good feeling and confidence.

FILE 15

Unit 14 p. 99 Conversation practice
Student A

FILE 16

Unit 3 p. 25 Speaking

Student B (customer)
You are a group of four people. You have one or more of the following in your group:
a baby, a young child, someone who's disabled, someone who has a food allergy, someone who doesn't eat a certain kind of food because of their beliefs

You haven't booked a table. Respond to the waiter's suggestions. Make a request based on the people in your group. When the waiter shows you the menu / asks for your order, ask for more information about two of the dishes on the menu. Then order your starter and main course. Respond as you wish to any other questions the waiter asks.
When you're ready, ask for the bill and pay.

FILE 17

Unit 15 p. 105 Conversation practice

Student B
You are from a country called Lidland, which is somewhere in northern Europe.
- Invent exactly where it is.
- Decide what the quality of life is like there and give at least two reasons for this.
- Decide how the economy is doing and give at least two examples.
- Say you are thinking of moving. Explain when / where / why.

FILE 18

Unit 5 p. 37 Conversation practice

Student A	Student B
Ask what B wants to do while here.	
	Give some ideas. Ask if A has any plans for you both while you are here.
Suggest doing activity.	
	Be positive, but ask to borrow something you need for the activity.
Agree.	
	Ask questions to find out details of activity.
Answer.	

FILE 19

Unit 12 p. 83 Conversation practice

Student A	Student B
Act dialling a number.	
	Answer.
Ask for someone.	
	Explain they're not there.
Leave a message.	
	Check contact details.
Leave details. Check when they'll be back.	
	Answer.
End conversation.	

FILE 20

Unit 8 page 55 Conversation practice

Student B
You want to go to the following places. Ask for directions and mark the places on your map.
- a bookshop
- the post office
- the police station
- the museum
- the ABC cinema

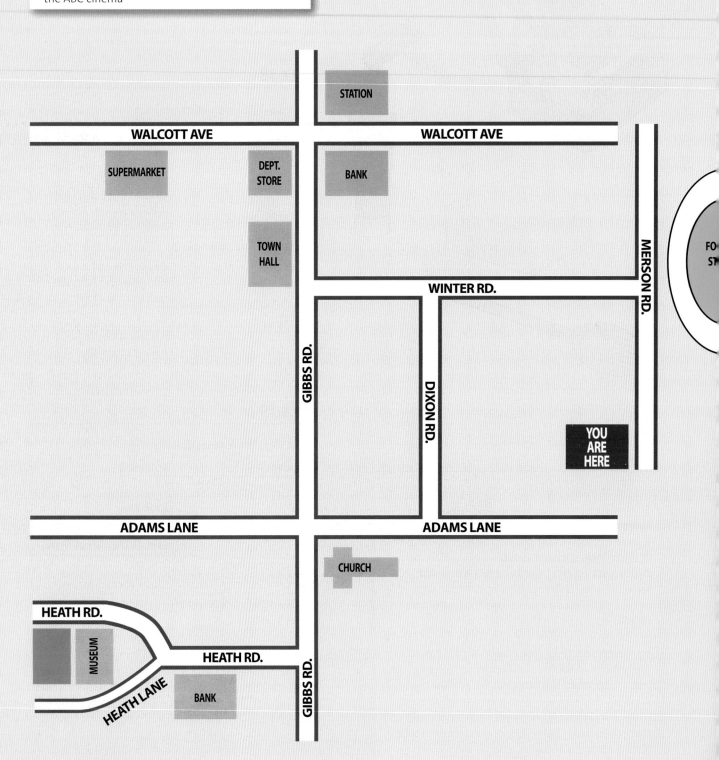

FILE 21

Unit 4 page 26 Vocabulary

(a) actor

(b) journalist

(c) engineer

(d) designer

(e) pilot

(f) sales manager

(g) photographer

(h) politician

(i) lawyer

(j) soldier

k) policeman

(l) secretary

(m) nurse

(n) builder

FILE 22

Unit 2 page 18 Reading

Two people were injured in London yesterday when a new low-cost clothes store opened. Hundreds of people gathered outside Primark in Oxford Street after reading stories on the Internet that all the items in shop had a 50% discount. Managers at the shop called the police to control the crowd and in the end they opened 15 minutes early. When the doors were opened, several people fell and there was some fighting as people ran to get clothes. Two people were taken to hospital for minor injuries. The rumours of a sale were, in fact, completely false, but most people were still happy they went. 16-year-old Tina Wilson said, "Primark is my favourite shop. I got this great coat for just £30. They do great fashion at great prices".

AUDIOSCRIPT

UNIT 01

🔊 1.1

L = Laura, M = Maya, A = Anna

L: Maya

M: Hi Laura. Sorry I'm a bit late.

L: That's OK.

M: How long have you been here?

L: Oh, not long. Ten minutes.

M: Sorry. The traffic was bad.

L: Are you looking for something?

M: Another chair. Oh ... there's one.

L: So who else is coming?

M: My friend Anna from Poland.

L: Oh yeah? How do you know her?

M: I met her on an exchange trip.

L: When did you do that?

M: Year 10 at school. Here. I've got a picture of her on my mobile. She's the girl in the middle.

L: Oh, wow! She's very pretty.

M: Yeah.

L: So is she just visiting?

M: No, she's studying here. She's really clever as well as being pretty and she's good at sport! Some people are so lucky!

L: Yeah. So who's the guy? Is that her boyfriend?

M: No! That's my brother!

L: Really? You don't look very similar.

M: I know. He's quite dark – but look at the nose and mouth.

L: Let me see. Yeah, I guess. So what does he do?

M: He's a nurse. He lives in the States.

L: Really? Why did he go there?

M: He's married and his wife's from there.

L: Really? How old is he?

M: 24

L: OK. That's quite young.

M: I guess.

L: Do you get on well?

M: Yes, we're quite close. He's very caring – and generous too. Obviously, I don't see him very often now. Actually, the last time I saw him was when I took this photo. It was over a year ago, but we email and talk on the phone quite a lot.

L: Do you have any other brothers or sisters?

M: Yeah – a younger sister.

L: Is that the other girl in the picture?

M: No, she's a friend from my Spanish class.

A: Maya!

M: Anna! How are you? We saved you a seat. Anna – I don't think you know my friend Laura. She's a friend from work. Laura, this is Anna.

A: Nice to meet you.

L: Hi – I've heard a lot about you.

🔊 1.2

1 Where do you live?

2 Do you know anyone in this class?

3 How long have you known him?

4 Why are you studying English?

5 Have you studied in this school before?

6 Are you enjoying the class?

7 Did you have a nice weekend?

8 What do you do?

🔊 1.3

1 A: Where are you from?
   B: The Czech Republic.

2 A: Have you got any brothers or sisters?
   B: Yes. Two brothers and six sisters.

3 A: Are you the oldest?
   B: No. I'm in the middle.

4 A: Do you see your grandparents much?
   B: No, not much. They live in a different city.

5 A: Do you get on with your brother.
   B: No, not really. He's quite annoying.

6 A: Where did you meet your girlfriend?
   B: At university. We were in the same class.

7 A: Do you like sport?
   B: No, I hate it, but I walk a lot to keep fit.

🔊 1.4

Speaker 1 – Trent Simons

People think identical twins have the same tastes and personalities, but my brother and I are very different: I'm keen on sport and I'm really fit and active; he hardly ever does anything. I'm confident, I go out, I'm captain of the football team, but he's really quiet. He has friends, but they're a bit strange and they always play video games together. We're probably different because we go to different schools and my parents don't treat us as 'the twins', you know, as one person. Apart from our appearance, I think the only thing that is genetic is having poor sight. But then he wears thick glasses and I wear contact lenses!

Speaker 2 – Angela Martinez

Being adopted, I occasionally wonder where my character comes from. I get good grades at school and people say Chinese are good students and very determined. But then so are my adoptive parents. My dad's clever and mum has a clothes shop in Madrid. I've learnt lots from them. Also I want to be a doctor like my uncle and I know I have to study to do that. I sometimes get frustrated if things go bad and I get really angry. Both my parents are very calm and patient – they never shout. Maybe my anger is because of my genes – but my gran says it's because I have no brothers or sisters and my parents are too liberal!

Speaker 3 – Justinia Lewis

Being a biologist, I obviously think genes are important – it's how evolution works. However, genes are only a small part of who we are: we humans share 30% of our genes with bananas and 98% with chimpanzees. Genes play a part in heart disease and other illnesses, but having a healthy lifestyle is more important and we learn that behaviour from our parents. Now I'm pregnant, I think about my character and my childhood. Neither of my parents are scientists, but they both read a lot and, they talked to me about lots of different things.

Also, none of us in our family are neat and tidy. I tell my husband it's genetic and that's why I don't put things away, but it's not true!

🔊 1.5

1 neat and tidy

2 calm and patient

3 kind and caring

4 open and friendly

5 fit and healthy

6   the cooking and cleaning
7   salt and pepper
8   try and help
9   go and see
10 scream and shout

UNIT 02

🔊 2.1

K = Keira, C = Claire, D = Dan

K: Did you have a nice weekend?

C: Yeah, it was good.

K: What did you do?

C: Oh, nothing much. I went for a walk with some friends round Sutton Park yesterday.

K: Oh, nice. It was a lovely clear day.

C: Yeah. It was a bit cold, but it was great. I was taking photos with my new camera.

K: That one? Let's have a look. Wow! That's really neat. Where did you get it?

C: In Jessops in town. I'm really pleased with it. It's really good quality and it's got quite a few different functions.

K: Really? Is it complicated to use?

C: No, not really. There are a few things I don't know yet, but it's OK.

K: Yeah. Well, the pictures look good and it's nice and light as well.

C: Hmm, yeah. It's cool, isn't it? Anyway, what about you two? Did you do anything?

D: Yeah, we went shopping.

C: Oh OK. Did you buy anything nice?

K: Well, I got these earrings.

B: They're lovely! They look quite old.

K: Yeah they are. I got them in a second-hand shop near here. They've got all kinds of things there – books, CDs, clothes. Dan got that jacket there.

C: Really? I love it. It looks really nice and warm.

D: Yeah, it is. It's pure wool and it's nice and thick. And it only cost fifteen pounds.

C: You're joking! That's fantastic. It really suits you as well. It's a great style and colour!

D: Thanks.

C: Did you get any clothes, Keira?

K: No, there were some really nice things, but I didn't find anything that fitted me. Everything was either too big or too small.

🔊 2.2

Conversation 1

A: Is that all you have?

B: Yeah, it is.

A: Well, do you want to go first?

B: Are you sure?

A: Of course. I have lots of things.

B: Great. Thanks.

Conversation 2

C: Would you like it wrapped?

D: Um ... what's the paper like?

C: It's this green paper.

D: Hmm, it's a bit plain. Do you have anything a bit prettier? It's a special present.

C: Well, there's quite a big selection in the stationery department. Do

you want to choose something and bring it here and I'll wrap it for you?

D: Really? You don't mind?

C: Of course not.

D: Thanks

Conversation 3

E: Yes sir. How can I help you?

F: I bought this the other day and it's damaged. When I got it home and took it out of the box, I found the button was loose and it's damaged here. Look, you see?

E: Are you sure you didn't drop it or anything?

F: No, of course not!

E: It's just that this kind of damage doesn't happen unless you do something. It's not a manufacturing fault.

F: Honestly, when I got home I took it out of the box and it was already damaged.

E: Have you got a receipt and the box?

F: I didn't bring the box. I've got the receipt, though.

Conversation 4

G: Is there anyone serving here?

H: Yes, but I don't think you can pay here.

G: That's OK. I just want to find out if they have something in stock.

H: Well, there was a guy here and he said he would be back in a minute, but that was ten minutes ago.

G: Oh right.

H: It's typical! The service is always terrible here.

G: Hmm.

H: Hatton's is better really. Their service is much more reliable and their things are generally better quality.

G: Really? Well, why didn't you go there?

H: Well, I do normally, but I saw in the window they had a sale here.

G: Ah!

H: There he is! About time!

I: Sorry.

H: That's OK.

Conversation 5

J: Excuse me. Do you have one of these in a smaller size? This one's a bit big.

K: I'm afraid not. That's why they're at a reduced price.

J: Never mind, Timmy. You'll grow into it.

L: But I don't like it.

J: Don't be silly. You look lovely. It really suits you.

🔊 2.3

There were two stories about fights connected with shopping this week – one to annoy the anti-shopper and one to make them happy. The first was the riot at the opening of the Primark store in London. How stupid can people be? It amazes me that people will wait for hours outside a shop because they think they will get a coat or T-shirt five pounds cheaper. Then they injure each other by pushing and fighting to get a coat or T-shirt that they probably didn't need anyway. Even when the shoppers discovered there were actually no discounts, they still bought things.

The second story was about a group of Chinese tourists in Macau. They started a mini riot because the tour guides were trying to take them to too many shops and they didn't want to buy anything. I can totally understand how the tourists felt. When I go into my city centre, I often think there are too many shops. There are 30 shops that just sell shoes! There are five that just sell socks! Of course, the Chinese group wanted to go and see the sights instead of going shopping – they were on holiday after all! When you go on holiday, you want to relax. You want to do something different, like go to the beach or visit beautiful buildings – temples and cathedrals, museums and galleries. Why does anyone want to travel a long way to buy things you can almost certainly buy in your own country anyway?

2.4

1 I'm not paid very well.
2 It's sold in most shops.
3 They're supplied by a firm in India.
4 We were charged 100 Euros for it.
5 Luckily, no-one was injured.

UNIT 03

3.1

A: Are you hungry?
B: Yeah, a bit.
A: Do you want to get something to eat?
B: I'd love to, yeah. Where are you thinking of going?
A: Well, there's a really nice Thai place just down the road. Do you know it?
B: I've seen it, but I've never eaten there. I don't really feel like spicy food today, though, so ... .
A: OK. No problem. I'm happy to go somewhere else.
B: There's a great steak restaurant near the big department store in the centre of town. How about that?
A: To be honest, I don't really like red meat.
B: Well, we could go to Sofra instead. Have you been there?
A: No. I've never heard of it. Where is it?
B: It's about fifteen minutes' walk from here. It's just round the corner from the bus station.
A: Oh, OK. And what kind of restaurant is it?
B: It's Turkish. It's really good. I go there almost every week.
A: Really?
B: Yeah, the food's delicious – and they've got a really good selection of dishes, so there's plenty to choose from.
A: Oh, it sounds great.
B: Yeah. The only problem is that it gets really busy. Sometimes you have to wait to get a table, so maybe we should phone and book.
A: Yeah. That's probably a good idea.

3.2

C1 = male diner, C2 = female diner, W = waiter

Conversation 1
W: How many people is it?
C1: There are three of us.
W: And have you booked?
C1: No. Is that a problem?
W: No, but do you mind waiting?
C1: How long?
W: Maybe ten or fifteen minutes.
C2: OK. That's fine.
C1: Could I change the baby somewhere?
W: I'm afraid we don't have any special facilities. You can use the toilet. It's not very big, though.

C1: That's OK.
W: It's just at the end there, down the stairs.

Conversation 2
W: Is this table here OK?
C1: Yeah, this is fine. Thank you.
W: Would you like a high chair for the little girl?
C1: That'd be great. Thanks. He's actually a boy, though!
W: Oh, I'm so sorry! Anyway, here are your menus. I'll get the chair.

Conversation 3
W: Are you ready to order?
C1: Not quite. Could you just give us two more minutes?
W: Yes, of course. (slight fade out / fade in again)
C2: Right. OK. Could I have the grilled squid for starters, please? And for my main course, I think I'll have the chicken.
W: And what kind of potatoes would you like?
C2: Roast potatoes, please.
W: OK.
C1: I'll go for the aubergines stuffed with rice for my main course, please. And the country stew? Does it contain any meat? I'm vegetarian.
W: Yes, sorry. It's got lamb in it. I could ask them to take it out.
C1: No, it's OK. I'll just have the tomato and avocado salad. And can we get some water as well?
W: Of course. Sparkling or still?
C1: Just tap water, please, if possible.
W: Sure.
C2: And could we have a small plate for our son? We're going to share our dishes with him.

Conversation 4
C1: Oh, dear – what a mess!
C2: I'll get the waiter. Oh, excuse me. I'm really sorry, but could you get us a cloth, please? My son's dropped some water on the floor.
W: Certainly madam. I'll just go and get one.
C2: Thank you.

Conversation 5
W: Would you like to see the dessert menu?
C1: I'm OK, thanks. I'm really full, but if you want something.
C2: No, no. I couldn't eat another thing. It was lovely, though. Could I just have a coffee, please?
C1: Me too. An espresso.

Conversation 6
C1: Could we have the bill, please?
W: Yes, of course.
C1: Great. Thanks.
C2: That's very reasonable, isn't it? Shall we leave a tip?
C1: No, look. Service is included.
C2: Wow. Then that really is good value for money. We should come here again sometime.

UNIT 04

4.1

Conversation 1
A: So what do you do? You haven't told me.
B: I'm an engineer.

A: Right. Where do you work?

B: Well, the company I work for is based in London, but I travel around quite a lot. I'm actually working in Scotland at the moment – in Glasgow. They're building a new stadium there and I'm working on that.

A: Really? Where do you live, then?

B: In London, but I'm renting a flat in Glasgow while I'm there. I usually come down to London every two weeks, if I can.

A: And do you enjoy it?

B: Yeah, it's great. I don't really mind the travelling and the money's good – and I don't really have much time to spend it!

A: Really? What're the hours like?

B: Oh, I work hard. I often do a 60-hour week.

A: Really? That's a lot.

B: Yeah, but it's OK and I get on really well with the other people I work with.

Conversation 2

C: So what do you do?

D: Well, I work for a small company back in Korea, but I'm actually a student at the moment.

C: Oh OK. What are you studying?

D: I'm doing a Master's in Marketing.

C: Is that what you do in your company? Marketing?

D: Yes, more or less

C: So how long have you worked for them?

D: About two years.

C: Only two years and they're sending you abroad to study! That's fantastic!

D: Yeah, well, actually my father runs the company and he wants me to become the marketing manager.

C: Oh right. I see. So how do you get on with the other people you work with? Is it difficult being the boss's daughter?

D: Maybe a little bit sometimes.

4.2

Speaker one – Claudia

I graduated in Germany two years ago with a degree in Media Studies and after that I applied for jobs in film and television. I know it's a competitive area, but it was depressing, because I didn't get one interview! Everyone wanted me to have work experience, but how can you experience work if nobody gives you a job?

In the end, I took unpaid work with a public relations company. To begin with, I hated it. I only did boring jobs like making coffee for people and photocopying, but recently I've started doing more interesting things. At the moment, I'm helping to advertise a German film.

I'm not happy working for no money, and sometimes I think the company is exploiting me. If they don't offer me a paid job soon, I'm going to start looking for something else!

Speaker two – Jerome

I worked as a doctor in a small town in Switzerland for almost thirty years and I retired five years ago. To begin with, I enjoyed it, but I soon got bored. I saw an advertisement for the Voluntary Service Overseas and applied. I got a job in Sierra Leone and I've been here for nine months. They pay my rent, but basically I'm working for nothing.

It's the best thing I've ever done! People here live in very difficult circumstances, but have a really positive attitude. Now, I'm doing some training with local doctors and advising them how to improve

services. My contract ends in three months, but I'm planning to stay here for another year, if I can.

Speaker three – Sulochana

I belong to an organisation that's fighting for the rights of housewives in Kerala, in the south-west of India. We're hoping to make the government pay us a salary and a pension for the work we do in the home. Something similar is already happening in Venezuela. Women play an important part in building the nation. Without mothers and wives at home, how can men work? But men don't appreciate this and that's why we're organising ourselves.
We're planning to start a website to tell more people about our situation and if we don't get what we want, we're thinking of stopping work and going on strike. Let's see how men survive without our help then!

4.3

1 I'm going to sort it out tomorrow.
2 They're going to do an English course.
3 He's going to rent a small flat.
4 I'm going to talk to my boss about it.
5 What're you going to do?
6 She's not going to go to university.

Review 01

R1.1

/æ/	gran
/eɪ/	grade
/ɑː/	dark
/ə/	arrest
/eə/	share
/ɔː/	saw
/iː/	treat

R1.2

1 /æ/ brand, hat, value, wrap, terrace
2 /eɪ/ behaviour, debate, creative, steak, establish
3 /ɑː/ argue, aunt, heart, smart, complicated
4 /ə/ annoying, pregnant, unreliable, facilities, active
5 /eə/ airline, caring, repair, wear, research
6 /ɔː/ cause, fault, install, warm, persuade
7 /iː/ colleague, disease, steal, neat, healthy

R1.3

1 share your seat
2 wear a smart jacket
3 argue with my aunt
4 cause a lot of laughter
5 be treated for heart disease
6 accuse him of charging too much
7 have a rare steak with cream sauce
8 have a debate with my colleagues about it

R1.4

1 Simm's has really good quality fruit and vegetables – and they have a really good fish counter where everything's very fresh. I always buy seafood from there. There are a couple of shops near me, where I can buy things if I've forgotten something, but the food's not as cheap and of course there's a much wider selection of

everything at Simm's.

2 I occasionally work from home, but I prefer it here really. I like to be able to chat to colleagues and I think they contribute to my work as well and I don't have a problem concentrating when I need to. I've got a big desk and the building is lovely and bright. There's also a nice café for staff and clients can use it when they visit too.

3 When I started university, it was quite far from my town, so I moved to a place with two friends. It's OK, but it's quite small and my flatmates are a problem sometimes. Neither of them put things away. My room is the only part which is neat and tidy. They're also both quite noisy so it's difficult to study sometimes.

4 It's lovely in the summer, because they have a terrace, which has a lovely view over the city. The menu doesn't have much choice, but the food they do is delicious. We don't always go there though, because it gets very busy and you need to book. Also because the waiters are going in and out all of the time and the tables are close together, the service is quite slow.

UNIT 05

 5.1

C = Corinne, M = Maribel

C: So what are you going to do while you're here?

M: I'm just going to take it easy. I might go shopping tomorrow. You're working tomorrow, aren't you?

C: Yes – and Saturday morning, I'm afraid.

M: Oh dear.

C: I'm sorry, but some important clients are coming and I need to go and meet them at the airport and make sure everything's OK.

M: Right. What time are you going to be back?

C: Hopefully about 2.

M: That's OK, then. I don't usually get up before 11 anyway and I've brought my trainers, so I might go for a run. Is there anywhere to go near here?

C: There's actually an athletics track just down the road.

M: OK. To be honest, though, I'd prefer a park or somewhere like that.

C: Hmm. There's not much near here. I usually just run on the streets.

M: OK. Well, I'll see. Have you got any plans for us over the weekend?

C: Well, a friend is having a party for his birthday on Saturday night, if you'd like to go.

M: Yeah, great. You know I always like a dance!

C: And the forecast is really good for Sunday, so we're thinking of going for a walk in the mountains near here.

M: Oh right. That sounds nice.

C: Yes, it's great there. There's a lovely river we can go swimming in.

M: Oh right. I haven't got my swimming gear with me.

C: That's OK. I'm sure I can lend you something.

M: Isn't the water cold?

C: A bit, but you soon warm up.

M: I must admit, I'm a bit soft. I like a heated pool.

C: Honestly, it's not so bad and the water's really clear. It's just beautiful with the mountains and everything!

M: So what time are you thinking of leaving?

C: Well, it's two or three hours by car, so if we want to make the most of the day, we need to leave about 6 o'clock.

 5.2

Last night I watched the big game in England between Liverpool and Chelsea. I was one of 1 billion people watching in places as far apart as Peru, Saudi Arabia and Vietnam. It was a nil-nil draw and perhaps the most boring game I've ever seen. Football may be the most popular sport in the world, but it's difficult to know why when you see a game like that. Knowing that the players earn millions a year just makes it worse! So why do we watch when there are plenty of alternatives? The Olympics contains thirty-five sports; other countries have different national sports such as cricket; and new sports are being created all the time.

Maybe it's because football is the simplest game to play. Does anyone really understand the rules of cricket? Football doesn't need expensive equipment. In fact, it requires hardly any gear at all and you need no real skill to play – who can't kick a ball? So nearly everyone has played at least once in their life and once you've played a sport, you appreciate it more. Finally, football's different every game. Last night's game was boring, but next time Chelsea might win five-four, with a goal in the last minute! You never know.

 5.3

1 These days, people are married on average for eleven and a half years, but the longest marriage lasted eighty years!

2 English must be one of the easiest languages to learn.

3 We wanted to go there because they said it's the nicest place to eat.

4 It's the prettiest village round here, so there's often a shortage of places to stay.

 5.4

In Spain, people typically work from nine in the morning till seven in the evening, though some start even earlier and finish even later. When people go out and relax, they often book a table in a restaurant for around ten at night or later and people frequently stay out till two, three or four in the morning. How do they do it?

In the past, the answer was the siesta – a short nap after lunch at around three or in the early evening. Recent research on sleep suggests the Spanish were very wise. A short nap of between 20 minutes and an hour sometime between 1 and 3 pm can increase energy levels and improve your mood and creativity.

However, nowadays more and more Spanish people are working longer and longer hours, and the siesta is becoming a luxury outside the summer holidays. At the moment, late nights are still common, but some academics say people are going to suffer from not having enough sleep if lifestyles don't change.

Strangely, this comes at a time when other countries are finally showing more interest in the siesta. One group in Britain has launched a campaign called National Nap at Work Week. They aim to inform people of the benefits of napping – and say that workers who take naps aren't lazy. In fact, exactly the opposite is true – people who nap during work time actually work better than those who don't sleep. Tired people lose concentration and make more mistakes. Naps also bring increased happiness, and happy workers are more productive.

Elsewhere, a New York-based company called Metronaps has created a special hi-tech room for business people to nap in during the day. They are hoping to install the rooms in businesses everywhere. And in Europe a lot of offices are buying a specially designed bed, called the Ready Bed, which can be easily folded and put away.

But remember, napping isn't only about being able to work better. Research also shows health benefits. People who nap regularly are apparently less likely to have heart attacks – maybe because they're more relaxed. A nap also means you can stay awake to do the things you really enjoy instead of falling asleep in front of the TV because you're so tired after a long day's work.

UNIT 06

 6.1

Conversation 1

A: Where are you from?

B: Italy.

A: What part?

B: Treviso

A: Where's that?

B: It's a small city in the north-east. It's about 40 kilometres from Venice. So say that's Venice, Treviso is just here to the north.

A: Oh OK. So what's it like?

B: It's great. The centre is very old with some beautiful old buildings, but the city's also quite modern. You know Benetton? The clothes?

A: Yes.

B: Well, Benetton's based in Treviso.

A: Oh wow! OK. So where do you live? In the centre?

B: Not exactly, but everything is quite near. It's small. It's easy to get round. I live near the river. You can walk along there – and there's a park. It's nice.

Conversation 2

C: Where are you from?

D: Oman.

C: Oh, OK. Oman. I'm sorry, but where is that exactly? My geography isn't very good.

D: It's in the Middle East – on the Indian Ocean. So you've got Saudi Arabia here and the UAE up here and Oman goes down here to the right.

C: Oh, OK. And where do you live?

D: The capital, Muscat, it's in the north of the country.

C: What's it like? Is it a big city?

D: Quite big – it's about a million and it spreads along the coast quite far.

C: It sounds nice.

D: It is. It's beautiful because you have the sea and the mountains behind. And it's a very exciting place because lots of people from different countries live there and, you know, there's lots to do there.

Conversation 3

E: So where are you from Chuck?

F: Texas.

E: Whereabouts?

F: I doubt you'll know it. It's a little town called Harlingen. It's right in the south – by the Mexican border.

E: Yeah, I know it. In fact, I've been there! I have a friend who lives in Port Isabel.

F: Port Isabel! Wow, that's real close. So did you like it?

E: Yeah, it was lovely. I mean, it's a bit quiet, but for a holiday it was great.

F: When were you there? What time of year?

E: February, but the climate's lovely. It's so warm. We went to the beach quite a lot.

F: Sure.

E: And we took a boat along the coast a couple of times and went fishing.

F: Did you catch anything?

E: Not much, but it was just nice to be on the sea.

F: So what's your friend called?

E: Harry Dancey

F: You're kidding me! Skip Dancey? I went to high school with him!

E: No! Really? What a small world!

 6.2

I'm from Harbin, in the north-east of China, but I moved to Wales last year to do a Master's. It's the first time I've lived away from home, it hasn't been easy. The culture is different and I have to speak English all the time as well, which is tiring. The place I'm living in is nice, though. I have my own room with a basin to wash in, but I have to share the bathroom and kitchen with five other students.

The best thing for me now is the freedom. I can do whatever I want – whenever I want. I can come home late if I want to and I don't have to answer questions about where I've been. The hardest things are learning how to live on my own – I have to do everything for myself now – and living in a block with so many other students. It can be very noisy sometimes!

 6.3

1 We can walk there in ten minutes.

2 Do you have to pay extra for the bills?

3 I don't have to pay my parents rent.

4 Friends can stay at my house if they want to.

5 She doesn't have to do any housework at all!

6 You don't have to cook for everyone in the flat.

7 I have to help with all the cooking and cleaning.

8 I can talk to her about anything.

9 They have to find a bigger place.

 6.4

H1 = host father, M = Maksim, H2 = host mother

H1: Hello there. Come in, come in.

M: Hello. I am Maksim.

H2: Hi. I'm Isabel and this is Oliver. How was your journey?

M: OK, but very long.

H1: I can imagine. Anyway, you're here now. Do you want me to take your coat?

M: Oh, yes. Thank you.

H1: And you can just leave your bag and things over there for now.

H2: Would you like a cup of tea or something to eat, Maksim?

M: No, thank you. I'm fine. Maybe just some water.

H2: Yes, of course. I'll just go and get some for you …
There you are.

M: Thank you. Oh, I almost forgot. I brought you this. It's traditional. It's from my country.

H2: Oh thank you. That's very thoughtful of you. It's … um … very … um … interesting. I'll go and put it … um … somewhere.

H1: I'll show you around the house in a minute, Maksim, but first I'll just tell you a bit about the house rules.

M: OK.

H1: We'll give you your own key, so you can come and go when you want. If you come home late, though, please try to be quiet. And make sure you lock the front door.

M: From inside?

H1: Yes. here, look. Like this.

M: Ah, I see. OK.

H1: And no overnight guests are allowed in the house.

M: Guests?

H1: Yes. Um ... no-one can sleep in your room apart from you, so no friends or ...

M: Oh, OK. yes. Don't worry. No problem. No problem.

H1: And breakfast is served between seven and eight. You know we're vegetarian, don't you?

M: Veg ...?

H1: Vegetarian. We don't eat any meat.

M: No meat?

H1: No. Didn't they tell you? Oh well. Anyway, that's more or less everything, I think. I'll show you to your room. I'm sure you're very tired.

M: Yes. And I have to get up early tomorrow. Do you have a watch I can borrow?

H1: An alarm clock, you mean? Yes, I'm sure we can lend you one.

M: Thank you.

H2: And then tomorrow morning, we'll show you how to get to your school.

M: OK. One question. Do you mind if I smoke in my room?

H2: Smoke? Well, actually, I'd rather you didn't, if you don't mind. I'm sorry.

6.5

1 Do you mind if I open the window?
   No, of course not. It is quite hot, isn't it?
2 Do you mind if I use your computer?
   No, of course not. One minute. I'll just log off.
3 Do you mind if I borrow your phone for a minute?
   Well, actually, I'd rather you didn't. I don't have much credit.
4 Is it OK if I leave class early today?
   Yes, of course. Just make sure you remember to do your homework.
5 Is it OK if I close the window?
   Yes, of course. It is quite cold, isn't it?
6 Is it OK if I stay a few more days?
   Well, actually, I'd rather you didn't. My mother is visiting tomorrow, you see.

6.6

1 I'll call you later.
2 I'll see you tomorrow.
3 I'll help you with that.
4 I'll go and get some.
5 We'll be there at 6.
6 She'll email you.
7 He'll bring it with him on Monday.
8 They'll probably forget.

UNIT 07

7.1

Conversation 1

A: Hi, how're you?

B: Not very well, actually. I think I'm getting the flu.

A: Oh no! Your poor thing! Are you sure it's not just a cold?

B: It might be, I suppose, but it doesn't feel like it. I've had it for a few days now. I just feel really weak and tired all the time and my muscles ache a lot.

A: That sounds horrible. Maybe you should go home and get some rest.

B: Yes, maybe you're right.

A: No-one will thank you if you stay and spread it!

B: That's true. Could you tell Mr. Einhoff I'm sick?

A: Yes, of course.

B: Oh, and would you mind giving him my homework? Thank you.

A: That's OK. You take it easy and get well soon.

B: I'll try! Bye.

A: Bye. See you.

Conversation 2

C: Bless you!

D: Oh! I am sorry! That's the fifth time in as many minutes!

C: That's OK.

D: I always get like this at this time of year! It's awful, because I hate winter, but then as soon as the sun comes out I can't stop sneezing! And my eyes really water as well. I really want to rub them, but that just makes them worse!

C: Oh, that sounds horrible. Are you taking anything for it?

D: Yes, I went to the chemist's last year and they recommended these tablets, so I take four of these every day, and they do help, but they don't stop it completely.

C: Why don't you get some sunglasses to protect your eyes a bit?

D: That's not a bad idea, actually, but I think I'd feel a bit funny walking round in sunglasses all day!

C: Yeah, I know what you mean, but maybe you ought to try it. You never know. It might work for you.

7.2

Conversation 1

A: Are you OK?

B: Hic! Yeah, I've just got hiccups. Oh gosh! Hic! It's really annoying.

A: Here. I know a cure. It never fails.

B: Hic

A: Take some water in your mouth, but don't drink it.

B: Mmm.

A: Now put your fingers in your ears. Bend down and put your head between your knees and swallow the water slowly.

B: Mmmm?

A: Swallow the water (said louder!)

B: Mmm.

A: OK. You can breathe now. Have you still got them?

B: Um, no. No, I don't think so.

A: You see. It works every time.

B: Maybe, but I wouldn't want to do it in public! People would think I was mad!

Conversation 2

C: Yes. Can I help you?

D: Yes, I would like something for a bad stomach, please.

C: Does it hurt or have you been sick?

D: Not sick. It's more gas. It's uncomfortable.

C: OK. It sounds like indigestion. It's after you eat, right?

D: Yes.

C: And you're going to the toilet normally? No diarrhoea?

D: Diarrhoea? No.

C: OK, so I think these are what you need. They're indigestion tablets. You mix them with water and drink them after your meals. They're the most effective, I think.

D: OK.

C: What flavour would you like? Orange or blackcurrant?

D: Oh, orange.

C: That'll be four twenty five. Don't take more than four tablets a day – and if they don't deal with the problem, consult your doctor.

D: OK. Thanks. I will.

Conversation 3

E: The burn's not too bad. We'll give you some cream for it, but you'll need some stitches in that cut. It's quite deep. What happened?

F: Well, I cut my head dancing with my son.

E: I'm sorry?

F: I was dancing with my five-year-old son and I stepped on one of his toys and I fell and hit my head on the side of the table.

E: Oh dear. What about the burn, then?

F: Well, my wife came in when she heard me shout and while she was helping me stand up, she knocked a cup of coffee off the table and it went all over my leg.

E: Oh dear, I am sorry. I shouldn't laugh!

F: Don't worry. It was very stupid!

E: Nurse, could you dress the burn after I've done these stitches?

G: Of course.

Unit 08

◆ 8.1

Conversation 1

A: Listen, we're obviously lost. – ask this guy.

B: OK, OK. ...Sorry. Do you speak English?

C: Sure.

B: Oh, great. Do you know the way to the museum from here?

C: Yes, but it is far. It's better to get a bus.

B: OK. So how do we get to the stop?

C: Down this road. Take the second road on the right then cross, turn left and then left and it's directly opposite the town hall.

B: OK, great.

C: No problem

B: So did he say second right or second left?

A: I don't know I wasn't really listening I thought you were! What bus did he say we should catch?

B: No idea! Listen, it's down here somewhere anyway.

Conversation 2

B It's your turn. Ask that old lady.

A: Excuse me. Is this the right bus stop for the museum?

D: Eh?

A: The bus? Brmm ... To the museum?

D: Eh?

A: To the museum?

D: Eh?

E: You want the number 67 bus.

D: Oh thanks.

E: You have to go over the road. This stop, it goes the wrong way. Go over the crossing. It's after the traffic lights.

A: I see it. Thanks.

E: They come often.

A: Thanks.

Conversation 3

A: Excuse me, sorry. Do you speak English?

F: Sure I do. How can I help?

A: Do you know where the museum is? Is it near here?

F: Yes, quite near, but you got off at the wrong stop, really. Go down this road until you come to a church. Then turn left. It's quite a big road. You'll go past a monument and a football ground. Just keep going. It's maybe half a mile. It's on the right. You can't miss it.

B: I told you that was it! Why do you never listen to me?

◆ 8.2

the Black Forest

the Great Wall

the Mediterranean

the Indian Ocean

the Great Barrier Reef

the Canary Islands

the Alps

the Amazon

the Nile

the Eiffel Tower

the equator

the Sahara

the Andes

the Thames

the Pyramids

the Caribbean

the Arctic

the Himalayas

◆ 8.3

M = Mark, L = Lisa

M: In a moment we'll be with Ellen McArthur, interviewing her about her latest adventure – sailing round the globe on her own – so if you have any questions for her, ring 9873–7373 or email us at may@bbd.net. But first, the travel news from Lisa Verity.

L: Thanks Mark, Not much good news, I'm afraid. Getting anywhere today is going to feel a bit like sailing round the world for many people. Terrible problems in a lot of places at the moment.

Starting with the airports. The air traffic controllers' strike in France is continuing to cause complete chaos. Many flights are being delayed and quite a few cancelled because only a few planes can fly over France and others have to be diverted to avoid French air space. Passengers who are flying at any time in the next few days are asked to ring their airline or consult their airline's website.

A lorry has crashed on the A516 entering Milton Keynes and lost its load of watermelons. Lanes in both directions are shut at the moment while police try to clear up the mess – a big mess I would imagine too! Avoid the area, if you can.

The M6 motorway between junctions 5 and 6 is completely closed for repairs. A diversion is in operation, but expect delays all day there. Traffic moving very slowly, so best to take other routes.

Large sections of the Northern Line in London are closed today because of continuing repair work to renew the underground. A replacement bus service is in operation. And

East Ham station is closed because of a flood. A burst water pipe there.

Better news elsewhere. The rail service between London and Birmingham is now running normally after a fallen tree was removed from the line. And there aren't any more problems on the A6 now that the traffic lights are working again at the crossroads with the B761. The traffic's moving freely there.

Finally, two events tonight to tell you about. Just to remind those travelling to Wembley for the big concert there – there's no parking in or around the stadium. Police will be operating in the area to remove cars, so go on foot or take public transport. And lastly in central London, a demonstration by cyclists is likely to cause some traffic problems from 5 o'clock, so avoid driving or leave work early. That's all from me – back to Mark.

M: That's pretty awful for those going on holiday. Any idea when the air traffic controllers might end their strike?

L: Well, negotiations are continuing, but there's little hope of a deal yet. We'll give you more news when we have it.

M: OK, thanks. Well, strikes were probably one thing she didn't have to deal with, but she had plenty of bad weather, storms, ten-metre high waves and more. Ellen McArthur, it doesn't sound like much fun! Why do you do it?

REVIEW 02

R2.1

/ɒ/	golf
/uː/	pool
/ʌ/	lovely
/ə/	spectator
/ɔː/	shorts
/ɜː/	work
/ʊ/	put
/əʊ/	throw
/aʊ/	out
/ɔɪ/	boy

R2.2

1 /ɒ/ concentrate, forest, cough, foreign, couple
2 /uː/ loser, remove, statue, mood, wood
3 /ʌ/ countryside, budget, brush, month, move
4 /ə/ season, recognise, contain, freedom, swallow
5 /ɔː/ forecast, score, court, shortage, factory
6 /ɜː/ burst, murder, worst, survey, cause
7 /ʊ/ put, pull, full, wool, flu
8 /əʊ/ mouth, boat, ocean, shoulder, progress
9 /aʊ/ doubt, allow, town hall, ground, launch
10 /ɔɪ/ noisy, annoy, voice, avoid, coincidence

R2.3

1 score a goal
2 hurt your shoulder
3 bounce up and down
4 drop the ball on the ground
5 reduce pollution from factories
6 the forecast is for snow
7 brush the dust from the floor
8 a good cure for an upset stomach

R2.4

1 We went to the mountains with some friends. It was lovely to be in the countryside and we parked by a lake, swam in the cold clear water and then we had a picnic. It was late when we went back home and when I was driving, I found it difficult to keep my eyes open. At one point, I just avoided going off the road and crashing into a tree. We stopped for an hour and I had a sleep to recover, and I was fine after that.

2 I made a mistake when I arrived because I didn't take my shoes off when I went in to the house. But after that there were no problems. The host family were really kind and generous. They gave me a spare key so I had a lot of freedom and they allowed me to use one of their bikes so I didn't have to spend any money on buses or trains. I spent most of my time cycling around the city, which was beautiful – especially the historic old town.

3 I didn't go to the meeting in the end. It was hot, I had hay fever, I had a headache, my eyes were watering and I felt bad. Maybe that's why I lost concentration and missed the stop. I got off and I didn't recognise where I was. I asked several people for directions, but no-one knew the place. So I crossed the street and got the 73 back home.

4 I forgot to set my alarm clock and I woke up at 8 and my flight left at 10. I called a taxi and went to the airport as quickly as possible. I had to run to the desk with my bags and when I got there, I was really sweating and out of breath. The woman at the desk then told me the flight was delayed and I then waited for four hours!

UNIT 09

9.1

Conversation 1

A: Did you read this article about bees?

B: No.

A: They're all dying for some unknown reason.

B: Really? That's terrible!

A: I know. It's really bad news because we really depend on bees. If bees become extinct, we won't have any fruit or vegetables.

B: I hadn't thought about that. They should do something – fund research or something.

A Absolutely.

Conversation 2

C: Did you see the forecast for tomorrow?

D: No.

C: It's going to be nice – really hot and sunny.

D: Really? That's great!

C: I know. It's good. It's been so wet and windy recently.

D: We should go out, then – go to the beach or somewhere.

C: Yeah, that's a good idea.

Conversation 3

E: Did you hear what they want to do in Morovia?

F: No. What?

E: It said on the news that they're going to pull down a lot of the horrible houses they've built along the coast and create a national park instead.

F: Really? That's great.

E: I know. It's good news.

F: They should do more to protect the countryside here too.

E: Definitely. We need more green spaces.

Conversation 4

G: Did you see they've discovered a new way to kill the mosquitoes that spread malaria?

H: No.

G: Yeah, it said it could save millions of lives.

H: Really? That's great.

G: I know. It's really good.

H: It makes a change to hear some good news.

G: Absolutely.

9.2

The people who were the teachers believed that the learners were receiving real electric shocks, but, in fact, there were none. When the 'teacher' pressed the electric shock button, it simply turned on a light in front of the 'learner'. After a while, the actor who was playing the 'learner' started to bang on the wall between him and the 'teacher' and to shout in pain. At one point, the 'learner' – who was an actor, remember – then complained about having a heart problem. Then, as the false shocks got stronger and stronger, the 'learner' went silent.

Some of the 'teachers' began to laugh nervously or show other signs of stress when they heard the screams coming from the 'learner'. Many people asked to stop the experiment and wanted to check that the learner was OK. However, the 'scientist' told them to "please continue". When the 'teachers' asked the 'scientist' if he was sure, the 'scientist' said that the experiment required them to continue. He then said it was absolutely essential that they continued. Finally, the scientist told any people who still complained, "You have no other choice. You must go on".

At the end of the experiment, 65% of participants had given the final 450-volt shock, although many were very uncomfortable doing so; at some point, every teacher stopped and questioned what the purpose of the experiment was, but only one person out of the forty absolutely refused to give shocks before reaching the 300-volt level – a level which could still kill you.

9.3

So what was the real purpose of the experiment? During the Second World War, soldiers had participated in some terrible crimes that caused the deaths of millions of innocents. People couldn't understand it. How could they all be so cruel? Why didn't anyone stop the killing? Milgram wanted to investigate these issues.

The experiment showed that people found it very difficult to say no to people in authority – people more important than them and who wore a uniform. All the ordinary people who took part in Milgram's experiment agreed to cause pain to another person just because a 'scientist' in a white coat told them to. Most continued long enough to kill someone.

UNIT 10

10.1

Conversation 1

A: So how's school, Ollie? Your father told me you're doing well.

B: It's OK, I suppose. Some bits are good.

A: Yeah? What're your favourite subjects?

B: Spanish and Art. And History's OK as well.

A: And what year are you in now?

B: Year Nine.

A: So how long have you got left?

B: Two more years.

A: What are you going to do when you finish? Have you got any plans?

B: Well, if I can save enough money between now and then, I'll try and take a year off. Dad doesn't want me to, though.

A: No?

B: No, he just wants me to stay in the system and go straight to university and study Business or something and graduate and become just like him.

A: Yeah, well. He's probably just worried about you.

B: Yeah, right. Whatever!

Conversation 2

C: So what course are you doing, Pep?

D: Pure Mathematics.

C: Wow! OK. That sounds hard.

D: Yeah, it can be, but I'm really enjoying it. To be honest, the most difficult thing for me is doing the whole degree in English, but my tutors are great. Everybody has been very supportive.

C: What year are you in?

D: My third, unfortunately. I've got my finals next April!

C: Oh, OK. Well, good luck!

D: Thanks!

C: What're you going to do after you graduate? Any plans?

D: Well, if I get the grades I want, I'll probably do a Master's somewhere.

C: Oh, OK. What in? The same subject?

D: Maybe. I'm not sure. I'm thinking of maybe doing Astrophysics, actually.

C: Oh, right. Have you applied anywhere yet?

D: No, I haven't, actually – not yet. But I probably should!

Conversation 3

E: ... So did you go to university, Dhanya?

D: Yes, I did. The Paul Cézanne University in Marseille. It's one of the oldest universities in France.

D: Oh, OK. What did you study?

F: International Law.

D: And did you enjoy it?

F: Yes, up to a point, I suppose, but to be honest, it was quite theoretical. It wasn't very practical and I think I've learned much more since I started working.

D: I know what you mean! I mean, I left school at 16 and started working straight away. To begin with, I did lots of horrible jobs, but I learnt a lot as well and it made me hungry for success. I was running my own business by the time I was 22. I'm not sure many university graduates can say the same!

F: You can't beat the university of life, eh!

10.2

Geography

Mathematics

Sociology

Economics

Chemistry

PE

History

Physics
RE
Biology
Latin
IT

🔊 10.3

I = Interviewer, R = Rebecca

I: So how did you find school when you came here?

R: A bit mixed. I made friends quickly. I knew a bit of Spanish and people were friendly, but I remember that to begin with, my brother just stood in the corner of the playground watching everyone play. It was sad!

I: But he made friends in the end?

R: Yeah.

I: So you could speak Spanish?

R A bit, but in class I hardly understood anything. It was horrible, but I sat with a girl that had an Australian dad and she sometimes translated for me.

I: That's lucky. Were classes very different?

R: Primary was. For some reason, I did the last year of primary here, although I'd already done it in England. Maybe it was because they have five years of secondary school in England, but there are only four here. Sorry, what was the question?

I: Were classes different?

R: Oh yeah. Basically, in primary in England we had the same teacher all day, but here we changed teachers. I liked some, but some – like Don Miguel – were really boring! He just read from the book. We didn't use textbooks much in England – we did more group work and arty things.

I: Right.

R: And we had lots of homework! I hardly had any in primary in England – maybe some reading or sums and once a term we did a project. Here, I had loads – maybe an hour or more each night. I remember really crying about it. My friends in England complain when they have to do 45 minutes in secondary school and I often have two hours – and we study for tests all the time.

I: So which do you prefer?

R: It's difficult to say. Now I'm at instituto …

I: Instituto?

R: Sorry, secondary school. We finish at two o'clock every day and then we get almost three months off in the summer whereas in England my friends finish at four and they only get six weeks' summer holiday. I chat to my friends in England on Messenger and they say school is boring too and they get stressed when they have assignments, but then they have this thing here, where if your teacher fails you some subjects, you have to repeat the whole year! I don't like that stress.

🔊 10.4

You hear politicians and parents here saying education is bad, but you get the same complaints in Britain where there are generally more resources. Parents send their kids to private schools or move house to be near good state schools.

From what Rebecca says, Spanish teachers are generally more traditional in their approach, but that's OK. Students probably learn to listen and concentrate better and get more knowledge. It all depends on the teacher – and the students, of course. There's good and bad everywhere. Luckily, Rebecca's very responsible and she has some great teachers. She's happy and the school has a good atmosphere,

small classes and there's no violence or bullying – that's the most important thing.

The only policies I don't like here are books and holidays. I spend 400 euros on books every year. In Britain, they're free. Schools buy the books and the students borrow them. Then in summer here, it's difficult looking after the kids for three months when both parents work.

UNIT 11

🔊 11.1

R = receptionist, D = David

R: Hillborough hotel.

D: Oh, hello. I'm ringing on behalf of a colleague. He wants some information.

R: Sure. What would you like to know?

D: Um, well, do you have any triple rooms available in August?

R: I'm afraid not. We only have doubles.

D: Oh right. Is it possible to get a double with an extra bed? They have a small kid.

R: That should be possible.

D: And how much would that be per night?

R: 110 euros per night, with a supplement for the cot.

D: Sorry. Does that includes the cost of the extra bed or not?

R: It does include it, yes.

D: And breakfast?

D: I'm afraid breakfast is extra. What dates are they thinking of coming?

D: Um, Tuesday the 12th to the 17th.

R: OK. Let me just check our availability. Hmm, I'm afraid we're fully booked that weekend.

D: So does that include Friday night?

R: That's right, yes. Sorry.

D: And what if they came earlier? Would that be better?

R: Again, the previous Saturday we're full, but we have rooms available from the Sunday night.

D: So that's the 10th, right?

R: That's correct.

D: OK. I'll need to check with them about that. And just a couple of other things.

R: Sure.

D: Do you have Wi-Fi or Internet access?

R: There is Wi-Fi in rooms for a fee.

D: So you have to pay, right?

R: I'm afraid so. It's 12 euros a day, or four euros for half an hour.

D: And do you have parking facilities?

R: Not at the hotel itself, but we have an arrangement with a local car park. They offer a reduced rate of 15 euros per day.

D: And what if they wanted to rent a car once they're in Dublin? Could they do that through the hotel?

R: I'm afraid not, but there are several car hire places nearby, or they could try through the Internet.

D: OK – and what about getting from the airport?

R: There's a shuttle bus, which serves a number of hotels including ours. It costs three euros – or they could take a cab.

D: OK. Let me just talk to my friends. Could you tell me your name if I call back?

R: Yes, it's Jackie, but any of my colleagues can deal with the booking.

D: Oh wait, sorry – one last thing. Will they need to make a payment when they make the booking?

R: Yes, we'll need to take a 10% deposit on a credit card.

D: So if for whatever reason they didn't come, they'd lose that money?

R: If the cancellation was made within two weeks of the arrival date, then yes, that's right.

⚙ 11.2

/iː/

/eɪ/

/e/

/aɪ/

/əʊ/

/uː/

/aː/

⚙ 11.3

R = receptionist, D = David

R: OK, so can I take your credit card details for the deposit?

D: Sure.

R: What kind of card is it?

D: Visa.

R: And the name on your card?

D: Mr D E Gwaizda. That's G - W - A - I - Z - D - A.

R: OK. That's an unusual name.

D: Yeah, it's Polish originally.

R: OK. And the card number on the card?

D: 1003 6566 9242 8307.

R: And the security number on the back of the card – the last three digits there?

D: 718.

R: And the expiry date?

D O – 6 Seventeen

R: And can I just take a contact number in case there are any problems?

D Sure. 0044 796 883 412.

⚙ 11.4

R = receptionist, M = Manager, L= Lady Zaza

R: Hello. Reception.

M: Hi. I'm calling on behalf of Lady Zaza, in the presidential suite.

R: Oh yes. It's a real pleasure to have her in the hotel.

M: Yeah, well, there was no way we could stay in that last place. The service there was a joke!

R: (nervous laugh) Well, I hope everything's OK with our rooms. We really didn't have much time to prepare them.

M: Yeah, everything's fine, basically, but there are just a couple of things she's asked for.

R: OK.

M: Well, first, can you ask room service to send some fresh flowers to the room? Lady Zaza enjoys arranging them. It relaxes her, you know? She'd like a hundred bunches of red flowers, eighty bunches of white and fifty bunches of yellow.

R: Certainly. I'll send someone up with them in a minute.

M: And tell them to bring more of her favourite chocolates too, please. With the peanut ones removed. There were two left in the ones that were in the room, and she almost ate them! She has a really bad nut allergy!

R: I'm so sorry to hear that. I'll sort that out at once.

M: Oh, and no green ones either, please. She can't stand the colour green!

R: Of course.

M: She'd also like the light bulbs in her room changed. She said it's too dark. And can you bring her a kitten?

R: Er, a kitten?!

M: Yeah, a white one.

R: I ... um ... well, I'll see what I can do.

M: Oh, and one last thing. Can she get a wake-up call at four a.m., please? She'd like to use the gym.

R: Well, the gym doesn't usually open until 6, but I'm sure we can organise something for her.

M: Great. That's it for now. Oh, wait. Just one second. She's saying something.

L: They did it again! You've got to do something!

M: Yeah, OK. OK. Hello?

R: Yes, hello,

M: Lady Zaza can hear the people downstairs. They're talking or watching TV or something and she wants them to be moved.

R: Moved? I'm afraid that's just not possible.

M: Sure it's possible. You've got hundreds of rooms in this place.

R: I know, but I'm afraid we're fully booked. We don't have any other rooms available.

M: So you're telling me you can't move them?

R: I would if I could, but I'm afraid I can't. I'm terribly sorry.

M: Well, that's just not good enough. I'd like to talk to the manager.

R: He's not here at the moment, I'm afraid, but I'm sure that if he was, he'd tell you exactly the same thing.

M: Is that right?

R: I'm afraid so, yes.

M: (long pause) OK. Well, I'll tell her ... but she's not going to like it.

UNIT 12

⚙ 12.1

Conversation 1

A: Hello.

B: Hi, it's Brendan. Is Neil there?

A: No, he's not up yet. Is it urgent?

B: No, it's OK. Just tell him we're meeting earlier – at seven, not eight. And tell him he's very lazy! 12 o'clock and still in bed!

A: Well, he was out late last night. Has he got your number, Brendan?

B: Yeah, he has. So what time will he be up?

A: I imagine in about an hour. He didn't get back home till four.

B: Oh right. Well, I'll see him later. Thanks.

A: That's OK. I'll give him your message. Meet at seven, not eight.

B: Yeah.

A: Bye now.

Conversation 2

C: Good morning, DBB. How can I help you?

D: Yeah hi. Could I speak to Jane Simpson, please?

C: Of course. I'll just put you through to her.

D: Thanks.

E: Hello.

D: Hi, Jane?

E: No, it's actually Poppy. I'm afraid Jane's out visiting a client. Would you like to leave a message?

D: Yeah, could you tell her Diane called. I've already spoken to my boss and he's fine with the price, so we can go ahead with the work. Can you ask her to phone me when she gets back so we can sort out the details?

E: Of course. Has she got your number?

D: I don't think she has my mobile. It's 07729–651–118

E: OK. 07729–651–118. And what was your name again? Sorry.

D: Diane Lincoln. L-I-N-C-O-L-N. So when will she be back?

E: Probably later this afternoon. I think she said she was going for lunch.

D: Oh right. Well, hopefully I can speak to her today. I'm actually away on holiday from tomorrow.

E: Oh right. Well, I'll let her know anyway.

D: OK. Thanks. Bye.

E: Bye.

12.2

Hello – and welcome to the World Mail enquiry service.

If you require general information about any of our products, including international mail, or need a redelivery service if you are moving house, please press 1. If you'd like to obtain a postal code or to check the status of a recorded or special delivery item, please press 2. If you need to talk to us about problems you're having with your mail or with one of our services, please press 3. To listen to information about what is available on our website, please press 4. To hear these options again, press 5.

12.3

H = help desk , J = Jaslyn

If you'd like to obtain a postal code, please press 1. If you'd like to check the status of a recorded or special ...

H: Hello. World Mail. How can I help you?

J: Oh hi. I'm trying to find out what's happened to two packages that my parents sent me from Singapore.

H: OK. How long ago were they sent, because obviously international mail can take a lot longer sometimes?

J: It's nearly two months now, and they were sent by registered airmail post, so they should be here by now, really.

H: Hmm. Yes, that does sound strange. Can I take your address, please?

J: Sure. It's Jaslyn – that's J-a-s-l-y-n - Wang and my address is Flat 13, 30 Bedford Way, Walford – that's W-a-l-f-o-r-d, London E25 4QW.

H: Right. Let me just check that on my computer. Yes. OK. I've got them. It seems they entered England on June the 16th, which is five weeks ago now and they're now being held in our main sorting office in Manchester.

J: OK. Do you know why?

H: I have no information on that, I'm afraid, but they're going out this week. They'll be with you by the end of the week, the 25th. Oh, and you'll have to pay eight pounds seventy for one of them as well, because of insufficient postage.

J: Oh, OK. That's strange. Thanks anyway, though.

12.4

H: If you can just wait one more minute. I'm just checking everything now. The system's a bit slow today, I'm afraid. OK. So one of your packages has been returned to Singapore and the other one is in our main sorting office in Manchester ...

J: No, that's not possible! Look, the last time I called, the man I spoke to said my packages had entered England on June the 16th, I think, and were being held in Manchester. He said they

were going out that week and promised me – promised me – that they'd be with me by the end of that week.

H: Ah, well ... I don't know what's happened, but obviously something has gone wrong. What I can do is I can ...

12.5

T = Trish, J = James

T: Hi there. Sorry I can't get to the phone at the moment, but if you'd like to leave a message, please do so after the tone. (Beep)

J: Hi Tricia. It's me, Jim. Sorry I haven't been in touch. I wanted to email you, but I'm having all kinds of problems with my Internet connection. I signed a contract with World Mail the other week, but they've been awful. They took about three weeks to deliver everything, and then the wireless box didn't work properly. I've tried calling them, but I always just get this automated system, which drives me mad! Then this morning I got a bill for £80. Thirty for installation and fifty for the first month! I couldn't believe it! It's so annoying. Anyway, sorry. I didn't mean to complain. Listen, I'll ... Oh. Um.

REVIEW 03

R3.1

/e/	pet
/iː/	retake, mosquito
/ə/	fisherman, authority
/ɪ/	rocket, windy
/ɜː/	term, first
/aɪə/	environment
/eɪ/	jail

R3.2

1 cancer / discovery
2 convenient / investigate
3 system / rocket
4 flowers / bunches
5 heated / trained
6 bee / reason
7 extracts / effects
8 finals / primary
9 redelivery / item
10 sight / witness
11 biology / meanwhile
12 introduce / identified
13 recovery / improper
14 assignment / responsible

R3.3

1 increase available resources
2 receive an urgent message
3 a poisonous species of snake
4 unbelievable success in business
5 a fixed minimum term
6 experiments by nuclear scientists
7 soldiers during the First World War
8 she went to jail on thirteen occasions

R3.4

1 I've just got back from a field trip with some of my year eleven students. The main aim was for them to identify and record the

different species of spider in the area. The wide variety of insect life there meant this was a real challenge for them. They now have to make Powerpoint presentations about their findings. The only problem we had was that one student got bitten and had to go and see a doctor! Apart from that, though, it was excellent.

2   There's a lot of social housing in this part of the city and the local council is the main landlord for over twenty thousand people. I have to report all the problems that people have with their flats. It can be quite difficult as some of the people who phone or come in to the office get really unpleasant, while I have to be patient and polite all the time! I get really stressed sometimes, but what can I do?

3   We still need to repeat the experiment before we can be sure of the findings, but we're possibly looking at an amazing discovery here that could save the government millions. The funny thing is that we only discovered the effects of heat on the material by mistake. It's amazing when you think about it.

4   I'm responsible for everything from organising the shuttle buses from the airport to sorting out babysitting in the hotels, from booking entertainment to keeping a record of all the payments and credit card details. If for whatever reason any of our clients are unhappy, I'm the person they come to. I like to make sure any complaints are dealt with straightaway.

Unit 13

13.1
A: What a boring lecture!
B: I know. It wasn't very good. I was starting to fall asleep near the end!
A: So what're you doing this afternoon? Have you got any plans?
B: Yeah, I'm thinking of going to see a movie and ... um ... listen, would you like to come with me?
A: Maybe. What's on?
B: Well, there's this film called Dust and Heat – directed by Umberto Collocini. It's supposed to be really good.
A: Yeah, I've seen it already, actually. I saw it the other day.
B: Oh yes? What was it like?
A: Not bad, but not as good as everyone is saying. The costumes were great and it's set in the Sahara, so it looks amazing.
B: Yeah, that's what I'd heard. So what was wrong with it?
A: Oh, I don't know. I just found it a bit too slow. I got a bit bored with it after a while – and the ending was very predictable.
B: Oh, right.
A: And that Scottish actor's in it as well. You know. What's his name?
B: Bryan McFletcher?
A: Yeah, that's him. I just find him really, really annoying. He can't act! Anyway, What else is on?
B: Um ... let me see. Oh, there's The Redeadening.
A: Yeah? What's that?
B: It's a new horror movie. It's supposed to be really scary.
A: OK. To be honest, I don't really like horror movies. I'd rather see something a bit lighter, if possible.
B: OK. Right. Well, how about this? It's A Love–Hate Thing. It's a romantic comedy set in Paris and New York and it stars Béatrice Binoche and Brad Schmidt.
A: That sounds more like it! Where's it on?

B: The Galaxy in Cambridge Road.
A: OK. And what time does it start?
B: There's one showing at 2.30 and then another one at quarter to five.
A: So shall we try the half past two one? We could go and have a coffee or something first.
B: OK. Great.

13.2
Speaker 1 – Peter
I'm a big fan of a Turkish singer called Sertab Erener. I first heard her in 2003 when she won the Eurovision Song Contest and I've liked her ever since then. I think she's got an amazing voice. She actually trained as an opera singer. I've got five or six of her albums and last year I went to Istanbul to see her sing live. In fact, I've been learning Turkish for the last two years because I've discovered Turkey through her music and want to spend time there – and I can understand her songs better. My all-time favourite song is Life doesn't wait – Hayat Beklemez. Excuse my bad pronunciation.

Speaker 2 – Gustavo
I've been playing the trumpet for ten years now with El Sistema, which is a programme that helps young people from poor backgrounds learn classical music. I really really love playing and without El Sistema I would probably be in a bad situation! When I joined, I was only eight, but I was already in trouble with the police. My favourite composers are Russian – Shostakovich and Stravinsky. We've been rehearsing The Rite of Spring recently for a concert. It's fantastic – the best.

Speaker 3 – Zelda
My favourite author is the Swedish crime writer Henning Mankell, especially his stories with the detective Wallander. The stories are good thrillers. They're unpredictable, but they're also about social issues, which makes them extra interesting. For the last few weeks, they've been showing a series on TV based on the books. It's OK, but the main character is different to the character in my imagination and, of course, there's less suspense because I've already read the books! I don't know if I'll keep watching.

Speaker 4 – Mary
I'm at art school, where I'm studying Fine Art. I've known I wanted to be an artist since I was three. I've always been more of a painter, especially people – portraits, but recently I've become much more interested in sculpture. I think my favourite artist at the moment is a Swiss sculptor called Alberto Giacometti. He does these beautiful, strange, thin sculptures. I saw an exhibition of his work last year. I don't know why I liked it so much, I just did – especially a sculpture called Cat.

13.3
business opportunity
security system
social life
heart disease
marketing manager
sunglasses
cash machine
swimming pool
tennis court

traffic lights
city centre
fast food

Unit 14

🔊 14.1

A: It's nice.

B: Yes, it is, but it's also very dirty !

C: I know. We'll have to give everything a good clean and sort the place out. Maybe we should go into town and buy some stuff.

A: Yeah, it's a good idea. One minute. I'll get a pen and we can write a list. OK. So ... .

B: Well, we need those things for cleaning. A brush and a ... I don't know the name. The thing that you put rubbish in. What's the name?

C: Do you mean a rubbish bin?

B: No, not that. You use it to get rubbish from the floor with the brush.

C: Oh, you mean a dustpan. A dustpan and brush.

B: A dustpan and brush. Yes, that's very useful.

C: And maybe we should get some cleaning stuff as well. Have we got any bleach?

A: What is bleach?

C: Oh, it's a kind of liquid that's really good for cleaning things, you know, like for cleaning the floor and the toilet. It's a kind of chemical. Quite strong.

A: Oh, we have some. It's in the kitchen. In the cupboard under the sink.

C: Oh, OK. I didn't notice that, but that's good.

B: We need to buy that machine that you use for the clothes. After you wash them. I can't remember the name. Oh, and I know this word as well.

A: You mean an iron?

B: Yes, an iron! And also the thing that you put the clothes on when you use the iron.

C: Yeah, an ironing board. OK. What else?

A: Oh, for the bathroom we need a thing for the shower. You know, the plastic thing that stops the water from leaving the shower – and the metal thing that holds it.

C: A shower curtain and a shower rail. Yeah, I noticed there wasn't anything like that in the bathroom. It's crazy, isn't it? Why doesn't the landlord provide things like that? It's so basic.

B: I know!

A: We should charge the landlord for these things.

B: Oh, one more thing. Before I forget. We need the machine that makes hot water – to make tea and coffee.

C: Oh, yes, of course. A kettle! I can't live without a kettle! I need my tea in the morning!

🔊 14.2

1 For my birthday this year, my big sister bought me my own website. She's really good with computers and I'm not, but the website has become something fun we work on together. I also loved the way she told me. She sent me an email where she gave me clues about the present for me to guess what it was, but I didn't know. Then she sent me another email with a link to a website. When I clicked on the link, I understood everything and I realised that the site was the present. I was really excited! It's my favourite ever gift because, as I said, it's something we do together.

2 I got a mountain bike for Christmas a few years ago and it's been one of the most useful presents ever. Over the last year, I've lived close enough to work to be able to cycle and so I've saved loads of money on petrol. A birthday present that also saves me money! Excellent. I'm also fitter and have lost weight.

3 One of my ex-boyfriends was the king of bad presents. One year, he gave me an iron for my birthday! An iron! I mean, what kind of message does that send about our relationship and the way that he saw me? The following year, he bought me a dress that HE really liked and told me that he wanted me to start wearing more clothes like that from then on – because they would make me more attractive. I couldn't believe it! A couple of weeks after that, we broke up!

4 A few years ago, I went out with a girl and as we were getting out of the taxi to go to dinner, she suddenly said, "I got you a present." I was quite embarrassed because it was our first date and I hadn't thought of getting her anything. Then she handed me a rock from a beach. I was confused. Why had she given me this thing? She said, "I wanted to give you something you'd never forget and you could tell your children about". I said thanks to be polite, but I actually thought it was a bit stupid and it was a bad start to the evening!

Now, though, I use that rock to stop papers on my desk blowing away and that girl is my wife!

Unit 15

🔊 15.1

L = Laima, A = Aidan

L: So how long have you been living here?

A: Almost two years.

L: Wow! You must like it.

A: Yeah, it's nice. I have a good quality of life here – warm climate, near the beach, not too much work.

L: It sounds fantastic.

A: Yeah, it's great, but I'm actually going back to Canada in a few months.

L: Forever?

A: Yeah, I think so.

L: Why? It sounds perfect here.

A: Well, the economy's doing quite badly at the moment. I mean, unemployment has gone up quite a lot over the last few months, so I'm not sure I'm going to have a job in a year's time.

L: Really?

A: Yeah, and also salaries aren't so high here, you know. I could get paid a lot more back home.

L: Sure, but I bet the cost of living's a lot higher in Canada as well. Everything's so cheap here. I mean, eating out is twice the price in my country. You can get a three-course meal for about six dollars here.

A: Yeah, that's true, but it used to be cheaper in the past. Inflation's gone up over the last two years and if it stays high, well, you know, it won't be so cheap

L: I know, but it's still a big difference, no?

A: Yeah, maybe, but anyway, in the end, I miss my family and friends and maybe money isn't so important, but I'll still have more opportunities back home, I think, so work might be more interesting there.

L: I guess so. It seems a shame, though. It's so nice here. Won't you miss the heat?

A: Yeah, probably, but I don't mind the cold weather so much. You get used to it after a while.

L: Mmm.

A: So what about your country? How are things there? Is it a good place to live?

15.2

The lawyer continued reading. It seemed Dad had actually been a good salesman. He earned quite a good salary, but he just preferred to save it. And he had been good at investing money too. The most expensive technology he had was a radio, but he bought shares in some camera and electronic shops. In 1965, the shares cost eight pence each and he sold them 35 years later for four pounds twelve each.

Of the 2.7 million pounds he was leaving, he had decided to give two million to a charity that looked after teenagers with problems. The rest was divided between me and my sisters.

For a moment, I felt angry. Why hadn't he said anything? Why had we lived like poor people? Why was he giving the money to other children? But then I thought, it's stupid to think like that. Really, I had a happy childhood and I'm very happy now. I remembered my parents reading us books they'd borrowed from the library and the hours we played cards together. It was fantastic what my parents had done. The love we had was more important than money, but now maybe the money they saved can bring some love to others.

The only problem I have now is what to do with a quarter of a million pounds – when I honestly don't really need anything!

15.3

1 Two million pounds
2 Seven hundred and eighty-one thousand
3 Six hundred and fifty-three
4 Nineteen Sixty-Five
5 Four pounds twelve.
6 Two point seven
7 A quarter

15.4

1 The minimum wage at that time was five pounds seventy-three an hour.
2 Inflation fell to three point four per cent last month.
3 The government is going to invest seven hundred million in schools.
4 Three-quarters of the population support own a car.
5 The new factory will create eight hundred and twenty-five jobs.
6 The house cost three hundred and sixty thousand euros.
7 We borrowed a hundred and ninety-four thousand from the bank.
8 We'll finally pay back the mortgage in Twenty Fifty-One.

15.5

Conversation 1

A: Yes, sir?

B: Can we get the bill, please?

A: Certainly. One moment.

B: Thanks.

C: How much is it?

B: Don't worry. I'll get this. It's my treat.

C: Are you sure? I don't mind paying half.

B: No, really. It's fine. After all, I asked you out.

C: Thanks. It's really kind of you.

B: Oh no!

C: What's up?

B: I've just realised I left my wallet in my other jacket. It's got all my credit cards and cash in it! I'll have to go and get it.

C: Don't be silly. It's too far to go. I'll pay today.

B: Are you sure? I'll pay you back as soon as I can, I promise.

C: No, it's fine. Honestly. Oh! Wow! Right. That's a lot! I hope they accept my credit card!

Conversation 2

D: That looks great on you.

E: Really?

D: Yeah. Really suits you.

E: Maybe. How much is it?

D: Well, it's vintage sixties.

E: Sorry?

D: It's very old. From the nineteen sixties. It's hard to find things like that in this condition.

E: Oh. Yes. So how much?

D: Let's call it two hundred.

E: Pounds?

D: Yes, of course pounds.

E: Two hundred pounds! But it's not in perfect condition. Look – there's a mark here.

D: OK. So let's say one eighty.

E: No, sorry. It's too much. Thank you.

D: OK, OK. The best price I can manage is a hundred and fifty. Any lower than that and I'll lose money.

Conversation 3

F: But if I don't buy it, someone else will.

G: So you've said, but a thousand pounds is a thousand pounds.

F: I know, but if I don't have a car, then I'll have to keep getting the bus into town. And that's not cheap either. Fares have just gone up.

G: OK, OK. Look, you did well in your exams and we'd be happy to help, but it is a lot of money. You're working now, so why don't you pay half?

F: I would if I could, mum, honestly, but I haven't managed to save much yet!

G: Well, maybe we can borrow some money from the bank.

F: Really? Oh, that'd be brilliant!

G: And you pay us half back when you have the money, OK?

Conversation 4

H: Your card was cancelled because of some irregular activity that we noticed.

I: Irregular activity? What do you mean?

H: Well, for instance, did you have lunch in Singapore last week?

I: No. I've never been there in my life.

H: Exactly. We suspect that your card was copied sometime last month and that someone then used it overseas.

I: Oh no! How did they manage to do that? And will I get a refund?

H: Everything is covered by your insurance and we're sending out a new card today. You'll receive your new PIN number after you get the card. They're sent separately for security reasons.

UNIT 16

 16.1

Conversation 1

A: Did you have a nice weekend?

B: Yes, it was great, actually.

A: Yeah? What did you do?

B: One of my oldest friends got married on Saturday, so I went to the wedding in the afternoon and then the reception later on. It was really good.

A: Oh yeah?

B: Yeah, they hired an old castle on the coast for it. It was an amazing venue. And they had a big buffet there, with really good food, and a DJ and everything.

A: That sounds great. What was the music like?

B: Excellent. I was expecting typical wedding reception music, but this DJ played lots of modern things as well. The dance floor was full all evening.

Conversation 2

C: Did you do anything last night?

D: Yeah, I did, actually. I went to a friend's house-warming. She's just moved into this new place. It's an amazing flat – in a converted church. It's a really impressive place.

C: Oh wow! So what was the party like? Was it good?

D: It was great to begin with, yeah. All the other guests were lovely. Everyone was really warm and friendly and very easy to talk to, but then my ex arrived with his new girlfriend.

C: Oh no!

D: Yes, and to make things worse, she was absolutely gorgeous! All the guys there couldn't stop looking at her.

C: Oh, you poor thing! That's awful.

D: I know. It ruined the night for me, to be honest. I didn't stay much longer after that.

Conversation 3

E: So what did you do last night? Anything interesting?

F: Yeah, I had a little dinner party.

E: Oh really? What was the occasion?

F: There wasn't one. I just felt like inviting some friends round and cooking for them.

E: Nice. So how did it go? Was it good?

F: Yeah, it was lovely. It was nice to see people and chat.

E: How many people came?

F: Twelve.

E: Wow! That's a lot of cooking.

F: I know! It took me ages to get everything ready.

E: Did you cook everything yourself?

E: Yeah.

F: You must be a good cook.

E: I don't know about that! I just follow recipes.

F: So what did you do?

E: Well, for starters, I did grilled aubergines covered in yoghurt and served with a slightly spicy sauce and then ...

16.2

1 From the 8th to the 15th century

2 From the 14th to the 16th century

3 The twelfth of April 1961

4 The twenty-third of April 1616

5 The twenty-fourth of December

6 July the fourth 1776

7 September the second 1945

8 November the ninth

16.3

1 I grew up in Mississippi in the 1960s and lived through some very hard times. As a black man, I was treated like a second-class citizen: there were places I was never allowed to sit, cafes and restaurants I couldn't enter and so on, so the fact that Barack Obama, a man of colour, managed to become President of the United States was truly remarkable. I'll remember the day he was elected for as long as I live.

2 My great-grandmother on my mum's side was Ukrainian. We never met as she died before I was born, but a few years ago my mum and I decided to go on a trip to the village that she came from. We spent a night in the house she'd been born in, which was very moving. The people were very welcoming and I felt a real connection with the place. It was incredible – a day I'll never forget.

3 August the Thirty-First will always be a very special day for me as it's the anniversary of the day that Princess Diana died. Her death in 1997 was a real tragedy and I still feel her loss today. Diana loved helping people and she touched the lives of millions of people all over the world. One of my biggest regrets is that I wasn't able to go to London for her funeral. I wanted to go, but I just couldn't afford to buy a ticket from Brazil.

4 When I was 23 or 24, I spent six months travelling round South East Asia. It was an amazing time in my life and I had lots of great experiences, but perhaps the day I remember best was when I climbed Mount Kinabalu in Malaysia, one of the highest mountains in the region. We started climbing at midnight, with a local guide, and we reached the peak just as the sun was coming up. It was incredibly beautiful.

5 March the 24th is a very special day for me as it's the anniversary of the day I had a special operation on my stomach to stop me gaining weight. Five years ago, I weighed over 150 kilos and wore size 50 trousers. Today I'm 75 kilos and I wear size 34! I go the gym every day now, I no longer have diabetes and I've even found a partner! Thanks to my surgeon, I've been given a second chance in life and I'll always be grateful for that!

REVIEW 04

 R4.1

1 region

2 weird

3 execution

4 voice

5 monarch

6 shame

7 shares

8 diabetes

9 charity

10 publish

R4.1

1 rehearse
2 technique
3 wealth
4 forecast
5 iron
6 duvet
7 vegetarian
8 execution
9 civil war
10 vacuum cleaner

R4.2

1   Hong Kong actress Kathy Chung stars as a detective in Eye Spy, which opens tonight at the Gate Theatre. The action begins with a terrible crime and Chung's character then tries to convince the five witnesses to talk about what they have seen. The plot is full of suspense and the unpredictable ending will be a real shock to everyone. Fans of Miss Chung should not miss this chance to catch her in action.

2   While the population of the city has grown over the last ten years, average salaries have gone down, unemployment has gone up and the pace of life has increased rapidly. All of these changes have created new social problems that are not yet really being dealt with. If elected, I promise to double investment in social programmes, so please: vote for change. Vote for Chapman!

3   The region declared independence last month, after experiencing many years of war. While the majority of citizens are opposed to the move, the king supports it, believing that allowing independence may be the only way of bringing peace to the country and its neighbours.

4   We have recently decided to ban this group. We believe they are a cult and that their activities are causing tensions between different groups in society. We reject the group's claims that their main activity only involves helping children from poor backgrounds. We think the reason they have founded a charity is to spread their ideas and to generate funds.

CREDITS

Although every effort has been made to contact copyright holders before publication, this has not always been possible. If notified, the publisher will undertake to rectify any errors or omissions at the earliest opportunity.

Photos

The publishers would like to thank the following sources for permission to reproduce their copyright protected images:

Alamy — pp10rb (David A. Barnes), 11lm (Art Directors & TRIP), 19b (Trinity Mirror / Mirrorpix), 20a (Image Source Black), 10b (Photo Japan), 20c (Peter Tsai), 20d (Alex Segre), 39a (Anthony Collins Cycling), 39c (Michael Jones), 39d (Nordicphotos), 44c (The Photolibrary Wales) 47br (Image Source Pink), 50bl (Cris Haigh), 59br (Andrew Woodley), 73b (Zefa RF), 80mr (JadroFoto), 92bl (Pictorial Press Ltd), 94d (Robert Landau), 103a (amana images inc.), 103b (Jim West), 103c (Blend Images), 113ml (North Wind Picture Archives), 159i (Penny Tweedie); **Associated Press** – 97mr (AP); **BBC** – pp94c (Leftbank Pictures); **Bossaball Sports SL** – pp39e (Bossaball Sports SL); **Cartoonstock** – 27bl (Edgar Argo), 53br (Phil Judd), 55br (Phil Judd), 81 (Clive Goddard), 133 (Steve Delmonte); **Getty** –pp12a (Maria Teijeiro), 44a (Robert Warren), 51bl/94a (Getty Images), 94b/97ml/113bl (AFP/Getty Images); **iStockphoto** – pp8–9t (Aldo Murillo), 12c (digitalskillet), 14–15t (Paul Piebinga), 20–21t (Saso Novoselic), 22 (Bedo), 23 (foodandwinephotoraphy), 24 (LyaC), 26–27t (Daniel Rodriguez), p28 (lisafx), 36–37t/122t (Anna Bryukhanova), 36b (Marcus Lindström), 36c (Carmen Martínez Banús), 37b (fotoIE), 40b (Kayfish), 42–43t (Justin Horrocks), 44d (Charles Benavidez), 45 (skynesher), 48–49t (Krzysztof Chrystowski), 54–55t (Robert Churchill), 56bg (skodonnell), 58b (Christoph Ermel), 64-65t (morganl), 64bl (Michel Lizarzaburu), 64br (Mooneydriver), 66c (Ricardo Reitmeyer), 66d (Lee Torrens), 66e (Gewoldi), 70-71t (Tomaz Levstek), 72mr (Chris Schmidt), 74b (Kristian Sekulic), 76-77t (Catherine Yeulet), 76b (rognar), 79b (Marilyn Nieves), 79c (Skip Odonnell), 79e (Dr. Heinz Linke), 80ml (Reuben Schulz), 80br (Kemter), 81-82t (Izabela Habur), 85ml (Terry North), 84br (David Haynes), 85tr (Blade_kostas), 87br (Diego Cervo), 92-93t (Stephanie Phillips), 94e (Alija), 98-99t (Roman Milert), 100a,b (anouchka), 100c (sjlocke), 100d,e,f (RapidEye), 104-105t (Andrey Volodin), 106b (DNY59), 109bl (Susan H. Smith), 110-111t (José Luis Gutiérrez), 112mr (Eduard Kim), 115b (Vernon Wiley), 120-121t (Soubrette), 122bl (gecko753), 122-123t (Rahul Sengupta), 125t (Exkalibur), 126t (Wolfgang Amri), 127t (pertusinas), 128-129t/130-131t (alvarez), 129b (Klubovy), 132-133t (Brad Killer), 134-135t (CapturedNuance), 123ml (Don Bayley), 159a (Slobo Mitic), 159b (Sandy Jones), 159c (Ron Hohenhaus), 159d (Wojtek Kryczka), 159e (1001nights), 159f (Angel Herrero de Frutos), 159g (iofoto), 159m (ranplett), 159n (Eric Hood); **Shutterstock** – pp12b (Scott Milless), 18b (magicinfoto), 25 (Jaimie Duplass), 29 (Anja Greiner Adam), 30icons (Eduard Andras), 36a (Karen Struthers), 37a (Petr Nad), 39b (Suzanne Tucker), 39f (Margo Harrison), 41br (Brandon Blinkenberg), 42br (Liotru), 44b (Monkey Business Images), 57b (Regien Paassen), 65bl (Four Oaks), 66a (bluecrayola), 66b (Miroslav Hlavko), 66f (Maslov Dmitry), 69br (Helen von Allmen), 69b (Laurence Gough), 79a (Avalon Imaging), 79d (Dima Kalinin), 80bl (Seleznev Oleg), 86br (Juriah Mosin), 103d (VojtechVlk), 111a (Sean Prior), 111b (Corepics), 123br (Christopher Futcher), 127 (Yuri Archurs), 130ml (PixAchi), 130br (casinozack), 131br (Johnathan Larsen), 132ml (Stefan Ataman), 159h (R. Gino Santa Maria), 159j (Timofey), 159k (Lisa F. Young), 159l (Eau Claire Media).

Cover photo: Shutterstock (Viktor Gmyria)

Illustrations: p52a,b – John Pritchett / pritchettcartoons.com; p52c – Patrick Latham / 3rd Man Cartoons; p122 – Mark Draisey; p126 – Clive Goddard; all others – KJA artists.